THE COMBAT ZONE

OTHER BOOKS FROM BRIGHT LEAF

House Stories
The Meanings of Home in a New England Town
BETH LUEY

Bricklayer Bill
The Untold Story of the Workingman's Boston Marathon
PATRICK L. KENNEDY AND LAWRENCE W. KENNEDY

Concrete Changes
Architecture, Politics, and the Design of Boston City Hall
BRIAN M. SIRMAN

Williamstown and Williams College
Explorations in Local History
DUSTIN GRIFFIN

Massachusetts Treasures
A Guide to Marvelous, Must-See Museums
CHUCK D'IMPERIO

Boston's Twentieth-Century Bicycling Renaissance
Cultural Change on Two Wheels
LORENZ J. FINISON

Went to the Devil
A Yankee Whaler in the Slave Trade
ANTHONY J. CONNORS

At Home
Historic Houses of Eastern Massachusetts
BETH LUEY

Black Lives, Native Lands, White Worlds
A History of Slavery in New England
JARED ROSS HARDESTY

At Home
Historic Houses of Central and Western Massachusetts
BETH LUEY

Flight Calls
Exploring Massachusetts through Birds
JOHN R. NELSON

Lost Wonderland
The Brief and Brilliant Life of Boston's Million Dollar Amusement Park
STEPHEN R. WILK

Legends of the Common Stream
JOHN HANSON MITCHELL

I Believe I'll Go Back Home
Roots and Revival in New England Folk Music
THOMAS S. CURREN

Minds and Hearts
The Story of James Otis Jr. and Mercy Otis Warren
JEFFREY H. HACKER

Letters from Red Farm
The Untold Story of the Friendship between Helen Keller and Journalist Joseph Edgar Chamberlin
ELIZABETH EMERSON

THE
COMBAT
ZONE

**MURDER,
RACE, AND
BOSTON'S
STRUGGLE
FOR
JUSTICE**

JAN
BROGAN

BRIGHT LEAF
Amherst and Boston
An imprint of University of Massachusetts Press

The Combat Zone has been supported by the Regional Books Fund, established by donors in 2019 to support the University of Massachusetts Press's Bright Leaf imprint.

Bright Leaf, an imprint of the University of Massachusetts Press, publishes accessible and entertaining books about New England. Highlighting the history, culture, diversity, and environment of the region, Bright Leaf offers readers the tools and inspiration to explore its landmarks and traditions, famous personalities, and distinctive flora and fauna.

ISBN 978-1-62534-609-4 (paper); 608-7 (hardcover)

Designed by Deste Roosa
Set in FreightText Pro and Berthold Akzidenz Grotesk
Printed and bound by Books International, Inc.

Cover design by Deste Roosa
Cover art: *City Censor, City of Boston,* CC BY 2.0, https://creativecommons.org/licenses/by/2.0, via Wikimedia Commons, Background art detail from photograph by Spencer Grant, 1977.

Library of Congress Cataloging-in-Publication Data
Names: Brogan, Jan, author.
Title: The Combat Zone : murder, race, and Boston's struggle for justice / Jan Brogan.
Description: Amherst : Bright Leaf, an imprint of University of Massachusetts Press, [2021] | Includes bibliographical references and index.
Identifiers: LCCN 2021016940 (print) | LCCN 2021016941 (ebook) | ISBN 9781625346087 (hardcover) | ISBN 9781625346094 (paperback) | ISBN 9781613768846 (ebook) | ISBN 9781613768853 (ebook)
Subjects: LCSH: Puopolo, Andy (Andrew P.), 1956–1976—Death and burial. | Harvard University—Students—Crimes against. | Murder—Massachusetts—Boston. | Murder victims—Massachusetts—Boston. | Trials (Murder)—Massachusetts—Boston. | Discrimination in criminal justice administration—Massachusetts—Boston. | Red-light districts—Massachusetts—Boston. | Boston (Mass.)—Race relations—History—20th century.
Classification: LCC HV6534.B6 B76 2021 (print) | LCC HV6534.B6 (ebook) | DDC 362.88/2930974461—dc23
LC record available at https://lccn.loc.gov/2021016940
LC ebook record available at https://lccn.loc.gov/2021016941

British Library Cataloguing-in-Publication Data
A catalog record for this book is available from the British Library.

To the memory of Andy Puopolo
and all murder victims,
as well as the families and friends
who never stop mourning them.

CONTENTS

A NOTE ON LANGUAGE

The 1970s is a particularly difficult time for racial issues in Boston, and racial language was prevalent. Some of the actual language used in this time period has been altered, when possible, without glossing over the relevant history.

THE COMBAT ZONE

CHAPTER ONE
A Night in "the Zone"

ON A COLD night in November 1976, at the end of an up-and-down season, the varsity football team gathered at the Harvard Club in accordance with tradition. Under crystal chandeliers, the students dined on roast beef and green beans as they listened to speeches about brotherhood and accepted awards for their accomplishments.

Princeton Heisman Trophy winner Dick Kazmaier gave the principal address, and Robert F. Kennedy's widow, Ethel, made a special trip to present an award in honor of her husband. But the more powerful speeches came from inside the team, from the coaches and the captain, who talked about the special bonds formed over double sessions, bus travel, and games that did not go as planned.

Everything about Harvard football was steeped in tradition, from the century-old rivalry with Yale to the little red flag waved each time the Crimson scored. It reminded the boys of the storied history of Ivy League football and the privilege of playing for Harvard.

Andy Puopolo, one of the seniors who had hung up his shoulder pads for the last time, ate the roast beef and sipped a Coke. He'd been pulled from Saturday's game against Yale with a mild concussion and had to be careful about how much alcohol he drank. It didn't matter. According to his friends and family, he was not much of a drinker.

He had dark hair that fell below his ears in the overgrown style of the seventies and green eyes often described as intense. Although relatively short for a football player at five feet ten, he was muscular from long hours spent in the gym. Originally scoffed at by the Harvard interviewer when he said he wanted to play football, he'd worked hard to bulk up and had fought through injuries to win a starting position. But now, his playing days were over and he was looking to the future. After the game

loss on Saturday, he had surprised his parents by announcing
he received his first acceptance to medical school.

Andy had had his share of glory—two interceptions in the
game against UPenn and a mention in the *New York Times*—
but it had been a disappointing season for the team. Picked
as the favorite to win the Ivy League championship, Harvard
had ended up not just behind the two cochampions, Yale and
Brown, but tied with Dartmouth for second place.

After dinner, the students went downstairs to the vaulted
ceiling and dark Tudor wainscoting of the lounge. They milled
around, drinking draft beer and bantering as they watched the
highlight reels. By the end of the official Harvard banquet, they
were ready to shake off defeat.

Just under fifty of the football players left the hallowed halls of
the Harvard Club and descended on Boston's Combat Zone. They
went to the Naked i, a strip club best known for its "All College
Girl Review" and its logo, an eye that winked over a backside
view of upside-down and bare female legs. One of the teammates
was related to the manager and had arranged to reserve the
private room in back for their own show. By all accounts, the
teammates, who arrived dressed up in their three-piece suits and
loafers, had a great time. After two of them climbed on stage
to dance with the stripper shortly before last call, the bouncers
announced it was time for the boys to go home.

A night in "the Zone" was an end-of-season tradition for
Harvard's football team, as well as a common end-of-year practice by other Boston college football teams, but the timing this
year was extremely questionable. The Combat Zone, which had
made headlines for police corruption and escalating crime only
the week before, was at the peak of its lawlessness.

Restricted by law to a four-block area between the Downtown Crossing and Chinatown, the red-light district was
crammed with strip clubs, X-rated movie houses, adult bookstores, and a gay bathhouse. Years before the advent of the
videocassette recorder (VCR) and a decade before the internet,

FIGURE 1. The Naked i in Boston's Combat Zone, August 1977. Photograph by Spencer Grant.

men formed long lines outside the peep shows where a quarter kept the porn reel going. Prostitutes swarmed the streets and created a gridlock on weekends as they stopped cars and fondled men through open car windows.

Dealers sold pot and heroin curbside. Mobsters and cops drank together at the bars as the muggers rolled drunks on the alleys outside. But the recklessness of the Zone, the unpredictability, was part of its allure. The neon marquees cast both a glow and a shadow over littered sidewalks that pulsed with excitement, crime, and danger.

As the Harvard students spilled out into the street, they broke into smaller groups, heading for taxis and cars. One of these groups, six Harvard students, accompanied by the Harvard equipment manager, passed by the Carnival Lounge on the way back to the Harvard van. Although they were dressed like lawyers, these men were young and loud and, at least one, drunkenly off-kilter.

Two of the young women standing outside the Carnival Lounge had prior arrests for both prostitution and theft. Cassandra McIntyre, still a girl at sixteen, was barely five feet tall and had a keloid scar running the length of her right cheek. Naomi Axell, the veteran at twenty-two, was long and lean, wearing a wig and a long, rust-colored leather coat. They approached the eight men passing by.

The two prostitutes were Black, and the three Harvard football players at the front of the line were also Black. They regarded the women stonily. In the second year of court-ordered busing, racial tension in this segregated city was at its peak. As one of these three men would recall years later, they wanted no trouble with the cops or with anyone else on a Boston city street. They told the prostitutes to get lost and encouraged their teammates to do the same.

But Naomi and Cassandra were already weaving between the other young men, reaching for their crotches. Recent publicity in both the city's two largest newspapers about the Zone's pickpockets who lifted wallets while they fondled genitals made a couple of the other boys wary. But not all of them.

As a few of the students would later testify, a conversation began. Rates were discussed. The two women followed the boys back to the Harvard equipment van.

Neither Andy Puopolo nor Tommy Lincoln were a part of this group. Both premed students, they were facing exams later that week and were halfway down the street, almost a block away, anxious to get home. Offered a ride by a fellow teammate, they made it back to his Chevy Nova. Andy would even get inside, taking a seat in back.

But within fifteen minutes, as hell broke loose on Boylston Street over a stolen wallet, these two football players were stabbed—Andy, critically. Three Black men were arrested at the scene and charged with assault with intent to murder.

The news of this violent end to the Harvard football season went around the country, horrifying parents of college-aged children.

The early headlines would focus on the outrage over crime and violence in the out-of-control Combat Zone. But this was the year when Boston established its reputation as the most racist city in the nation; when angry parents rioted in the streets and pelted buses full of schoolchildren with rocks; when a Black student stabbed a white one in the high school library; and when student demonstrators attacked a Black businessman with an American flag. Race was a part of every story, every argument.

The stabbings would lead to the cleanup of Boston's controversial red-light district and be an important factor in its eventual demise. The trials would change the way juries were chosen in Massachusetts and influence a federal Supreme Court decision on jury selection years later.

The Andrew Puopolo murder was the most highly publicized murder story in Boston in the 1970s. Wildly varying verdicts only two and a half years apart would reflect changes in the city and prove that criminal trials aren't always about the victim, the accused, or even the crime when the forces in play are trying to right a completely different wrong.

FIGURE 2. Andy Puopolo in 1976, taken his senior year at Harvard, to submit with his medical school application. Courtesy of Danny Puopolo.

CHAPTER TWO
Combat Medicine

IN THE EARLY morning, as doctors worked on Andy Puopolo, the emergency room lounge at Tufts New England Medical Center began to fill with football players, who had followed the police cruiser from the Combat Zone, and with cops, who lingered in the hallway as a hospital administrator tried to impose order on the growing crowd.

Decades later, Danny Puopolo, who had just turned nineteen, would recall being awakened from a deep sleep when the phone rang. His mother's cry jolted him awake. He heard footsteps in his parents' bedroom and his father's voice on the phone. Within seconds his father was at his doorway, telling Danny to get up: Andy was in the hospital. He'd been stabbed in a fight, and it was bad.

Only twenty-two months apart, the two brothers were extremely close. They had shared a bedroom since infancy in the family's tiny North End apartment and through adolescence, when they had moved to the three-bedroom, multilevel house in Jamaica Plain. Even when their older sister, Fran, married and moved out, leaving an extra bedroom, the boys opted to stay together.

Andy, who came home from Harvard nearly every weekend, had slept in the matching single bed just two nights before as he recovered from a concussion he'd suffered during the Harvard-Yale game. Now, groggy from sleep and spinning into shock, Danny refused to believe the news.

His first act was to throw on sweat pants and grab the keys to the 1975 Cutlass he and Andy shared. He wanted to get to the hospital to convince himself that his brother's injuries weren't that bad. But at the front door, his mother's cries made him stop and turn. Helen Puopolo, already dressed, stood at the top of the half flight of stairs, her eyes fearful. She didn't want her youngest, barely awake and in shock, careening through the city streets at this hour. She begged Danny to wait for them so they could drive together.

His father appeared behind her and asked Danny to call his sister and her husband and tell them to meet at the hospital.

The knife wounds were deep. The emergency room doctor had to cut open Andy's chest and massage his heart to revive him. The hospital's top cardiac and thoracic surgeons had been summoned from their homes, and when the family arrived at the hospital, Andy was about to be moved upstairs for more permanent repairs to his lung and heart.

Andrew Sr., a quiet man who carried himself with the bearing of a former Marine, asked if he could just see his son. He recalled that a nurse escorted him into the trauma room and allowed him a fleeting glance. Unconscious on the stretcher, Andy's packed chest was covered by a bloodstained hospital gown; tubes came out of his throat, groin, and neck.

Andrew Sr. steadied himself and returned to the waiting room. He told Helen and Danny what the doctors had told him: They were lucky. Police had gotten Andy to the hospital just in the nick of time.

The lounge in the emergency room grew loud as teammates and friends continued to swarm in. A hospital administrator pulled Danny and his parents aside and guided them through the emergency room to a lounge in the Pratt/Farnsworth Building, near the intensive care unit where Andy would be moved after surgery. Built into the corner of the building, the semihexagonal room was called the Solarium. Large windows dominated three angled walls and looked out onto the dark and silent street.

For the next several hours, the family waited in the oddly shaped room that was furnished with two small couches and a dozen hard-backed chairs. Helen Puopolo sat stiffly next to her husband. Normally a stylish woman, well coiffed, she was a young-looking forty-seven, but tonight, her eyes, the same green Andy had inherited, were aged with fear. A deeply religious woman, she'd had no time to grab her rosary beads, which later would become a fixture. She prayed silently, her empty hands white knuckled, while her husband tried to keep her calm by assuring her that their son would make it through.

Andrew Sr. had been an athlete in his youth—a boxer in the Marines. He was still fit at fifty-two and sat at attention in the uncomfortable chair, sipping weak coffee from the vending machine. Fran and her husband, Paul, driving in from the suburbs, arrived half an hour after the rest of the family. Although all three children looked alike, the resemblance was striking between Andy and Fran, who had the same intense eyes and sharp cheekbones.

Fran was the firstborn, the built-in babysitter, and she still worried about her younger brothers. She told the *Boston Herald* that she'd been having bad dreams about Andy before the stabbing, that a woman pointed to him and said, "You will be killed." When she told Andy about the dream, he'd assured her with "Don't worry Fran, I can take care of myself."

Danny took his sister by the arm and steered her out of the Solarium and down the hall so he could explain what happened out of earshot from their mother, who didn't need to hear it again. Unshaven and rumpled in the sweatpants and sweatshirt he'd found on the bedroom floor, Danny was a couple of inches shorter than Andy, stockier, and barrel chested. He wasn't the same kind of athletic star as his brother, lacking the intense focus, but he was strong and quick. An avid recreational boxer, he'd taken down more than one opponent with his fists. Since the call from the hospital, he'd been cursing himself for not having been with Andy that night.

He told his sister that Andy had asked him to meet up with the football players at the strip club for drinks and he'd refused. Fran couldn't understand why either of them would want to go to the Combat Zone. Danny explained that after the breakup dinner, the Harvard football team always went to a Combat Zone strip club for one last drink together. That it was tradition.

At this hour, office doors on either side of the hospital corridor were sealed tight. The only sounds came from the nurses' station and the hum of machines in the ICU as Danny explained why he hadn't agreed to meet up with Andy that night—he'd wanted him to enjoy a last night out with his team without having to look out after his younger brother. But now he was convinced that if he *had* gone, Andy would have been so worried about him that he would have gotten the two of them out of there at the first sign of any fighting.

Across town at Massachusetts General Hospital, surgical residents surrounded Tommy Lincoln in the trauma room and debated exploring the wound to determine the extent of damage. Later, when he himself was a doctor, Tom Lincoln—no longer called Tommy—would recall how, luckily, an older, wiser attending surgeon had been called in to examine the wound. It was just below the liver. The attending advised against an unnecessary surgery.

Still charged with adrenaline, Tommy had little pain and was confused about why the doctors didn't just let him go home. He also didn't understand why uniformed police officers were in the hallway, guarding him.

Because he'd been dispatched to Mass General in an ambulance before the police had caught any of the three men who would be charged, Tommy had no idea that the police were actually there to guard thirty-three-year-old Eddie Soares, who had been transported to the same hospital for treatment of knuckle scrapes he'd gotten while fighting Andy. Tommy was stunned when the police brought the short, stocky man, his hand bandaged, to the end of his hospital bed, along with another Black man, thirty-six-year-old Richie Allen, a muscled powerhouse who worked as a bouncer at the Carnival Lounge. The police asked Tommy if he could identify the men as being involved in the brawl. He could.

Twenty minutes later, another set of police officers brought Leon Easterling into the hospital room for Tommy to identify. He had no doubts that this man in the long leather jacket and diamond earring was the one who had stabbed him outside the MBTA public transport station on Tremont Street.

At this hour, Tommy didn't know the extent of Andy's injuries. He was more worried about his father, an oral surgeon who worked upstairs at this very hospital, finding out that he'd been in the Combat Zone that night. He wondered if he might be able to keep it from him and asked one of the cops if the arrests would make the news.

He recalled the way the cop looked at him, not bothering to mask his amusement. "Are you kidding?" he asked. "The whole world is going to know about this."

As daybreak brought a dim gray light through the Solarium windows, the Puopolo family jolted to attention. Three doctors entered the Solarium. They had just come from the surgery. Dr. Joseph Amato took the lead and did all the talking. The family circled around him.

Because of Tufts New England Medical Center's proximity to the Combat Zone, staff doctors saw a lot of gunshot and stab wounds and were considered the city's experts in the newly emerging field of "combat medicine." Still, Dr. Amato, a cardiac and thoracic surgeon in his early thirties, expressed shock and disgust at how viciously Andy had been cut up.

The first stabbing had punctured Andy's lung; the second attack penetrated his thick, muscled chest wall and gone deep into his heart. Andy had nearly bled to death and had arrived at the emergency room with no pulse. It was only because he was such a strong, young athlete that doctors had been able to restart his heart. Andy *came back*, Dr. Amato told them, in a tone of amazement. The young man's revival had impressed the entire medical team.

Although the brain could only survive without oxygen for five to six minutes before sustaining permanent damage, doctors were optimistic. Andy's pupils had responded to light. He stood a good chance of recovery because of the fast action of the police, who had gotten him to the hospital within minutes of the stabbing.

Dr. Amato told the family that they should go home and get sleep—or at least shower and eat something. Andy wouldn't be out of recovery for a while. None of them wanted to leave, Danny recalled, but after another hour or so, a new shift of nurses arrived and insisted it would be many, many hours before Andy regained consciousness.

From the Solarium window, Danny could see reporters below, already starting to gather with their notebooks and tape recorders. Television vans from all three of the Boston stations were parked on Harrison Avenue. The hospital administrator, a woman with glasses hanging from a chain around her neck, explained that they didn't have to talk to anyone in the media. Doctors would meet with the press to explain the medical procedures and update them on Andy's condition. Security would escort the family members directly to their cars, so they would not be harassed.

The family was still in shock, exhausted from anxiety and lack of sleep. They didn't understand why so many reporters were interested in Andy. Later, they would get used to the press waiting at the front door of the hospital, at their home, and at the courthouse. But that first morning, Danny would later recall, "we were just kind of numb. We didn't get that this wasn't even about my brother."

That evening, the afternoon newspapers and all three local television stations featured the story. The next morning and in the months to come, more than three hundred newspapers—from as far away as Butte, Montana, to Biddeford, Maine, including big-city papers in Las Vegas and small-town dailies from Indiana, Mississippi, and Texas and even the *Pacific Stars and Stripes* in Japan—would report and follow the account of the two Harvard football players stabbed in Boston's Combat Zone. Many newspapers splashed photos of Andrew Puopolo and Thomas Lincoln across their front pages.

The story had everything: Ivy League victims, prostitutes, and police heroes who saved a life by whisking a football hero to the nearest hospital in time to restart his heart. It was a cautionary tale about what happened when well-bred boys walked on the "wild side," but it was also a story about Boston's social experiment.

Across the nation, cities were dealing with what *Time* magazine had called America's "Age of Porn" in an April 1976 cover story titled "The Porno Plague." Dominated by organized crime, pornography was a new and deeply controversial growth industry in a culture of rapidly changing social norms.

There were two trends upsetting the public. The first was a new social acceptability of pornography in this era. Recent Supreme Court decisions had made it difficult to ban adult entertainment outright, and about 780 theaters in the nation were suddenly showing X-rated movies to growing audiences. The former prostitute Xaviera Hollander, best known for her memoir *The Happy Hooker: My Own Story*, had sold nine million copies of her numerous paperbacks. Linda Lovelace, of *Deep Throat* fame, had graced the cover of *Esquire* magazine. *Penthouse* publisher Bob Guccione had been honored at a fundraiser by Brandeis University.

The second trend getting attention was the increasingly violent content of these films. Graphic sadomasochism (S&M) plots included rape, murder, and decapitation as part of the sexual thrill. The 1975 film *Story of O* featured sexual abuse and whipping of a woman by multiple men. In 1976, *Snuff*, a softcore film with a Charles Manson cult–inspired plot in which a woman was sawed to pieces, purported to include a real-life murder. Although it turned out to be a marketing hoax, the film galvanized feminists who picketed the film across the nation.

Feminists objected to this flood of violent pornography as antifemale. "Pornography, like rape, is a male invention, designed to dehumanize women, to reduce the female to an object of sexual access," wrote the feminist Susan Brownmiller, author of the 1975 book *Against Our Will*. But everyone got involved in the discussion: English professors, social psychologists, political scientists, psychiatrists, First Amendment advocates, and even *Playboy* publisher Hugh Hefner weighed in on where this new pornography was taking the nation, with comparisons made to the fall of the Roman Empire.

Cities across America scrambled as officials tried to figure out how to cope with the sleazy new industry overtaking their downtowns. It wasn't just a morality play. In the mid-1970s, cities across the nation struggled in the recession. Only the year before, the nation's largest and richest city, New York, billions in debt, had teetered on the brink of bankruptcy, forcing massive municipal cutbacks that were epitomized by the tons of rotting garbage that piled up on city streets. Boston wasn't doing much better. The proliferating X-rated bookstores and theaters in the heart of the downtown area hardly improved property values.

Boston's solution to the pornography problem, the Combat Zone, both fascinated and rankled the nation. Ironically, the puritanical city best known for banning everything from Walt Whitman's poetry collection *Leaves of Grass* in 1882 to the 1967 Swedish film *I Am Curious (Yellow)* had decided to officially zone an "adult entertainment district."

The official zoning was actually a containment strategy, meant to appease the city's more well-to-do neighborhoods by limiting the industry to that four-block area, but it was widely viewed as progressive. To critics of the plan—and there were many within the city as well—this official zoning only made the problem worse by condoning a new social acceptability of sleaze.

A story about the stabbing of two Harvard football players proved just how misguided that social acceptability really was. The sensational fact that the victims were white Harvard students and the suspects identified as Black pimps didn't hurt newspaper sales either.

CHAPTER THREE
A Sexual Disneyland

IN A STRAIGHT-LACED city like Boston, where "puritanical" actually meant founded by Puritans, the existence of a red-light district downtown had always been rife with conflict. Boston had managed to rid itself of its original red-light district, Scollay Square, by bulldozing the area of barrooms and burlesque halls in the early 1960s to make way for the new Government Center. But Boston would soon learn that when it came to adult entertainment, city planning was no match for market forces.

Lower Washington and its side streets, an area of low-rent storefronts and deteriorating old theaters about a dozen blocks away, provided inexpensive real estate for the setup of newer, more risqué strip clubs, modern X-rated movie houses, adult bookstores, and the innovative coin-operated peep shows of the era. The essence of Scollay Square, also known as "the crossroads of hell," would evolve with the times, growing wilder and more dangerous in its new location.

The new neighborhood had informally been called "the Combat Zone," since the 1950s because of all the uniformed soldiers and sailors who hung out in its bars and nightclubs and got into street fights. A 1964 exposé by Jean Cole and other reporters at the *Record American* about rising crime in the new red-light district got the credit for making the nickname stick.

By the 1970s, twelve strip clubs and a total of more than thirty-five sex entertainment businesses operated in the Combat Zone. Terrified that the flourishing sex industry would spill into nicer neighborhoods and sully upscale Back Bay or Beacon Hill, city officials felt the need to act. Demolishing buildings clearly hadn't worked, and federal high court decisions regarding First Amendment rights in the early 1970s prevented the city from banning these businesses.

The city's novel response the following fall, approving a zoning amendment to officially establish the four-block area for adult entertainment next to Chinatown, which had little political voice and was promised a thriving restaurant climate as well as two new housing projects for not objecting, according to Michael Liu's *Forever Struggle: Activism, Identity, and Survival in Boston's Chinatown, 1880–2018*. The housing projects, along with other promises by the Boston Redevelopment Authority to dress up the neighborhood, never materialized, but meanwhile, the sex industry swiftly boomed. Mixed among the topless bars, strip clubs, peep shows, and X-rated movie houses was a gay bathhouse, the occasional drag show, and gay hookup spots. Soon, the *Wall Street Journal* would describe Boston's adult entertainment district as a "sexual Disneyland."

The Zone wasn't devoid of social value. In fact, it was known as a refuge for the offbeat, artistic, and liberal minded—one of the few places in the 1970s where gays were accepted, where Blacks and whites drank at the same bar, and where an interracial couple could share an apartment without rocks coming through the window. The area, a hot spot for big band, jump, jazz, and rock and roll in the 1950s and early 1960s, featured live music throughout the 1970s, making it a haven for young musicians.

But if the Zone came of age in an era of cultural revolution, it also came of age in an era of urban poverty and escalating crime. The national recession hit Boston hard at a time when violent crime had more than quadrupled between 1960 and 1970.

In the Combat Zone, crime wasn't just up—it was in your face. On weekend nights in 1976, as many sixty streetwalkers clogged the short block of LaGrange Street outside Good Time Charlie's. The pimped-out Cadillacs lined up one after another on the streets, according to former Combat Zone police detective Billy Dwyer. Sexual encounters could be had in the backrooms of certain clubs, in X-rated theaters, in the alleys and parking lots. One nightclub even found a way to let customers charge oral sex on credit cards.

On weekends, suburban clients showed up, driving around the block—the "drive through" as it was called—until it was their turn to pick up pot or cocaine from corner dealers. Nearly everything was a cash transaction, and nearly everyone was high on something. Wallets were ripe for picking.

Garrett Byrne, a six-term district attorney for Suffolk County, which has jurisdiction over Boston, had led the office since the end of World War II. An ardent opponent of the Combat Zone and an unapologetic prude, he maintained an activist vice squad that raided every porn house and bookstore in search of obscenity violations. But the city of Boston was decidedly less aggressive in policing liquor violations, prostitution, or street crime. A public outcry occasionally led to a crackdown, but often the police appeared nonchalant.

Some believed that Boston's lax policing of the Combat Zone was simply benign neglect. After all, the city grudgingly provided vital services, including street maintenance and building code inspection, in this part of town. Others attributed the neglect to embarrassment, as if by ignoring the Combat Zone, the city could negate its existence. But most saw it as license: an anything goes policy—as long as "anything" stayed in the Zone.

As it turned out, it *was* a kind of a license, although not official and not from the city itself. Police weren't just "lax" in the Zone, as many complained, they were utterly corrupt. The public learned about it from the police commissioner himself.

Robert diGrazia, a controversial "radical" reformer who had led police departments in the San Francisco area and St. Louis County, Missouri, had been recruited in 1972 to clean up the city's police department. At six feet four, he was ruggedly handsome and welcomed public speaking. He quickly made his voice heard throughout the city.

In an interview, shortly before he passed away in 2018, diGrazia said that while he had known he was hired to tackle corruption, he was still surprised to discover the extent of it. Soon after his arrival, he became convinced that Boston had the most corrupt police force in the entire nation. District

One, which included the Combat Zone, the North End, the waterfront, and Back Bay, was the epicenter of that corruption.

In a historic 1919 police strike, the entire Boston police force had been replaced with young recruits all about the same age. Since then, nearly the entire force had retired and was replaced pretty much in unison. In the early 1970s, the members of the force were, on average, forty-four years old—the oldest force of any major city in the nation—and deeply entrenched in the status quo.

The new-to-town police commissioner supported the 1974 zoning change that gave the Combat Zone its official status with the understanding that the zoning change would be coupled with radical reform in District One. But reform wasn't easy for diGrazia, who was the first non-Irish police commissioner in the city's modern era. Many in the rank and file didn't like him and considered him a grandstander. As an outsider, he soon found himself navigating a labyrinth of political connections and one of the most militant police unions in the nation. He decided that he needed proof to demote and replace a corrupt command and ordered a secret investigation into daily operations in District One.

That secret investigation lasted more than thirty-three months. DiGrazia was a man not afraid to make headlines. Perhaps too many headlines. In the 1975 mayoral election, the new police commissioner's extreme popularity with voters was noted as a factor in Kevin White's reelection. Shortly after the election, the mayor asked diGrazia to a breakfast meeting to smoke out his police chief's political ambitions. Despite diGrazia's assurances that he had no interest in challenging the mayor in the next election, the relationship between the men deteriorated. DiGrazia said he felt the mayor's cold shoulder keenly. He accepted a new job in Maryland.

After delaying the results of the secret investigation for more than a year, diGrazia said he began to worry that it would never get publicized. A week before his departure for Maryland, the police commissioner released the report directly to the *Boston*

Globe and the *Boston Herald American* (which was what it was then). It didn't appear coincidental that he chose a day that the mayor was out of town.

These were the peak earning years of the Mafia's Angiulo crime family, which controlled gambling and prostitution in Boston. Four years after the first *Godfather* movie was released, Boston mobsters were flush with glamour and payoff money. According to diGrazia, at least half of all the cops who policed the Combat Zone were on the take.

Known as the Special Investigation Unit (SIU) report, the 572-page secret document conservatively estimated that at least 40 percent of the adult entertainment businesses in the Combat Zone were mob owned, according to the *Boston Globe*, which did a comprehensive spread on the report. It exposed both trivial and wide-scale corruption and broke it all down in painstaking detail.

One of diGrazia's earliest actions in District One had been to end the popular practice of allowing police to make extra money working detail for the Combat Zone clubs. Critics—and there were many—complained that the policy change reduced the number of uniformed police in the Combat Zone, which led to the spike in crime. But the SIU report made clear that the detail work, bought and paid for by the nightclubs, had compromised the police.

The Boston Globe's partial text of the SIU report revealed that investigators witnessed unnamed police officers drinking for free at the Combat Zone bars and strip clubs, off duty and on. Patrolman ignored obvious liquor violations, bookie operations, prostitution, public sex acts, and drug sales. They were witnessed standing idly on the street as the street hookers stopped traffic and reached into cars to fondle men's genitals.

The police allowed mobsters to double-park throughout the Zone and waterfront. But much worse, they sabotaged their own department's investigations by tipping off organized crime in advance, the report stated. In the ultimate symbol of corruption, District One police had provided an escort for the funeral cortege of mob leader Gennaro Angiulo's mother, with one of the city's top commanders directing the traffic himself and serving as an honor guard. In fact, the SIU report charged that police raided only low-level street bookies, prostitutes, and pimps when they needed to divert attention from Mafia-run crime or when forced to put up crime numbers to appease a public outcry.

Six officers were reported to have extorted sex from Combat Zone prostitutes. In one particularly cruel expression of the city's racism, two of these officers, dubbed the "golden boys," concluded a forced sexual encounter with a Black prostitute by shoving her out of the car in the all-white and notoriously hostile Southie, blowing the horn as they sped away.

The SIU report also drew attention to the growing problem of a pickpocketing scheme that had been plaguing the Zone for several years. It described "wolf packs" of young women dressed as prostitutes and sometimes referred to as "whorelets." They lifted wallets as they fondled the men leaving the clubs in an apparent solicitation. Key details from this report about how the scheme had evolved would influence the prosecution of the Harvard football player stabbing, most notably, a new element that developed in 1974.

Male protectors showed up and started working with the young women to rob the men. The report explained that these protectors stepped in if the victims became too vocal about being robbed or struggled to get away; they would typically loudly charge that the theft victim had insulted the girls and would attack or rob the victims themselves. Investigators called it the "robber whore" scheme.

In a 2017 interview, diGrazia revealed that he knew of several cops who participated in the scheme itself by looking the other way in return for a cut of the stolen wallet. One of the most depressing revelations about the Boston Police Department in those days was how little it cost to buy a cop, diGrazia said. Clean cops, and he estimated that about half of the force in District One was clean, were deeply discouraged. The morale of the Boston force was at an all-time low.

Dumped on the city as the commissioner made his exit, the SIU report elicited both praise and criticism, with some calling it a "vindictive," parting shot at the mayor. Although the report identified twenty separate instances of police misconduct, it was designed to identify wide patterns of corruption rather than provide evidence for prosecuting dirty cops. It did not name names and led to few prosecutions. But its timing was pivotal.

So swiftly followed by the stabbings of the two Harvard football players and the death of an off-duty state trooper after a fistfight in a Zone later the very same week, diGrazia's SIU report led to citywide consensus: Crime in the Combat Zone was out of control. The city could no longer turn a blind eye—or even a nearsighted one. Something had to be done.

To say that Boston police in District One were in need of some positive press would be an understatement. At a press confer- ence the morning after the two Harvard football players were stabbed, Sergeant Frank Sullivan stood at the podium before a standing-room-only crowd of print, radio, and television reporters with tales of heroics and other good news to share.

Tommy Lincoln, whose wounds were not life threatening, would be out of the hospital by the weekend. The prognosis for Andy Puopolo was hopeful, and best of all, doctors gave full credit to police for their "fast action."

As the cameras clicked and reporters scribbled into their notebooks, Sullivan explained why he had defied a standing department order that required him to wait for an ambulance to transport a victim and instead sent Andy to the hospital in the patrol wagon. "If I had waited for an ambulance," he told the press, "the kid would have died in the street."

That quote would be repeated in early and late editions, on radio shows and television that evening and the next day. Police had gotten Andy to the emergency room in under six minutes. It was only because of this smart and speedy delivery that doctors could resuscitate his heart and repair it.

"He's a lucky kid," Dr. David Rosenthal told reporters. He was the doctor on Tuft's staff who had sewn up the hole in

Andy's heart and restored his blood pressure. "I've known very few who have come back after that."

The new police commissioner, Joseph Jordan, had been sworn in just the day before but also got credit. One of his first acts had been to beef up the police presence in the Combat Zone. This was the reason police were able to swarm the area within seconds of the fight.

Not only had police saved the Harvard student's life, they managed to arrest not one but three men from Boston for the crime: Leon Easterling, 41; Richard Allen, 36; and Edward J. Soares, 33. Although witness statements identified Leon Easterling as the only one who stabbed both football players, Sergeant Sullivan made clear that all three men were equally at fault. All three men were charged with assault and battery with a deadly weapon, as if they had all thrust the knife.

Why all three? Sullivan explained that the Harvard boys were the latest victims of the robber-whore operation that reporters in the room already knew was a chronic Combat Zone problem. It was so chronic that the *New York Times* had reported on it. It was so long-lasting that local strip clubs and even other prostitutes had complained about it, because it took cash out of men's pockets and was bad for their business.

The defendants, who would be identified as "pimps" in some of the later stories, were initially called "protectors" in this first press conference. When one reporter asked if the wallet had been stolen during a solicitation of a prostitute, Sullivan waved off that suggestion, according to the *Boston Globe* reporting. There was absolutely no prostitution involved; the crime was pure larceny. "They do it a lot, they grab you, you get all excited, and zing, your wallet is gone," he explained.

As reporters attended press conferences, the Puopolo family returned home to Jamaica Plain. Nobody could sleep, Danny recalled. The doctors had told them that the first few hours would be crucial for Andy, and they wanted to be there when he awoke. They showered, attempted to eat breakfast, and drove back to the hospital.

That morning, doctors had been optimistic in interviews with the press. The knife wounds had just missed the heart's delicate network of nerve fibers that controlled Andy's heartbeat. And while there were risks to the brain when it was deprived of oxygen, they had a "hunch" that Andy's brain was not damaged. Early signs were encouraging.

But by the time the family returned to the Solarium, doctors had revised their prognosis. Dr. Joseph Amato and Dr. Richard Cleveland, the chief surgeon, greeted the Puopolos with jarring news: Andy had experienced muscle spasms when he came out of anesthesia. This could mean that his brain had lost too much oxygen.

Because of hospital rules, they were allowed into the ICU one at a time. Danny describes Helen Puopolo as a stay-at-home mother in the Italian American tradition. She enjoyed cooking big family dinners and took pride in still making both her sons' beds and folding their laundry. He recalled how his mother refused to look at her eldest son bandaged and unconscious with tubes running in and out of him. She would wait in the Solarium until his condition improved, smoking cigarettes for the first time in her life, praying for this nightmare to be over.

Fran went into the ICU first. She was petite like her mother but with long dark hair that she wore tied back in the hospital. Like Andy, she exuded intensity and had been an exceptional student, earning her bachelor's degree at Boston State College at nineteen. She quickly became the family's liaison with the medical staff, peppering the doctors with questions each day and updating Danny and her parents.

The hospital's ICU was more hectic in daylight. Phones rang in the offices and nurses were in and out of patients' rooms. At the end of the corridor the ICU was a large sterile room housing the hospital's most advanced lifesaving equipment. Andy's was to the left, the first of about twelve beds.

Andy was in the midst of a seizure, and nurses had to administer anticonvulsion medication. When he was stabilized, his father was allowed into the ICU. Danny was the last one in. He tried to focus on the peaceful expression on Andy's face, like he was asleep. But he wasn't asleep. Bandages covered his chest, where the knife had gone in—once, twice, twisting up to his heart, but what Danny remembered most vividly was his brother's arm, where the intravenous feeding tube was attached. Knife slashes scarred the skin above and below. He filled with anger as he imagined his brother trying to fight back with only his fists.

Danny was convinced that if he'd been there with his older brother, he could have found a pipe on the ground, a block of wood, anything to hurl at the attackers. If he had been there, as he should have been, none of this would have happened.

CHAPTER FOUR
You Can't Back Down

RATHER THAN A product of Harvard privilege, as he was sometimes portrayed to be, Andy Puopolo hailed from Boston's white working class. As both a rallying point and a target, he would become its symbol.

Given the affluence of present-day Boston, it can be hard to remember just how poor cities were in the late 1960s and early 1970s. Boston was in a postwar slump, with factory jobs disappearing and shipyards and military bases closing. By 1970, Boston had lost more than 160,000 residents to the suburbs, where federal housing policies made it easy to buy homes and where the new industrial parks were sprouting along the federally financed highways.

Left behind in the city was the working class, which had to fight for whatever jobs remained. As noted by Ronald P. Formisano, author of *Boston against Busing: Race, Class, and Ethnicity in the 1960s and 1970s*, the exodus of so many middle-class whites made it feel like the Black population, historically minuscule in Boston, came flooding in, seemingly transforming entire neighborhoods like Roxbury and Mattapan, which had been mostly Irish and Jewish, overnight.

But while the rate of increase in the Black population outpaced all but two other northern cities, the starting point had been only 3 percent of the population in 1940. Black residents were still only 16 percent by 1970, making it difficult for the community to have a voice—especially in an Irish-dominated city with a city council that was elected at large. Although Blacks would become slightly more than one-fifth of the population by 1980, this increase came in the midst of one of the city's worst recessions, thus ensuring conflict over what little opportunity there was.

Shut out of jobs by a strong patronage system and ethnic control of the unions, Black people had rioted for three days in Mattapan over excessive police force in 1967. There were more riots, although on a smaller scale than other northern cities, the next year, after Martin Luther King's assassination. The racial tensions that simmered throughout the 1960s grew worse during the 1970s recession.

If Blacks wanted opportunity, they soon learned, they'd have to go to the federal and state courts. Key court decisions mandating fairness in educational resources and hiring in the city police and fire departments created deep resentment. Long before busing exposed the city's racism to the world, the lines were drawn.

What made it worse was that Boston's white working class was fighting for its own survival. In the 1970s, the city had an unusually high number of immigrants struggling to get by. A full third of the city was foreign born or, like Andy Puopolo, the offspring of at least one foreign-born parent. The Lower End of Irish South Boston, crammed with housing projects, had the highest concentration of white poverty in the entire nation.

Until Andy turned fourteen, the Puopolo family lived in a two-bedroom apartment over a leather goods store on Salem Street in the heavily Italian North End. Fran slept on a Castro Convertible in the parlor until she was sixteen. Although cramped for space, the family considered itself lucky because the apartment had its own bathroom, Danny said. In many North End buildings, multiple families had to share a single toilet in the hall and bathe in the public bathhouses.

Rents tended to be high in the neighborhoods because federal urban renewal projects of the 1950s and 1960s had wiped out the West End entirely and decimated the housing stock in other neighborhoods. The Puopolo family was better off than many others, as Helen's father owned the apartment building the family lived in. He also owned J. Gandolfo Inc. on Commercial Street, a grocery and liquor store and wholesale importer and distributor.

Andrew Sr. worked seven-day weeks loading trucks as well as making sales calls at restaurants, but he always had a job. Others couldn't find work in the depths of the 1970s recession, when unemployment reached 15 percent in some of the white working-class neighborhoods and 20 percent in Black Roxbury.

The North End, one square mile on the waterfront, is one of the oldest sections of Boston. Aging brick buildings lean into the narrow streets. Corner markets, pastry shops, cafés, and restaurants offer an old-world charm that now make it a destination for tourists. Paul Revere's house is a major attraction.

In the 1960s and early 1970s, it was a family neighborhood. Hordes of children played on the streets and alleys, neighbors watched over one another's kids, and shopkeepers lingered on sidewalks waving brooms. It was a safe and tight-knit community, and residents were deeply suspicious of outsiders. At the waterfront playground where the young Puopolo boys played baseball and pickup basketball, no outsiders were welcome, Danny said. No Irish. And, certainly, no Blacks.

This was true throughout the city, which was divided into well-defended territories, with the Italians in the North End and East Boston; the Irish in Southie, Charleston, Dorchester, Hyde Park, and West Roxbury; and the Black community in Roxbury, Mattapan, the South End, and parts of Dorchester. Ethnic divisions were hardly unique in northern cities, but the geography of Boston made it more pronounced. Boston Harbor acted like a moat, separating Charlestown and East Boston from the rest of the city and surrounding Southie on three sides. The Central Artery highway—another urban renewal project—had physically cut off the North End from the rest of the city. Neighborhoods felt like nations unto their own.

Poverty and the sheer number of young baby boomer males ratcheted up the tension between white working-class neighborhoods. Ethnic pride and neighborhood pride were deeply intertwined. Just crossing the bridge between the North End and Charlestown was considered a provocation and routinely attempted for sport. Celtics games, North End festivals, or a Southie-Eastie high school football game were all potential venues for a fistfight.

It was an era of ethnic violence and gangland wars. The Irish fought it out among themselves, with the survivor being the notorious Winter Hill gang, eventually commandeered by Southie's infamous Whitey Bulger. And they vied for power with the Italian Mafia, which had its Boston headquarters in the North End.

From their Prince Street headquarters, the Angiulo brothers, underbosses for the Patriarca crime family in Providence, Rhode Island, ran bookmaking and loan-sharking rackets. During the 1960s, they established a lucrative crime empire that at its peak collected the equivalent of more than half a million dollars per week.

In the tight-knit North End neighborhood, it was not uncommon for civilians to have at least some kind of connection to the Mafia: a neighbor, in-law, or family member who knew someone or knew someone who knew someone. Andrew Sr. had come to the North End as a five-year-old immigrant from Naples and gone to high school in Boston with Donato Angiulo, the capo of the organization. He was on greeting terms with all the Angiulo brothers, four of whom would be convicted in 1986 on various counts of racketeering in the state's longest-ever organized crime trial.

When Andrew Sr. returned from World War II as a decorated marine who had seen action in Iwo Jima, Okinawa, and Guam, he was approached by Donato Angiulo and offered his own "corner." Andrew Sr. said he respectfully declined this entrée into the crime organization. He was straitlaced and didn't even like to gamble.

He had other ideas for his family. An authoritarian father in a traditional Italian American sense, he kept a tight rein on his children, focusing the boys on sports to keep them away from those very corners where he didn't want to work. He and Helen prioritized religion, education, and family above all else. The former Marine also emphasized loyalty. He wanted the boys to look out for each other. They marched around the apartment to "The Marine's Hymn" and took "Semper Fi" to heart.

Both boys were coordinated athletes, but Andy was taller, faster, and the unrivaled star of the family from an early age. Deciding from the age of five that he would be a doctor, Andy

felt he had to excel at everything. Danny was more easygoing.
There was a surprising lack of jealousy or rivalry between the
two brothers so close in age.

In the Boston neighborhoods in the 1960s, young boys
grew up learning how to use their fists. Danny recalled that
once, when he was about ten years old, he accused another
kid of cheating during a stickball game. As he and the alleged
cheater started exchanging curses, a group of older boys gathered around them, egging them on. Danny was terrified as they
all headed to Stillman Street, where all disputes were settled.

As they walked past the variety store, Danny saw Andy
hanging outside with his friends and asked him what he should
do. Andy was firm: "You can't back down," he told his younger
brother, but he offered to follow along to make sure the fight
was fair—that none of the other older kids jumped in. Danny
knew that while he would have to fight his own battles, his
brother would always be looking out for him.

Once in another fistfight, Danny fell and landed on a rock,
he recalled. The cut was bad enough that Andy stopped the fight
and took Danny home to clean up the wound. The blood was
everywhere. Andy decided that he had to avenge his younger
brother, but he had a code about these things. He couldn't fight
Danny's opponent, because he was Danny's age. That wouldn't
be fair. But neither could he let an injustice of this magnitude
slide. So Andy went out to fight the kid's older brother, who was
actually one of his own best friends. For little boys all across
the North End looking for something to fight about, blood was
thicker than water.

In those years, most Blacks were fearful of stepping foot in
the North End, thus the young boys didn't encounter actual
racial incidents until their teens, Danny said. But once, when
they were about ten and twelve years old, the two boys attended
an outdoor dance performance that was part of the mayor's
Summerthing series, a citywide arts program designed to alle-
viate racial tension and unrest. The crowd grew ugly when a
Black dancer showed up with the troupe. The North Enders
tried to shout him off with racial insults.

At home, Danny and Andy's parents didn't allow to them to say the N-word, although they heard it plenty on the streets. Their older cousin, also named Daniel Puopolo and nicknamed Boonie, stood up to the Summerthing crowd and insisted that they shut up and let the Black dancer perform. Danny said that his cousin was harangued by his friends and neighbors for months afterward.

Nevertheless, the boys grew up proud of their North End roots. When the family moved to Jamaica Plain, which was more mixed ethnically, the boys wanted everyone to know their pride in their Italian heritage. When *The Godfather* movie came out in 1972, they pinned a movie poster to the wall of their new bedroom beside the hockey star Bobby Orr and the actor and martial arts icon Bruce Lee. They also returned frequently to the old neighborhood to visit their two sets of grandparents, play youth baseball and pickup basketball at the waterfront park, and work weekends and summers bottling olive oil at their grandfather's company, Danny said.

Loyalty to the old neighborhood was a religion. It ran deep, especially for Andy, who would never lose his distinct North End accent. Nor would he apologize for any of the neighborhood characters who occasionally showed up at Harvard parties in their matching track suits and gold jewelry. The proudest day of his football career, he once told Danny, was when he looked up and saw two rows of Harvard Stadium filled with friends and neighbors from the North End.

The strong connections the Puopolo family maintained in the North End would cause endless rumors about mob revenge for the Combat Zone stabbing. These rumors, some of them true, would prove important later on.

Both the Puopolo boys attended Boston Latin School. The oldest public high school in the nation claims five signers of the Declaration of Independence as alumni—although Ben Franklin, technically, was a dropout. Akin to an exclusive private school, Boston Latin is as much of a feeder school to

Harvard as are Phillips Academy in Andover and Trinity School in New York and was a rare source of upward mobility for the children of the city's working class. Competition has always been fierce: who gets in and who doesn't was and remains a subject of great controversy.

In the late 1960s and early 1970s, Boston Latin was both white and all male. The school didn't admit girls into the freshman class until 1972. The federal court desegregation instituted racial quotas at Boston Latin, but not until 1976, and these were overturned by a lawsuit two decades later. The school, which has seen Black enrollment decline since then, still struggles to match the diversity of the city's population. In 1973, when Andy graduated, there were only a handful of African Americans in a class of 237.

If Boston Latin was lily white in the early 1970s, it was, at least, a place where those boys from warring neighborhoods met peacefully. Boys who used to beat in each other's heads found themselves studying side by side and playing on the same sports teams. Andy forged friendships with boys from Chinatown, Charlestown, Brighton, and Dorchester that would deepen when they all went to Harvard together.

The few African Americans in the Andy's class didn't always feel welcome, recalled Greg Mazares, Andy's best friend. They tended to stick together socially, sitting together in the cafeteria apart from the white students. But the dividing line was less clear-cut in athletics, and Andy—as he would continue to do at Harvard—made a point of making friends with all his teammates.

At Boston Latin, Andy also became friendly with Greg McBride, a Black student from the South End, who was in the grade above him. The two, both gym rats, often found themselves working out together. Later, one of the coaches pitted them against each other in a footrace. Greg, who was Boston Latin's track star, was expected to win and did, but Andy made it a close contest, and the two developed a mutual respect.

Greg said he often wondered if Andy, who weighed less than a hundred and forty pounds in high school, felt underestimated because of his size, which made him inclined not to underestimate or prejudge anyone else. But Danny didn't believe it was Andy's size. He said when they grew up, the Irish in Boston looked down on the North End Italians, and Andy had a chip on his shoulder about being called a "Guinea." It made him relate to anyone he saw as an underdog.

At Harvard, Andy made close friends with several Black teammates and bunked with them in the preseason football camp. He also befriended and championed the sole Black player on the baseball team who struggled with a coach always trying to cut him. Jim "Catfish" Hunter said that Andy's support for him irritated the coach and may have cost Andy his own chances on the baseball team in their sophomore year. "Pound for pound, he was the best friend I had at Harvard College," Hunter said.

Andy was intense about everything, Academically, he would worry excessively about a test result everyone knew was going to be an A, Mazares recalled. In sports, he was a three-season athlete who could be a little over the top in workouts, devising a nine-mile jogging course up and down Boston Latin School halls and stairways and around the perimeter to "warm up" before basketball games.

In the heat of battle, Andy had a temper and argued with the refs. Even as a sports fan, he did not accept defeat graciously. Both his younger brother and father recalled how when listening to a game, he would chuck the radio across the room if his team—the Celtics and Red Sox—lost.

But the trait most often mentioned by friends from both Boston Latin and Harvard was loyalty—to his family first, his friends, and his team. His downfall was fearlessness combined with an overdeveloped sense of what was right and wrong. If he perceived an injustice, he didn't hesitate to confront someone— and he never backed down, said Kevin McCluskey, one of his close friends. It came as no surprise to anyone that he jumped into the battle that night in the Combat Zone and fought for his teammate.

*

The tiny number of Black students admitted to Boston Latin in the early 1970s meant there was little overt racial conflict inside the school. But there was plenty of racial tension sizzling outside the door.

More than a decade before the city erupted into conflict over busing, Black parent activists and civil rights leaders had been fighting the city over its segregated schools. As early as 1961, the National Association for the Advancement of Colored People (NAACP) complained to the Boston School Committee, then an elected board that ran public education in the city, about the unfair distribution of resources. Black schools were overcrowded and underfunded, with inferior textbooks, supplies, and physical facilities. The state passed the 1965 Racial Imbalance Act, which attempted to create more equity in the schools, but the School Committee fought the law and resisted any attempt to acknowledge segregation or mollify protestors.

Having awarded jobs in the school system as political patronage for decades, the Boston School Committee also turned a deaf ear to demands for more Black teachers. At Boston English, an all-male school that was more than 50 percent Black, only three of seventy-seven faculty members were Black. Students held protests in 1968 and 1970 and occupied the assembly hall in 1971 over disciplinary actions taken against a Black student. The school of twelve hundred students shut down for five days because of the ensuing violence.

Black students' grievances spread over the next month, and there were Black student boycotts in several city high schools, even where Blacks were a minority. Reports of Black students beating whites during these boycotts—some true, others invented—helped fuel growing white resentment.

Boston Latin was elite. The top of the academic heap. The students were hated by all the other public high schools, white or Black, but tension with Boston English, directly across the street, was enough of a constant that the schools staggered their dismissal times: Boston Latin students were released forty-five minutes earlier than Boston English to avoid fistfights on the way home.

Frustrated by the city, Black activists had taken their grievances to federal court, and as the legal battles for desegregation intensified in the early 1970s, the racial tension increased. By 1973, Andy's senior year, one basketball game at Tobin Gym grew especially ugly.

Danny recalled how the gym, one of the largest in the city, was packed with the home crowd of more than a hundred, almost entirely Black. Boston English High School boys, their girlfriends, neighbors, and a handful of parents sat shoulder to shoulder on the wooden bleachers, fifteen rows deep. Others huddled by the scoring table and milled around the locker room doors.

On the visitors' side, only about eight spectators had come to root for Boston Latin, which was usual for a game in Roxbury, Danny said. He went to all his brother's game and sat right behind the Boston Latin bench, talking to an Italian friend he knew from Eastie, a talented starting guard who stood only five feet seven.

The Boston English players, all Black, had a winning team record and a serious height advantage over Boston Latin. They were expected to win, but Boston Latin made it a tight game with speed and hustle. Everyone in the stands on both sides was shouting for their team and swearing at the refs. In the last minute of the game, Boston Latin stole the ball, scored, and won by a basket. Danny recalled that he and the Eastie starting guard rose to their feet clapping and shouting. The pure elation of victory lasted for about a minute. Boston English fans began to stamp their feet, thumping on the wooden bleachers. The thumping grew louder and louder. Rhythmic. "Latin Pussies!" It was a common refrain.

This was nothing new, Danny said. Winning in anyone else's gym, whether it was Roxbury or Southie or Charlestown, could lead to a fight. The Eastie guard pulled out a straight edge razor that he kept in his gym bag for protection and offered it to Danny, warning him he'd never get home alive otherwise.

Just then, Andy, coming off the court, swooped down on them, waving away the razor blade and grabbing Danny by the neck. He insisted that Danny would be coming home with him and led his brother swiftly through the angry crowd, as they followed the Eastie guard toward the visitors' locker room.

Danny recalled that about five Black kids stood blocking the door. As the Eastie guard tried to pass by them, a six-foot Black kid jumped him. Andy immediately launched himself at the Black kid, landing punches.

Coaches from both teams ran over to break up the fight. The Boston Latin coaches ordered the team players to go below to the locker room and take time as they showered so things could cool down.

About twenty minutes later, when the Boston Latin team emerged from the locker room dressed in street clothes, the boys headed for the door. The first teammate to reach it pulled the door halfway open and jumped back. A brick thudded into the base of the door, followed by a shatter of bottles hitting cement.

The coaches locked the door and called the police. Danny estimated that more than sixty Black youths—male and female—stood outside the gym and on both sides of the street shouting threats at Boston Latin. Danny said he didn't want to think about what would have happened if he had tried to get home on his own, armed with only the razor blade. He couldn't stop thinking about the fearlessness with which Andy had thrown himself into the fight. Danny both admired his brother's heroics and worried about it.

The cops responded right away, but it took more than an hour for them to disperse the crowd, Danny said. Barricaded inside, the Latin boys had to wait for the police to decide it was safe enough to leave the building and go home. In the scheme of the racial violence in public schools that lay ahead, this was a mere warm-up.

CHAPTER FIVE
The Sleaze Factor

AT THE TIME, the advice for family members of coma patients was to try to stimulate their brains back to activity. Danny recalls how by day, he and Fran took turns sitting by Andy's side in the ICU, talking to him around the clock. In the evenings, their father, who had to return to work, joined them. Helen Puopolo arrived at the hospital every morning and stayed late, but she sat in the Solarium, chain-smoking, or she went to the chapel at St. James Church nearby to get on her knees to pray.

Music was supposed to tap a different part of the brain than language, Danny had heard, so he tried it as a way to get through to his brother. He recorded singles from all of Andy's favorite groups: the Stylistics, Earth, Wind & Fire, Tavares, the Temptations, the Isley Brothers, and the Spinners. He brought the cassette deck from their bedroom to the ICU and installed it next to Andy's bed. He watched his brother's face intently, often desperately, for some sort of recognition as the music played softly day and night. There was no change. No flicker.

Family, friends, teammates, and Harvard faculty squeezed onto the sofa and hard-backed chairs in the Solarium. It was always crowded, Danny said. The lounge smelled of coffee and cigarettes in the mornings and of pizza boxes at night. It became something of a scene. Priests from the Greek Orthodox Church joined the pastor of nearby St. James in the Solarium to pray for Andy. Boston's Father Edward McDonough, "the healing priest," who had a national reputation for bringing the sick out of comas, also came to pray.

Very early, the doctors could see that it was hopeless. They tried to take Andy off a respirator for thirty seconds at a time, but he couldn't breathe on his own. His eyelids didn't blink when touched; he had no reaction when doctors stuck him with a pin or put ice water in his ear.

One week after the stabbing, doctors gave Andy a brain-wave test, using an electroencephalograph (EEG) machine. It recorded a flat line: cerebral silence. The family refused to accept the test as conclusive, but the Suffolk County prosecutor's office did. The prosecutor began to prepare for a murder indictment against the three defendants, upping the charges from assault with intent to commit murder. Thomas J. Mundy Jr. went to court trying to double the bail amount, quoting the doctors as saying, "The chances of a neurological recovery are virtually nonexistent."

Even after further tests confirmed Andy had no brain activity, Andrew Sr. was determined that their prayers would not be defeated: "I will never give up as long as there is an ounce of breath in his body. If people keep on praying, their prayers and our prayers will bring him back somehow. God will answer our prayers," he told the *Boston Globe*. He had good reason to believe that people from all over the world *were* praying for Andy. Letters poured in from as far away as Australia and Italy. Complete strangers from all over Boston sent cards with dollar bills inside them, even though no money had been requested.

City politicians began to drop by the Solarium. Senator Ted Kennedy sent a poem and a personal letter of support. From Rome, the pope blessed a medal that was pinned to Andy's pillowcase. Uninvited, two psychics, a husband and wife team, showed up in the Solarium and predicted a recovery.

But not everyone in the city rooted for the Harvard boy.

Locally, the media covered every change in Andy's condition, every special service held to pray for him, every tribute. When the Boston Latin football team dedicated its Thanksgiving victory to Andy and delivered the game ball to the hospital, it made the sports page.

But the real subject was the Combat Zone. The day after the stabbing, Ray Flynn, the state representative from South Boston who would become the next mayor of Boston and, later, an ambassador to Rome, launched a grassroots campaign to pressure the city to "purge" the Combat Zone of crime. Interviewed three decades later, Flynn said he was motivated by childhood memories of the Lower Washington neighborhood in the days when the theaters provided vaudeville and family entertainment. He'd been opposed to the adult entertainment zoning from the start.

Flynn had been a star college basketball player, then briefly in the pros, and he'd spent time working with youth in various parts of the city. He'd coached Andy personally and said that he couldn't get the image of the young boy, the aspiring athlete, out of his head. He stood on the corner of Boylston for three days collecting signatures of people who were fed up with Combat Zone crime. He recalled being threatened by the local thugs and calling for police protection. Flynn also circulated a petition to clergy and to legislative, business, and labor leaders demanding action in the Zone and personally dropped it on Mayor White's desk.

Later, Cardinal Medeiros, a powerful man in an overwhelmingly Catholic city, added his voice to an ever wider, louder, and reverberating demand to clean up the Zone. The *Boston Globe*, which had previously supported the concept of an authorized adult entertainment district, now questioned its implementation. The editorial demanded the mayor provide better police protection against the "notorious mode of robbery" that had led to the Puopolo stabbing or face "the need to close every bar, theater and bookstore in the Zone."

The new police commissioner, Joseph Jordan, assigned a vice control unit to "saturation" duty in the Zone. When an off-duty state trooper, a father of seven, died of cardiac arrest after a fight in a Zone variety store later that same week, police completely blanketed the red-light district. There were cops "every ten feet," many working fourteen- to sixteen-hour shifts. The Zone was being guarded, as one cop told the *Boston Globe*, "like the Berlin wall."

The furor and outrage did not abate. By the end of the month, the new police commissioner and the Suffolk County District Attorney's office held a press conference to officially declare the

Combat Zone experiment a failure. Law enforcement had concluded what was now becoming crystal clear to everyone: the clustering of adult entertainment together in a few downtown blocks was a huge mistake. The illusion of license led to an increase in all kinds of crime from prostitution to muggings to murder.

National television networks sent their cameras to Boston to focus on the failure of the Combat Zone as a strategy of "containment" and the true societal costs of pornography. Along with New York and Detroit, ABC included Boston in an April 1977 special entitled "Sex for Sale, the Urban Battleground."

In addition to the police crackdown on prostitution and other crime in the Zone, the Suffolk County District Attorney's office and city licensing boards teamed up, vowing to aggressively prosecute liquor violations and ferret out mob ownership of the strip clubs. The assistant district attorney who unveiled the plan also proposed banning nude dancing entirely to lessen the allure of the Combat Zone and make it "dull and boring."

The police saturation, as well as nonstop media attention, brought business in the Combat Zone to a screaming halt. The owners of strip clubs, theaters, and bookstores gathered forces to fight back. Their advocacy group, created years before to support the city's zoning change and cleverly named "BAD," for the Boston Adult District, was represented by a twenty-seven-year-old spokeswoman who had a knack for generating headlines.

Debra Beckerman, a former night club dancer who would eventually return to the stage, was, not surprisingly, an attractive brunette who knew how to command the spotlight. She'd had public relations experience and was adept at firing up publicity both locally and nationally. She provided well-spoken strippers for press interviews and talk show appearances and defended the Combat Zone as "a haven of sorts for the socially dispossessed." Beckerman launched an entirely new city investigation by alleging that an attorney for one of the state agencies owned a blind interest in one of the clubs and received preferential treatment by law enforcement. It turned out to be true.

Beckerman charged that Boston patrolmen were too "uptight" about sex to adequately police the Zone and that their disdain of

"Sodom and Gomorrah" made them ineffective. Then she went further. Even though Andy wasn't dead yet and his family was still praying for a miracle, she specifically blamed the Boston police for his "murder" because they had ignored club owners when they had complained about street crime in late summer.

Cleared out of their territory, prostitutes swarmed into upscale Back Bay, where the residents immediately complained. In little more than a month, police arrested more than 150 prostitutes. They responded by holding a "cake-bake" sale to raise money for their two-year-old union, Prostitutes Union of Massachusetts (PUMA), which wanted to legalize prostitution in the state and would succeed in getting the issue before the state legislature the following spring. Prostitutes began granting interviews using first-name aliases, all of which made for sympathetic and lively news stories.

Prostitutes said that they, too, were furious about what cops called the "robber whore" or "whorelet" scheme but what they called "robber-baron" schemes. They wanted the public to understand the distinction between "honest" prostitution and the "rip off variety." The local president of the National Organization of Women (NOW) came to the defense of the "legitimate" prostitutes, saying that were merely trying to survive in a male-dominated society that didn't accept responsibility for its own violence, cruelty, or sexuality.

A woman who identified herself as a retired prostitute named Virginia told the *Boston Globe*, "Robbery, assault and killing are crimes. Providing pleasure at reasonable costs shouldn't be. The market is there, it wants us." Lois, another retired prostitute featured in the *Globe* story, complained that politicians were over-reacting to the stabbing. She said in print what many people in the city were thinking: "If it had been anyone else that was stabbed the whole incident would have been overlooked by the media and the police."

Lois had a point. Although the Police District One report and the death of the off-duty state trooper also played a role in the crackdown, the sheer volume of the headlines reinforced the suspicion that the city and the nation were outraged about crime in the Combat Zone chiefly *because* the two victims were white boys from Harvard.

It took about a week after the Combat Zone stabbing for the story to be defined in racial terms. In a letter to the editor in the *Boston Globe*, Gordon Dalby from Newton condemned "our white arrogance and naïveté." He wrote, "Those who go into the Black community and treat the human beings there as objects of carnal appetite simply have no right to become indignant when one discovers his wallet stolen. And when the white boys reared in clean, quiet suburbs which box in that ghetto then chase after prostitutes into dark city streets, that's like the king's red coats charging into the forest after Yankee snipers."

Dalby was from one of the affluent liberal suburbs that the Boston working-class neighborhoods resented for its liberal attitudes and condescension. The Combat Zone wasn't actually a "Black community" but a commercial district that the Special Investigation Unit report had clarified was mob owned and operated. In fact, the Combat Zone's sleaze factor insured that it was condemned equally on both sides of the racial divide.

In the fall of 1976, the Black community did not rally around Leon Easterling, Richard Allen, or Edward Soares, nor did it argue that these men were innocent men falsely accused. Identified in the press as protectors for the women who stole the wallet, the men were portrayed as Combat Zone street hustlers. But neither was there much sympathy for the Ivy League victim. Both the *Globe* and the *Herald* had inaccurately reported that Andy had been among the football players who chased the prostitute down Boylston Street trying to get the wallet back. This led many to assume he'd been soliciting sex. The prevailing opinion was that the Harvard boy got what he deserved.

Robert, a Black man who retired after thirty years of working part-time jobs in the Combat Zone and did not want to identified with his last name, expressed what he said was a commonly held view: People who worked the Zone for a living did it because they had to; it was one of the few places where Blacks could get a job in Boston and make decent money with a little hustle. Harvard football players lived in a world of opportunity and could go anywhere they pleased. They had come to the Combat Zone for all the wrong reasons. "Those boys went there looking for one thing—trouble," he said.

Andy's Boston Latin School friend Greg McBride heard a similar reaction in his South End neighborhood. There was little to no sympathy in the Black community for the victims. "I had to explain to a lot of people, over and over, that Andy wasn't there soliciting anyone for sex, that he was there only because it was a team end-of-the-year ritual."

But that explanation didn't necessarily help. Eyebrows raised over an Ivy League ritual stupid enough to involve a trip to the crime-ridden Combat Zone. "And people blamed Andy because he was a Harvard student. They figured that meant that he thought he was better than everyone else," McBride said. "I had to explain that Andy wasn't anything like that. He was the least person like that. I kept saying this isn't a Black-and-white issue; it's a human issue."

But in Boston in 1976, nearly every issue was about race.

It was the third year of court-ordered busing, and the city was well on its way to earning the racist reputation that it would never shake.

Because the all-white Boston School Committee was considered a springboard for higher political office, its members grandstanded and won elections by fanning racial fury. The School Committee had spent nearly a decade refusing to acknowledge that the public schools were segregated and made only the most-feeble attempts to address the inequities between white and Black schools.

In the spring of 1974, U.S. District Court Judge W. Arthur Garrity Jr., a small, wiry man with large glasses and great conviction, ruled. He'd found clear patterns of segregation in the School Committee's policies, and he imposed busing as the solution. The plan, which began with reshuffling

FIGURE 3. Louise Day Hicks at antibusing rally at Thomas Park, South Boston, in 1975. Photograph by Spencer Grant.

nineteen thousand students between eighty schools, felt punitive. In some instances, Black students were shipped from an underperforming Black school to an even worse performing white one.

The first stage of the plan called for busing students between almost entirely Black Roxbury and white Southie, the Irish neighborhood known as the most hostile to Blacks. It didn't go well. When the first buses full of Black students rolled into South Boston High School in September 1974, they were met with angry whites with signs that read "N———Go Home."

At the end of the day, as the buses tried to take the Black students home, angry whites awaited on Day Boulevard. They launched beer bottles, soda cans, and rocks that shattered the bus windows and injured nine of the passengers. Mayor Kevin White pronounced the first day of busing "a success" because the violence had only been in Southie.

He was a little optimistic. The violence only got worse, much worse. Fights broke out between Black and white students in cafeterias in Southie and Hyde Park. Racial brawls initiated by Blacks at Boston English High School spilled into the streets and housing projects and injured thirty-eight by the end of one day.

Fifty Black students at Technical High School smashed more than a dozen windshields and set fire to a car that turned out to belong to a Black teacher.

Apparently encouraged by antibusing School Committee and City Council members, white students boycotted classes. The powerful antibusing group Restore Our Alienated Rights (ROAR) was led by Louise Day Hicks, a politician whose career had taken her from the School Committee during the sixties to the Boston City Council, to the U.S. Congress, and back to the Boston City Council.

Thousands of protesting parents marched through the South Boston streets to the Bunker Hill Monument in Charlestown, through the Boston Common, and at Government Center. Antibusing motorcades involving hundreds of cars drove out of the city to the private homes of anyone deemed somehow responsible: Governor-elect Michael Dukakis, who lived in Brookline; the president of the *Boston Globe* in South Natick; and Judge Garrity in Wellesley.

Pro-busing forces countered with rallies of their own. An organization called Assembly for Justice charged that Louise Day Hicks was responsible for "the blood of every Black child shed after being hit by a rock or broken glass," the *Bay State Banner* reported. A National March against Racism drew twenty thousand to the Boston Common and tandem rallies in cities including Seattle, San Francisco, Pasadena, and Portland, Oregon.

If busing failed utterly to integrate the races, it united the white working-class neighborhoods. They were united in resentment of the Blacks whose complaints had caused these problems; their fury at Judge Garrity, who was burned in effigy; and their hatred of rich liberal elites, inside Boston and out, who were trying to solve the city's social problems on the backs of working-class kids.

A theme that runs through historian Ronald P. Formisano's 1991 book, *Boston against Busing*, is that class was a major and often overlooked factor in Boston's reaction to busing. Boston's white working-class neighborhoods especially despised the liberals in Boston's rich white suburbs, particularly Brookline,

Newton, and Wellesley, convinced that they looked down on them as racists.

.Judge Garrity had earlier ruled against a metropolitan solution that would have expanded the breadth of desegregation beyond the city where poverty was concentrated to include these highbrow towns with their exclusive school systems. These suburbs patted themselves on the back for an entirely voluntary Metropolitan Council for Educational Opportunity (METCO) program, which didn't involve sending their children out of town but invited a small number of Black children in—an invitation not extended to Boston's poor white children. "If the suburbs are honestly interested in solving the problems of the Negro," Louise Day Hicks once asked, "why don't they build subsidized housing for them?"

In the poorest of Boston's white suburbs, Southie, the violence was the most extreme. At pivotal moments, helicopters flew overhead and hundreds of Boston police officers in riot gear stood guard over the high school. Some three hundred state troopers and one hundred Metropolitan District police were called. The U.S. Army and Air National Guard were activated. The neighborhood looked like an armed camp.

One morning in mid-December 1974, when state police were diverted to an uprising at the prison, a fight erupted. Outside the high school library on the second floor, a Black student stabbed a white boy, who collapsed and was rushed to the hospital. As the boy underwent emergency surgery for a punctured lung and liver, the news pulsed through the neighborhood. Within minutes, a crowd began to gather around the school. It soon grew to two thousand angry whites shouting racial epitaphs and an increasingly threatening chant of "Here we go, Southie, here we go!"

As the *Boston Globe* reported it, Black students huddled inside with teachers and administrators in fear of their lives. Distraught Black parents who learned of the siege waited anxiously in a nearby parking lot, protected by police. Tactical and mounted police forces were called in. A state helicopter flew overhead. Southie politicians and antibusing leaders were called to try to disperse the angry white mob.

Louise Day Hicks was highly respected by young and old in Southie for leading the decade-long battle against desegregation. A stout, well-coiffed former lawyer who dressed like a demure housewife, she was known as the Iron Maiden. She took the bullhorn and addressed the crowd, pleading with them to go home. They shouted her down with "Shut up, Louise!"

It took a dozen police units and a decoy plan involving mounted and motorcycle police to divert the crowd in front of the high school while the 125 Black students and teachers raced out the back door and into other buses. Furious that they'd been outsmarted, rioters smashed windows and overturned police cruisers, including the police commissioner's car. Fourteen civilians and eleven police officers were taken to the hospital.

City officials closed South Boston High School and debated making it permanent. As the judge and city officials wrestled over plans for the second phase of busing, the FBI and local police investigated a tip about an alleged antibusing plot to blow up five city bridges—a plot that was taken seriously by law enforcement but ultimately never confirmed by hard evidence.

The violence continued throughout the year, in the schools, around MBTA stations, and in housing projects. Each stoning, beating, knifing, or Molotov cocktail thrown by one racial group provoked a retaliation. The protesters complained vehemently that media coverage, particularly by the *Boston Globe*, focused on white assaults and underreported Black violence. It heightened the siege mentality of the white working-class neighborhoods, which harbored bitter resentment.

Fury only increased in the fall of 1975, in part because of the many absurdities of the second phase of the plan. According to Jim Vrabel's *A People's History of the New Boston*, these plans included allowing children on the odd-numbered side of a street to stay in their local schools while busing away those in even-numbered houses; busing siblings, even twins, to completely different schools; and sometimes busing students from racially diverse neighborhood schools to schools that weren't diverse.

The second phase of the busing plan now included Charlestown, another poor and insular Irish neighborhood, and swiftly, a new round of protests and violence erupted. That spring, a protest by Charlestown high school students at City Hall Plaza would manage to capture the entire world's attention.

Theodore Landsmark, a young Black lawyer in a business suit, was on his way to a business meeting in City Hall. He was twenty-nine years old, a Yale grad, with degrees in both law and architecture. He had had nothing to do with busing or education or the raging protests but happened to cross the plaza at exactly the wrong moment.

Two hundred and seventy white teenagers from Charlestown and South Boston High Schools had just left a meeting with Louise Day Hicks, now the City Council president. After a brief meeting, they wanted to appeal to Judge Garrity in person. They marched through City Hall Plaza headed for the federal court house, carrying placards, bicentennial banners, and American flags. All worked up after some heckling by a group that included Black counterprotesters, they spotted Landsmark just entering the plaza.

One student hit Landsmark from behind and knocked off his glasses. Another knocked him to the ground. While the businessman was down, other youths started kicking him in the ribs. He tried to struggle to his feet, once, twice. Just as he got up and attempted to wrestle off one of his accosters, another youth, a fifteen-year-old Charlestown boy, carrying the flag, turned it into a spear and came at him.

A *Herald* photographer, Stanley Forman, snapped the photo, which caught the white youth in motion as he was apparently about to impale a Black man in a business suit with the American flag. Shot on April 5, 1976, the photo captured the city's racism in a bicentennial year, illustrating just how little progress racial relations had made since the founding of the country. Entitled *The Soiling of Old Glory*, the photo ran on front pages across the country and eventually won a Pulitzer prize.

Landsmark broke free of the mob and found the police, who transported him to the hospital. The flagstaff, which appeared to be aimed directly at his heart in the photo but was not, glanced off his face instead. He suffered a broken nose and multiple face and head cuts. Appearing in in press conferences in bandages, Landsmark blamed the city politicians, who kept "stirring the pot of racism," not the kids themselves or their communities. Appearing calm and intelligent, he drove home the message that no Black, no matter how well educated, well dressed, or removed from violence, was safe in Boston.

Retaliation came a few weeks later. Like Landsmark, Richard Poleet, a thirty-five-year-old white auto mechanic, had nothing to do with busing or education or the raging protests. He was driving home to Jamaica Plain when a rock went through his windshield at a traffic light in Roxbury, forcing him to collide with another car. A group of about fifteen Black teenagers pulled him out of his car, went through his pockets, and beat his head with rocks. Poleet, a father of four, slipped into a coma and never regained consciousness. The *Boston Globe* reported "more than a dozen stonings" that night, most in Mattapan and "all involving gangs of black youths hurling stones at white motorists and pedestrians."

After the mayor, the governor, the police commissioner, and the head of the National Association for the Advancement of Colored People deplored the violence, pro- and antibusing leaders immediately blamed each other for inciting it. Representative Ray Flynn and other antibusing leaders lamented that the assault wouldn't get as much media attention as the Landsmark attack.

A week after the Combat Zone stabbing, the *Herald* published a story reminding its readership of that racial attack by comparing the deteriorating medical condition of the two coma victims. Andy Puopolo and Richard Poleet were both clinging "desperately' to life support. "Were it not for the mechanical assists that force vital fluids and air into them, they would surely die," the *Herald*'s medical editor wrote.

The comparison of the two cases, which would be made repeatedly as both came to trial, unified the two as white victims of Black assailants. This helped make Andy, who also had nothing to do with busing, education, or the raging protests, a symbol of white working-class Boston and the city's racial turmoil.

CHAPTER SIX
Loyalty and Revenge

THE DOCTORS AT Tufts New England had known from the first seizure that Andy's brain had gone too long without oxygen in those precious minutes between the stabbing and the emergency room. But when they agreed to repeat the tests, not once but twice more, they were not simply humoring the family. It had only been six months since the New Jersey Supreme Court's precedent-setting decision to allow the parents of Karen Ann Quinlan, who was in a "persistent vegetative state," to disconnect her from a respirator. Few hospitals had official policies or a committee process for "pulling the plug."

In the Puopolo case, the doctors had to be "extra careful" because of the pending criminal charges, Dr. Theodore Munsat, the hospital's neurologist in chief, explained to the *Boston Globe*. Just two years earlier, Boston City Hospital had run into legal trouble after removing a Medford man from life support. The defense attorney had argued, albeit unsuccessfully, that physicians were responsible for the man's death, not the defendant who had actually crushed the man's skull with a baseball bat.

As expected, subsequent brain scans on Andy showed a flat line—no activity. At first, Andy had appeared peaceful in repose but as the weeks passed, his body deteriorated rapidly, Danny recalled. His face began to swell. Conjunctivas infected his eyes. He contracted pneumonia and went into cardiac arrest—from which doctors resuscitated him. In early December, his kidneys began to fail, and doctors approached the family about taking him off life support.

"Not as long as there is an ounce of breath in his body," Andrew Sr. told the *Boston Globe* reporter. The miracle that had saved Andy from death in the emergency room and restarted his heart had made the family believe in miracles. They would pray harder.

But by mid-December, the decision was taken out of the Puopolos' hands. Andy's breath grew labored, even on a respirator. Doctors could see he was going fast, and they called the family to come in. In the artificial twilight of the ICU, they gathered at his bedside to say their goodbyes. Andy died shortly before four in the morning on December 17, still on life support.

His father was the last to leave Andy's bedside. For the rest of his life, he said, he would remember a silly argument he'd had with his son only a couple of months earlier. Andy had been getting ready to go to the photographer to get a headshot to attach to his medical school applications and came out of his bedroom wearing a polo shirt and slacks. Worse, he still had the horseshoe-shaped moustache that he'd grown over the summer that made him look like he was about to ride off with a motorcycle gang.

Andrew Sr. recalled ordering his son to go back to his room to put on a suit. Andy, who never paid attention to his clothes and also hated being told what to do, insisted the photo wasn't important, any decent medical school would accept or reject him based on his accomplishments, not on how he looked. After a heated argument, he refused to put on the suit, but he'd trimmed off the moustache.

As a tribute to his son, Andrew Sr. grew a moustache, he said, even though he had never wanted one. At his son's deathbed, he vowed he would never shave it off—a vow he kept. He recalled kissing Andy one last time and walking out to make the arrangements. As he headed to the telephone booth in the lobby to call the funeral home to pick up his son's body, Dr. Amato was waiting for him outside the elevators.

Dr. Amato was a young man in his early thirties who had shown great compassion for the family and would remain friendly with them for decades after the tragedy. On the night of Andy's death, he was there to offer condolences, but he also stopped Andrew Sr. from calling the funeral home. He told Andrew Sr. that it would have to wait until after the medical examiner established the cause of death.

Up all night and exhausted, Andrew Sr. wasn't sure he was understanding correctly. To him the cause seemed apparent: his son had been stabbed to death.

Dr. Amato gently explained that the state would have to do an autopsy. Andrew Sr.'s reaction was visceral. The way he saw it, his son was finally at peace after a brutal knifing, two surgeries, and thirty-one days attached to machines. He didn't want anyone else cutting up his son.

Dr. Amato told Andrew Sr. that neither of them had a say in it anymore. Years later, Andrew Sr. recalled the doctor's exact words: *your son's body is the property of the commonwealth now.*

The next day, a reporter tracked down Andrew Sr. at the funeral home, where he was delivering a blue suit that Andy would eventually be buried in. The reporter asked him if he wanted revenge against the assailants.

Caught at what had to be one of the worst moments in a parent's life, Andrew Sr. said that he didn't care about the police investigation or about revenge. "He was like a flower cut down," he said of his son. "We prayed and prayed that he would pull through. That's all I could think of for thirty-one days. Now the ordeal is over, but our prayers are just beginning." He continued, "Revenge is not going to bring Andy back or wipe the pain from my wife's face. We'll never be the same."

But if Andrew Sr. wasn't thinking about revenge at this moment, others were.

Andy had been the pride of his family, but he had also been the pride of the North End. His older cousin Daniel (Boonie), the same one who had stood up for the Black performer at Summerthing, told Harold Banks of the *Herald*, "To a lot of kids in the North End, he's a symbol. After all, not many kids who played Little League baseball for Bova's Bakery go on to Harvard."

The Italian community had coalesced around this tragedy for both good and ill. Decades later, the family still talked about the kindnesses. A North End family that owned Cuddemi Clothing in Chestnut Hill donated the blue suit that Andrew Sr. dropped off at the funeral home. Another North End businessman, Arthur Castraberti, owner of the Saugus restaurant

Prince Pizzeria, which could seat seven hundred, insisted on hosting the mercy meal following the funeral and refused to accept any payment.

While the thirst for revenge after a murder is a common human reaction the world over, the Italian "vendetta," which requires family members to avenge the death of a loved one, had recently gained new currency in popular culture. American crime films tended to glorify revenge in general, but *The Godfather* movie, released just four years earlier, had made Michael Corleone's duty to destroy his father's assassins a noble calling.

Many in the North End spoke openly of how the New England Mafia would certainly exact revenge for the fallen hero. Neighbors flagged Danny down when they saw him on the sidewalk or sent messages through one of his cousins to tell him his brother would be avenged. It was impossible that there would be no retribution, they insisted. This insult to the North End could not stand.

Danny said he believed it. He remembered one time when he and Andy had come to the North End park to play basketball; one of their friends from the neighborhood became so upset about Andy's being cut from the Harvard baseball team that he threatened to find the coach and "teach him a lesson." The friend already had a criminal record, and Andy was alarmed enough to stop the game and make the friend promise that he'd leave the coach alone. Afterward, Andy and Danny had joked about how you had to be careful about North End loyalty.

Aside from neighborhood pride in their Italian Ivy League football hero, the mob had a more monetary motive for revenge, everyone seemed to agree. The mob owned many of the adult entertainment businesses in the Combat Zone, and they had all taken a serious financial hit because of the stabbing. In fact, the local adult entertainment trade group, BAD, estimated that business in the strip clubs was off 30 percent since the stabbing.

The heat was on. A citywide "summit" between law enforcement and licensing agents was launched. Boston was in the midst of conducting special investigations into the straw ownership of clubs. Who knew where it was all going to end? Or what other damaging information would come up during the trial.

The neighborhood consensus was that the Angiulo brothers would certainly have Easterling, Soares, and Allen whacked in the Charles Street jail, where they were being held. The rumors were so pervasive that the day after Andy died, the radio station WEEI's investigative team reported uncovering "an underworld plot to kill the men." An Associated Press reporter asked the master of the Charles Street Jail about the safety of the three suspects and was assured that they were "secure." There was no need for additional protections because of Puopolo's death.

Rumors that the Mafia was going to kill the three defendants had even rippled into nearby towns, such as Brookline, where police heard it. Some speculated that the two prostitutes, who weren't arrested or charged, would be whacked on the street. Susan Wornick, the former Boston television newscaster who covered the Puopolo story for WBZ radio at the time, recalled that speculation about Mafia retaliation was so widespread that "no one thought there was going to be a trial."

She said admiration for the fallen football star was strong throughout the city. She added that while victims of a tragedy are often idolized at the outset, a more mixed picture eventually emerges, but not with Andy Puopolo. "Any reporter who tried to find anything negative on Andrew couldn't. Everyone said the same thing: Andy was a just a really great guy."

Andy's wake was packed. The line to get inside the John Cincotti and Sons Funeral Home wound around the corner and down Salem Street—a thoroughfare of butcher shops, vegetable markets, and cafes—with a three-hour wait to get inside the door. It wasn't just the North End, Harvard, and Boston Latin communities but also complete strangers from all parts of the city who had been following the story from newspaper and television reports.

When Andy was still in a coma, an African American woman believed to be a sister of Easterling and Allen came to the hospital with a box of Danish pastries but was shooed away by the doctors, who thought contact between the families would be inappropriate. Now, two African American women, also believed to be relatives of the defendants, walked into Cincotti's.

Danny recalled that the chatter of the funeral parlor grew dead silent as the two women slowly made their way up the aisle and knelt at the coffin to pay their respects. They did not approach family members.

Decades later Danny would say he had respect for those two Black women, who, in the city's worst year for racial violence, had the courage to come into the hostile Italian North End and into that funeral parlor. But at the time, he was furious. "It felt like an invasion—like what were they doing there?"

The funeral was held at St. Leonard's, a late nineteenth-century Romanesque Catholic church that was built to serve a one-time parish of twenty thousand Italian immigrants. The church held four hundred and was jammed, the *Herald* reported. People clogged the aisles and the entry, spilled out into the sidewalks and streets, stopping traffic.

Outside, mourners who couldn't get in made the sign of the cross as the coffin was wheeled back into the hearse. A procession of more than one hundred cars traveled out of the city to Holy Cross Cemetery in Malden, where Andy would be buried next to his two grandfathers. Danny estimated the crowd at more than one thousand.

Malcolm DeCamp, one of the students who had been in the van the night of the stabbing, was one of many Harvard students who delayed going home so they could attend the funeral. He was from rural Kentucky and had no familiarity with an urban ethnic community. He said he expected the funeral to be swamped with the Harvard students, professors, football coaches, and deans who filled the pews, but he hadn't anticipated the entire neighborhood—or what looked like the entire city—waiting outside the church during the service. He saw the crush of people still outside the church and lining the sidewalks, many of them crying, and was overwhelmed by the magnitude of it all.

Before the funeral, when family members had their last private moment with Andy before the casket was closed, Danny was the last to go. He remembered kneeling at the coffin to get a last look at Andy, at the hands that withered during the month-long coma, at the face that no longer looked anything like his brother. He promised Andy that he would take care of things. That he would get justice.

CHAPTER SEVEN
Ferocious Competitors

NINE HOURS AFTER Andy died, Leon Easterling, Richard Allen, and Edward Soares were indicted for murder in the first degree.

Assistant District Attorney Thomas J. Mundy Jr. was the natural choice to head this high-profile case. At thirty-nine years old, he was the top prosecutor at the Suffolk County District Attorney's office. He also led the Major Violators Division, a relatively new and extremely successful program designed to get the worst criminals off the street and behind bars as quickly as possible.

The tall, long-limbed, and broad-shouldered Mundy was a full-throttle kind of guy. Extremely athletic, he didn't just ski every weekend, he regularly won NASTAR (National Standard Ski Race) downhill races. He didn't just play handball, he won club championships. In 1976, he didn't just smoke cigarettes, he chain-smoked unfiltered Lucky Strikes, two packs a day, colleagues said.

Sandy-haired, with a just-beginning-to-recede hairline, he was of Irish descent and looked it. The son of a Boston police lieutenant, he graduated from Boston public schools—Brighton High—and went to Boston College for both undergrad and law school. Defense attorneys often wondered if he'd been a cop earlier in his career. He hadn't.

When Tom Mundy died in 1993 at age fifty-four, it was after a distinguished twenty-eight-year career in the Suffolk County District Attorney's Office: He prosecuted more than a thousand cases under three different district attorneys, was third in command of the office, served as chief trial counsel for ten years, and won the first ever state prosecutor of the year award.

But no long criminal justice career is without controversy. Mundy was a prosecutor's prosecutor, highly regarded by his peers and admired by the young prosecutors who worked under him, but he was hated passionately by more than one defense attorney who had to go against him in the 1970s. Some flat out despised him. A repeated complaint was that Mundy was miserly in the discovery process, which legally required him to share information with opposing counsel. In other words, he wasn't generous about turning over exculpatory evidence, which is evidence that might work in a defendant's favor.

Colleagues insisted he was tough but fair, motivated not by money or power but by a sense of duty to get justice for victims of crime and their families. He inspired numerous young prosecutors who decades later still felt an intense gratitude and loyalty to him.

Mundy was known for being prepared, with a mastery of both the law and the facts—the kind of lawyer who never missed a detail, said John Kiernan, an attorney and friend who worked with him in the prosecutor's office for many years. Mundy "played hard, but he played fair."

He was renowned for his closing arguments, which masterfully tugged at juries without ever violating evidence rules. They were so good that Boston College law professor Tom Carey, who had worked with Mundy in the Major Violators Division, sent his students to courtrooms to watch Mundy in action.

Even Mundy's harshest critics acknowledged that he was extremely effective in trying a case. But he was an "old school" prosecutor, which meant that the battle lines in court were firmly drawn.

He didn't make nice with the defense attorneys or chitchat during recess, recalled attorney Thomas E. Dwyer, who had also worked with Mundy in the prosecutor's office. Focused intensely on winning at trial, Mundy in his early career paid less attention to whether the win would hold up on appeal. In 1976, he was part of a culture in the prosecutor's office that was about to change.

The Suffolk County District Attorney's office, which employed upward of two hundred people, prosecuted nearly half of the murders in Massachusetts and almost 40 percent of the crime. The office had broad investigative powers and a strong working relationship with several police forces. A *Boston Globe* piece on the power of the office reported that while the district attorney had no legal authority to control which judges heard cases, the prosecution often managed to get a particular judge to sit on a particular case by asking.

The district attorney was considered the second most powerful job in Boston. In 1976, the job was held by Garrett H. Byrne, a former state representative and career politician who had already been in office twenty-four years. He was a veteran of the First World War, not the second.

He achieved national acclaim for his prosecution of the Brinks robbery and at seventy-eight was still considered effective. A husky man in glasses, he looked younger than his years but was known as an old-fashioned guy. An Irish Catholic and a family man, he had once prosecuted the musical comedy "Hair" for obscenity and appealed his losses all the way up to the U.S. Supreme Court. And he really, *really* hated the Combat Zone.

In addition to disliking the very notion of adult entertainment, Byrne had long known what the public didn't know— the full magnitude of Zone corruption. He had established activist units in white-collar crime, police corruption, and career criminals whose investigations had only increased his determination to shut down the Zone for good, recalled Dwyer, the prosecutor who led many of those investigations.

In the fall of 1976, Byrne's office, the FBI, and the IRS had all cranked up the heat on investigations into the true ownership of strip clubs and adult bookstores. The Suffolk County District Attorney's office was preparing subpoenas for seventy people to appear before the grand jury. By the end of December, the city ordered the Teddy Bear Lounge shut down permanently because it was being operated under "hidden ownership." And that would be only the beginning.

The Puopolo murder would be tried by the Major Violators Division, the special unit that was sponsored by the U.S. Justice Department to go after career criminals. Organized crime had learned how to exploit the delays in overcrowded courts to pressure for plea bargains and intimidate potential witnesses. To counter this, all Major Violator cases were moved to the top of the docket and tried while eyewitness testimony was still fresh.

The speed of trial—an average of only eighty-six days from arrest to conviction—gave mobsters less time to intimidate potential witnesses, but it also gave defense attorneys very little time to prepare their cases. In the seven months after its inception of the Major Violators Division in 1975, the Suffolk County Major Violators Division had won convictions in seventy of seventy-two cases—a success rate of 97 percent.

As head of this division, Tom Mundy had every reason to be confident about his chances in the Puopolo case. His boss, Garrett Byrne, who was leading the charge to clean up the Combat Zone, likely supported an aggressive prosecution, especially since it wasn't just an outraged city paying attention but an intrigued nation.

From the outset, Mundy had decided to charge each of the three defendants with first-degree murder. The prosecutor was applying the legal theory of "joint enterprise," also called "joint venture," that detractors criticized as "guilt by association." It stipulates that anyone who assists, is available to assist, or encourages the commission of a crime is as guilty as the instigator. The theory is similar to the felony murder rule that makes the person who drives the getaway car during a bank robbery as guilty of murder as the holdup man who goes inside the bank with the gun and pulls the trigger. Even if the driver had no idea that the holdup man was going to shoot someone, he was at the wheel, ready to assist a getaway by driving the car.

But to win a joint enterprise case, you had to be able to convince a jury that those who didn't technically commit the murder shared the murderer's intent. In this first-degree murder case in Massachusetts, it would mean putting three people away for the rest of their lives without the possibility of parole. This can make it a harder sell to the jury.

Joint enterprise can be controversial. Critics say it can be a "lazy law" overused by prosecutors to imprison as many people as possible, including some on the periphery of a murder. In the

United Kingdom, where it was used by prosecutors to fight gang violence and appeared to be targeting people of color, the High Court severely restricted its use in a 2016 landmark decision.

But even defense attorneys say it remains a perfectly legitimate legal theory in the right cases. In 1976, Mundy applied it to the Puopolo case. Leon Easterling was known as a pimp in the Zone, and the prosecutor had informants telling him that Easterling and his half-brother Richard "Richie" Allen worked as protectors for the two prostitutes who had several aliases and multiple previous arrests for pickpocketing. Witnesses said that Edward Soares had been punching Andy up until and even after the stabbing. This testimony alone could make him complicit in the murder.

Mundy was a meticulous prosecutor and dug into the case because he dug into all his cases, his colleagues agreed. But there was another factor no one mentioned. Mundy was in the running for an appointment to the judge's bench. A victory here, in this exceptionally high-profile case, couldn't hurt his chances.

Kiernan, who worked in the office at the time, insisted that Mundy was motivated by strong feelings for the victim— something that was said about him throughout his career. In this instance, he'd also taken a liking to the family, especially Andrew Sr., and he wanted justice for them. He also related to Andy as an athlete and as another city kid who didn't back down from a fight.

Both were ferocious competitors who didn't like to lose.

FIGURE 4. Defense attorney Henry Owens around 1972, shortly before he was elected to the City Council in Cambridge, MA. Courtesy of Henry Owens.

CHAPTER EIGHT
A Terrible Witness

HENRY OWENS HAD little faith that the three defendants charged with the Puopolo murder could get a fair trial in Suffolk County. Not when the victim was white. And not just any white kid but a Harvard football player. In his mind, that was the only reason the case had been sensationalized—why every newspaper in the country had reported it.

Owens was one of a handful of Black lawyers in private practice in Boston in 1976. It was a frustrating job. One day, he looked around a courtroom and noticed that all the defendants were Black and all their lawyers were white. In other words, Black defendants knew they stood a better chance with a white lawyer because the entire system was white: police, prosecutors, judges, and juries.

A graduate from Southern Connecticut State College and Suffolk Law School, Owens had grown up in an upper-middle-class family in Cambridge, the son of a businessman who owned a very successful moving company. Owens chose not to go into what was a lucrative family business because he was hell-bent on changing the status quo in Boston from the inside, he said. In the mid-1970s, the "inside" was in dire need of change.

A civil rights champion who would later be named among the nation's Top Ten litigators, Owens would make a reputation for himself exposing the brutality of Boston police in the 1980s and early 1990s. But his career wasn't without controversy. In 2001, he faced charges from the state Board of Bar Overseers of mishandling client funds, which friends and foes both said was wildly out of character and which Owens vehemently disputed. After a brief suspension, he returned to practice law well into his retirement years, remaining highly regarded. But in 1976, he had been out of law school only nine years, which meant that he was one year shy of meeting the criteria to win a state appointment as a defense attorney in a murder case.

Owens recalled first becoming interested in the case when one of Richard Allen's relatives phoned him in November and asked if he'd consider taking it. But that was soon after the stabbing when the charges against the defendant were assault and battery with intent to murder. With the charges upped to first-degree murder, he needed to be on the list of lawyers the state used to appoint representation for indigent defendants, and although Owens had plenty of experience in murder trials, he didn't have ten years' worth.

But he wanted in on this case. Badly. In his reading of events, Richard Allen was a mere bystander to the crime and should never have been arrested with the other two defendants. In his view, the stabbing had resulted from a spontaneous street brawl, and the state was casting "too wide a net" with its use of joint enterprise to include Allen in the charges.

And a Black man had very little chance of getting a fair trial in Boston in the best of circumstances, but in this case it was worse, he said. The day-in-and-day-out publicity had drummed up an aching sympathy for the victim while regularly demonizing the three defendants either as protectors of robber-baron pickpockets or as pimps.

Racial hatred was at a fever pitch, Owens said. The city's white working-class neighborhoods, from which the majority of the jury would be pulled, were in a fury over busing. Whites were in no mood to consider the constitutional rights of three Black defendants.

Owens had worked as an assistant prosecutor in the Middlesex County district attorney's office in Cambridge for two years before he went into private practice and had many friends in the legal community and in law enforcement. But he was not particularly popular among the prosecutors in Suffolk County. Opposing counsel complained that he was too dramatic, a bit of a grandstander. Even his staunchest allies said that his booming voice rattled blinds and could be heard two courtrooms away.

With so much local and national publicity about the murder and the Combat Zone, the commonwealth wanted a swift trial and certain conviction, Owens believed. He had a reputation as a relentless advocate of Black rights and was known to work around the clock for his clients. This would not make him the top choice in this particular case.

It would take some fast talking, but he was good at that. In addition to the deep voice, Owens also had a commanding presence. He'd been captain of both his high school and college football team and kept in shape running long distance. Tall and square-shouldered, with his hair worn in a conservative Afro, Owens was often told that he looked like O. J. Simpson—both when he was young and it was a high compliment, and later when he really got sick of hearing it.

Owens worked at One Boston Place, near the courthouse, but he recalled that by the time he got there, the judge had already appointed lawyers for the other two defendants. Wallace W. (Wally) Sherwood, another young Black lawyer, would represent Leon Easterling. Sherwood, who passed away in 2016, had a Harvard pedigree and had made the governor's short list for judgeships two years before. Although he had founded the Roxbury Defenders Project, he had little hands-on experience in murder trials.

But in Owens's view, the choice of attorney for Soares was worse. Walter J. Hurley, who passed away in 1993, was a "double eagle" who had gone to Boston College for undergrad and law school. While he was among the city's top criminal lawyers in 1976 and known for his integrity, he was in line for a judgeship, a politically sensitive process. Owens doubted that he would risk aggressively going up against the state's interest in this case.

The judge was about to appoint another lawyer to take Richard Allen's defense. Owens knew the lawyer pretty well and felt certain that he wanted the case solely for its publicity value. Owens stepped forward to interrupt the judge with an offer to take the case pro bono. This meant he was willing to work for free, an offer the judge couldn't refuse.

Owens said that he knew what he would be up against. He had battled Tom Mundy before and didn't like him. He considered the prosecutor a "law and order" guy with tunnel vision, who couldn't see anything from the defense's point of view. But

Owens had respect for his abilities. "To give the devil his due, the man could try a case."

There were other challenges. Because the Puopolo trial had moved to the top of the docket, jury selection began in early March. This gave the defense less than three months for a murder trial. Owens said that today, in this kind of a high-profile case, court-appointed defenders are typically given a year to prepare.

But what concerned Owens most was the judge who had just been assigned to preside over the case: James Roy, who was notoriously tough on crime. While prosecutors considered Roy a no-nonsense judge who was hard on everyone, Owens considered Judge Roy a flat-out racist who was especially "vicious" when defendants were Black.

Owens believed Judge Roy had been purposely assigned to the case to make sure the prosecution won. His certainty on this score helped him decide his legal strategy.

An examination of the evidence, which included the autopsy, witness statements, police records, and grand jury testimony, convinced Owens that he needed to separate Richard Allen's case from those of the other two defendants.

The facts of the case were strong against both Leon Easterling and Edward Soares, he said, and if the three defendants were tried altogether, those facts would work against his client. It didn't matter that Allen had had no physical contact with the victim. Or that he'd been urging the Harvard students to leave before the fight broke out. He would be tainted by the evidence against the other two.

Owens had another problem. He could not put Richard Allen on the witness stand. It was out of the question. He liked Richie Allen, whom he considered a "good-hearted kid just trying to survive," but he would make "a terrible witness." For starters, he wasn't very bright. On cross-examination, "Mundy would crucify him." Richie was also physically intimidating because of his size and muscle. And there was an air of unpredictability about him that wouldn't work in his favor with the jury.

But more important, Richie Allen had an extensive criminal record, the worst of the three defendants. His long and complicated relationship with Boston Police began when he was arrested as a runaway at age thirteen and continued through his twenties and thirties when he was arrested almost fifty more times. He'd already served four stints in the house of corrections.

Allen died in 1994, and it was impossible to find relatives to talk about him, but most of Allen's Juvenile Court charges, which began in 1953 when he was a runaway, were subsequently related to probation violations, according to Boston police records. As the years progressed, his crimes escalated to larceny, armed robbery, assault and battery with a deadly weapon, car theft, carrying firearms, and frequent possession of narcotics.

Former Boston police detective Billy Dwyer, who patrolled the Combat Zone in the seventies, remembered Allen as regular in the Zone, a street guy, who was often drunk or high and frequently getting into fights. "I always got along with him, but you had to be careful with him. The elevator did not go to the top floor."

Because of his size and toughness, Allen was sometimes employed by various nightclubs in the Combat Zone to keep the thieves and muggers away from the club entrance, Dwyer said. But the work was on a day-to-day basis, and Allen was always struggling to make a buck.

Mark Pasquale, who worked at his father's King of Pizza on the corner of Boylston and Washington Streets in the Combat Zone, remembered his father banishing Allen from their restaurant: "He never robbed anyone himself, but he was a bodyguard to anyone who did the robbing. The funny part of it is that a lot of the clubs knew him, and they knew what he was doing, but they couldn't do anything about it. You can't arrest someone who is just standing there offering protection."

Leon Easterling was five years older than Richard Allen, who is described as his half-brother in media coverage and identified as Leon's brother in his obituary. (Although police records, which can be inaccurate, do not indicate parents in common.) Of the brothers, Leon appeared to be a more complicated man. Although in 1976 he was slight, not quite five feet nine and 148 pounds, he'd previously been a successful amateur boxer who had taken a shot at going professional.

Before he died in 2014, Leon responded to an email and said he'd be willing to meet and talk about himself and his version of the Combat Zone fight, but he insisted on being paid for the interview. This was declined. His closest family members—his sisters, his wife, and daughters—refused to talk about him in the context of this book project.

Several former close friends, who agreed to talk only if their names were withheld, said he was a talented singer who sang as well as James Brown. While he had dropped out of high school, Leon Easterling was repeatedly described as well read. He was also good looking—a point several witnesses noted in their description of him in the police reports—well dressed and sharp.

He had a natural charisma that people said could charm anyone, especially women. But he also had an explosive temper when he drank. "He wasn't completely evil, but when he drank, the evil came out," said one friend.

In the 1960s he'd married a white woman and worked a straight job as a truck driver for several years in Philadelphia in the late 1960s. He legally adopted his stepson and fathered a daughter. He returned to Boston after the marriage fell apart. Reportedly, drinking and anger contributed.

Leon's mother had run off when he was fifteen years old, leaving him and one of his sisters on their own, according to one friend, who said that Leon and his sister Lillian, who lived in Boston, remained close. But he was also good at compartmentalizing alliances. When he lived in Philadelphia, he didn't talk about his half-brother, and when he returned to Boston in the early 1970s, he didn't talk about his Philadelphia family.

Ray Molphy, a bartender who worked at various Combat Zone clubs between 1968 and 1992, described Easterling this way: "He was unhappy and had a lot of anger, real or perceived disappointment with how he got to where he was and where he might have chosen otherwise. Leon was an older guy whose chances in life had diminished. He was a smart enough person that he was unhappy with his lot in life."

In the early 1970s, the two often played board games together at the bar, and Easterling helped Ray find an apartment
when he needed a new place. Easterling collected Ray's rent
each month and gave him the impression that he owned the
South End townhouse, although research at the Registry of
Deeds came up with no records of Leon Easterling owning
property under his own name. His arrest sheet lists his home
address as 274 Cambridge Street, which is on the back side of
Beacon Hill rather than in the South End, and he was provided
counsel as if he were indigent.

Leon was up front about being a pimp, Ray said, but he usually had only a couple of women working for him at a time, and
he wasn't flashy or boastful the way other Combat Zone pimps
were at the time. He described Easterling as an understated guy,
who could be menacing without flaunting how tough he was.

Easterling had been arrested more than ten times in his life
and served time in prison in separate stints in the 1950s and
early 1960s, according to Boston police records. The charges,
which begin in 1953 with larceny from a person, escalated to
robbery by force and violence, car theft, and two assault and
battery charges by means of a knife, through 1960. After a
ten-year hiatus, the charges against him in the early 1970s
included numerous vehicle violations, including a counterfeit
driver's license, and multiple drug possession charges: marijuana, cocaine, and heroin with intent to sell. He was also
charged with assault and battery, as well as maintaining and
earning money from a prostitute, but all these were continued
without a finding.

It's understandable how Easterling's and Allen's criminal
records, combined with the two women's history of pickpocketing charges, led Mundy to believe that the two men were
working as protectors in the robber-whore ring. But while one
assistant prosecutor involved in the case said Mundy had several sources in the Combat Zone that confirmed this view, not
all the incoming information supported this theory.

Billy Dwyer, the former Boston police detective who was
working in District One at the time, says he knew both women

involved in the wallet theft and that neither were regular Combat Zone prostitutes who had pimps to protect them. He described them as young girls with drug problems who had come to the Zone that night to rip off enough money to score drugs. In his view, Easterling and Allen were Combat Zone hustlers, but neither was organized enough to be running a pickpocket operation.

But the bigger problem was Eddie Soares. While several people remember Leon Easterling and Richie Allen as lower-level hustlers who hung around the clubs and streets in the late hours when prostitutes and pickpockets plied their trade, few people seemed to remember the short, stocky jewelry peddler originally from Cranston, Rhode Island.

Soares died in 1998, and despite many queries and help from the Portuguese community in Southeastern Massachusetts, none of his relatives could be located. Billy Dwyer recalled that Eddie Soares was friends with Allen and Easterling but added that he rarely saw him in the Zone at night. He saw Soares working only by day selling cheap jewelry from his cart.

Soares, who was thirty-three years old and of Cape Verdean descent, was also known to be religious. Although he had served time in the house of corrections for assault and battery and joyriding in 1960 and was also charged for unarmed robbery and receiving stolen goods in 1962, these offenses occurred during his teenage years. Except for a single charge of marijuana possession that was dropped, he had a completely clean record for fourteen years prior to the night of the Combat Zone fight.

Richie Allen's defense attorney, Henry Owens, believed the prosecution had little evidence to prove that the three men were running a robber whore operation together. He also thought that if their cases were tried separately, the facts supported a first-degree murder conviction for Leon Easterling, who had stabbed Tommy Lincoln before killing Andrew Puopolo, and a manslaughter conviction for Eddie Soares, who had been in a fistfight with Puopolo up until and, by one witness account, after the first stabbing. Richie Allen hadn't touched anyone.

Owens felt sure that if his client's trial could be separated from the other two, a jury would find him not guilty.

The judge denied Owens's pretrial motion to try the three defendants' cases separately and also rejected pretrial motions by both Owens and Sherwood to postpone the trial owing to all the publicity. The defense attorneys wanted the trial moved to the fall of 1977, when they hoped the furor over the Combat Zone would die down. Mundy argued that he had to try his case before his witnesses graduated from Harvard and dispersed across the country, and Judge Roy had seen it his way. Jury selection was set to begin in early March 1977.

CHAPTER NINE
Private Loss, Public Controversy

THE MONTHS AFTER his brother died were a blur, Danny said. He couldn't sleep. The twin bed in the room, untouched and unrumpled, made him miss the long late-night talks he used to have with Andy when he came home weekends. How he was always trying his boost his younger brother's confidence. Or his eyes would land on the athletic trophies on the bureau and remind him of how Andy routinely downplayed his own accomplishments. But mostly, he thought of all the times Andy had stood up for him and looked out for him and how he had failed his brother.

His thoughts whirled, the same regret over and over. He should have met Andy in the Combat Zone that night. Why hadn't he gone? Just said yes? Because he was a little uncomfortable hanging around Harvard people, was that it? He should have gone.

At Boston College, Danny's professors had been understanding and gone out of their way to allow him to complete the fall semester despite his shaky attendance. But after the holidays, which had been dismal, he couldn't settle his mind, couldn't think about anything other than the upcoming trial. He wasn't ready to go back to school for the spring term and face the looks he'd get in the cafeteria, people peering up from their sandwiches at him, wondering if he was the one whose brother was murdered in the Combat Zone.

He also worried about his mother. She wasn't able to look at Andy as he lay dying, and she didn't like to talk about what had happened. Although family, friends, and neighbors did their best to offer support, Helen's grief was a private, unrelenting affair. It didn't seem healthy. One day, in a silent, unexplained fury, she ripped up every letter of sympathy every stranger and every prominent politician had written her. But while Danny worried about his mother, the rest of the family worried about him. He talked about dropping out of college.

Experts now know that losing a loved one to murder is different from the grief of other death losses, both more acute and longer lasting. In her 1992 book *Shattered Assumptions: Towards a New Psychology of Trauma*, psychology researcher Ronnie Janoff-Bulman concluded that following the trauma of murder, survivors experience a drastically altered worldview and suddenly see themselves as helpless and weak in a violent, meaningless world. This changed worldview makes coping with grief a longer, more complicated process than when losing a loved one to natural causes.

Numerous studies in the decades since the Puopolo murder have confirmed that the shock of violence, the public nature of murder, and the criminal justice system itself all intensify the mourning process. Without intervention, many survivors of murder victims never recover from the loss.

After a murder, family members of the victim are forced to confront graphic details about the physical violence intentionally inflicted on their loved one: The thrust of the knife. The extensive damage to organs. In Andy's case, the Puopolos also spent a month hoping for a miracle as they watched a twenty-one-year-old at the prime of life deteriorate day by day until not even life support could keep him breathing.

And in the Puopolo case, the nature of the murder generated intense publicity, both locally and nationwide. Family members could not turn on a radio or TV without hearing some new angle on Combat Zone crime, which always referenced the murder. Politicians argued about who was at fault. Network news magazines produced special feature programs. Their private loss was a public controversy.

In the aftermath of any murder, there's also a strange, rarely understood stigma that surrounds the family, according to Dr. Stephanie Hartwell, a renowned medical sociologist who worked closely with survivors of homicide victims in Boston for many years. Because murder is such an unnatural thing, the survivors often feel that they are somehow blameworthy, she said, as if there has to be a reason why this rare and heinous tragedy is happening to them. Their reaction to this illogical stigma is anger. A lot of anger.

When someone is murdered, the public tries to find a reason why it happened, she said. If the victim was somehow at fault, goes the logic, this tragedy could never happen to me. In the Puopolo murder, the common response was, What was he doing in the Combat Zone anyway? This question, which even friends and neighbors felt free to ask the family, implied that Andy somehow deserved to be murdered.

Today, families typically receive something called "psychological first aid" in those first hours when they learn about the murder, and there are intervention programs that deploy professionals experienced with shock and grief in the earliest hours of the tragedy to try to mitigate the long-term side effects of experiencing such an extreme and life-altering loss. Survivors are guided to available social services that might help them cope with the trauma. But in 1976, there was no such thing. No one suggested grief counseling or support groups to the Puopolo family.

Survivors of homicide victims are angry, notes Hartwell. They are angry at the murderer. They are angry that they feel shame. And they are angry that the public wants to believe the victim somehow "asked for it."

While the criminal courts attempt to provide justice, the proceedings themselves add to the family's trauma, forcing them to relive the event from start to a not-always-satisfying finish. Life is for the living, and so is the criminal justice system. The questions by detectives, the cross-examination by defense attorneys, the decisions by judges to accept or exclude evidence—all seem to be about the murderer, not the victim. Survivors often feel that they have no power and, worse, that the system is about the rights of the defendant, not about the snuffed-out life of the victim.

Today, the families of homicide victims are encouraged to make a victim's impact statement in court before sentencing, which gives them the chance to speak for the victim and voice what the murder has done to the family. It allows them to directly address the judge and the people who have destroyed their lives. They have explicit rights, which include being notified about everything that happens to a convicted murder, including parole hearings or release dates from prison.

But it would take the escalating number of murders that decimated cities in the 1980s and 1990s before victims' rights and services became an expected part of social services and the criminal justice system nationally. In Massachusetts, these changes didn't happen until 1984, when the state passed the Victim Bill of Rights, which also provided the money so the courts could hire victim advocates.

Today, victims' families can also file a civil suit for wrongful death, as in the O. J. Simpson case. After a jury found the former football star and celebrity not guilty, the victims' families won a wrongful death suit of $33.5 million in civil court. If it were today, lawyers likely would be lining up to encourage the Puopolo family to file a civil suit against Harvard University, which employed the driver and owned the equipment van where multiple witnesses said the pickpocketing incident occurred. But in 1976, the Puopolo family never considered suing anyone.

Although the Suffolk County District Attorney's office had a victims' services coordinator in 1976, there were no advocates. It was up to Tom Mundy to prepare the Puopolos for the upcoming trial. Andrew Sr. had been summoned to the prosecutor's office immediately after the stabbing and again after the funeral. He was impressed with the prosecutor.

Tom Mundy lived only a block up the street from the Puopolo's comfortable split-level in Jamaica Plain, and as the trial approached, he began to stop by on his way home from work. Andrew Sr. and Helen were unfailingly gracious hosts, always inviting him in for coffee and pastries and, later, he and his wife for dinner. Mundy sat with them in their kitchen, with its immaculate counters and cabinets and painted mural of the Italian countryside, and explained the process and the likely courtroom scenarios.

The families of murder victims typically yearn for maximum justice, whatever that maximum is by state law. In 1976, capital punishment was not an option in Massachusetts. The punishment for first-degree murder was a life sentence with no possibility of parole. Told that all three defendants had played a role in the murder, making them all equally culpable, the Puopolo family wanted all three convicted of first-degree murder.

Outside the courtroom, Tom Mundy was more soft spoken. Nothing will bring Andy back, Mundy told them, but at least these men would never be able to do this to any other family, Andrew Sr. recalled. Both he and his wife were impressed with the prosecutor's compassion. They could hear the genuine sympathy in the prosecutor's voice and sensed that Tom Mundy would throw himself into the case "one hundred percent."

It was going to be painful, the prosecutor had warned. Extremely painful. They would have to listen to witnesses describe the stabbing of their son. The doctors would be giving the jury graphic descriptions of the medical procedures and why they failed to save Andy's life. Mundy would be telling the jury how much they had suffered, what it was like that month. How Andy deteriorated bit by bit, what exactly happened to his brain and organs.

They would hear a lot of lies from the defense, Mundy told Andrew Sr., and it was important not to get excited or upset. Family members couldn't show their anger in court, especially when the defense witnesses were lying. It was important to stay calm through it all.

By this point, Helen already knew she would never go into the courtroom. Andrew Sr. still felt it was his duty to be there.

Mundy told him that he'd make a sympathetic figure and a strong witness. He asked whether he'd be willing to get up on the stand and identify the clothing Andy was wearing when he was stabbed. Andrew Sr. had a temper, he knew that about himself. But he also knew that he could control it if it meant getting justice for his son. He agreed.

Mundy didn't encourage other family members to attend the trial because of how difficult it would be for them to control their emotions. Any outburst could give the defense grounds to call for a mistrial. That would mean starting over from scratch. Going through it all over again. Danny recalled.

He had reluctantly reenrolled at Boston College for the spring semester, but he still couldn't concentrate on his school-work. The only thing he cared about was making certain that the three men who murdered his brother were convicted of first-degree murder and put away for life. No chance of parole. No chance of getting back on the street. He didn't particu-larly care that the state had no capital punishment because he believed life imprisonment would be a worse punishment, but it was important to him that these three men paid for what they did with their entire lives.

He also didn't want his father to have to sit through the agonies of the proceedings alone. But mostly, he had to be there in the courtroom. He had to do this for his brother, who had always been there for him.

CHAPTER TEN
Wading through the Jury Pool

JURY SELECTION BEGAN on March 8 in the Suffolk Superior Courthouse, a sleek, elegant, twentieth-century high-rise. It had been built in 1939 as an annex to the original neoclassic, ornate, Louvre-like courthouse, renamed in honor of John Adams and home to the state's Supreme Judicial Court. The two stately granite buildings in sharply contrasting styles cast long shadows on Pemberton Square, a windy, crescent-shaped alleyway on the back side of Beacon Hill.

The goal of any jury selection is to find twelve jurors and four alternates "from all walks of life" who can separate themselves from any media coverage to render a fair, unbiased decision. But in Suffolk County in the spring of 1977, there were a few problems.

The jury pool had long ago ceased to represent an accurate cross section of the population. This was because jurors were required to serve an entire month, generally without pay, which meant everyone tried to get out of jury duty. And because it was asking for so onerous a financial commitment, the court was generous about excuses, especially for anyone normally making a good paycheck.

Suffolk County had fifty automatic exemptions, which included doctors, lawyers, nurses, accountants, public officials, and a host of other career professionals. This left the jury pool loaded with the young, the old, and lower end of the economic ladder: retirees, students, and the unemployed. Utility workers and others with union contracts that paid them for jury service were also overrepresented.

John Kiernan, the Boston lawyer and former prosecutor who worked with Mundy for many years, joked that the makeup of jury pools in the seventies was like the bar scene in the first Star Wars movie, the intergalactic cantina filled with weird and wild creatures from all over the universe. And he was not alone: conservatives and liberals both considered it seriously flawed.

The jury pool was overwhelmingly white, even in Suffolk County, which had one of the state's highest concentrations of minority residents. Jurors' names were pulled from lists of registered voters, and Blacks did not vote at the same rate as whites. Several attempts to fix these problems, including one failed effort just that fall, had stalled on Beacon Hill. The desperately needed reform of the system wouldn't happen until 1983.

According to the transcript, the first group of jurors in the Puopolo trial, about sixty in all, were herded into the courtroom for Judge Roy to emphasize their civic responsibility to serve and to outline the basics of the case at hand. They were the first group of 185 potential jurors interviewed.

Inside Suffolk Superior Court, built at the height of the Great Depression with federal Works Progress Administration money, the lobbies were massive, but the courtrooms cramped. Floor-to-ceiling cherry paneling absorbed what little sunlight the tall, narrow windows allowed in. Ornamentation was spare, and the interior was well worn. Except for the U.S. and Massachusetts flags on either side of the judge's bench, centered on the far wall, the courtroom was without majesty.

The court stenographer and prosecutor sat up front closest to the judge. The defense sat behind the prosecutor directly in front of the rail that separated the trial theater from the gallery, where spectators were already filtering in. The defendants sat apart from their lawyers, together in a defendants' box at left. The jury box was elevated along the front right wall.

After the jurors were briefed in bulk, they returned to the central jury pool. They were called back into the courtroom one by one so the judge could interview each individually in a hearing called "voir dire."

Judge Roy was a dapper man, with a fondness for bowler hats. Conservative and well to do, he had grown up in Indiana, graduated from Notre Dame University and Harvard Law School, and served as a navy lieutenant in World War II. Like

the Suffolk County district attorney, Judge Roy was no fan of
the Combat Zone. Only three years earlier, he had sentenced
the manager of an X-rated theater to two-and-a half years in
Walpole state prison on obscenity charges for showing the film
The Devil in Miss Jones.

Sometimes called "the hanging judge" for stiff sentencing,
Judge Roy was regularly assigned to trials involving the worst
crimes in the state, which were typically the ones that drew the
most publicity. Detractors like Henry Owens and others called
Judge Roy a racist, but he was also named among the most
admired judges in the mid-1970s, called "fair and impartial" by
his peers and "compassionate" by at least one court-appointed
defense attorney.

The purpose of voir dire was to find the requisite numbers
of jurors that both prosecution and defense could agree were
unbiased enough to provide a fair hearing of the case. A potential juror could be rejected two ways.

The first was "for cause." The judge could eliminate a juror
for reasons that included competing responsibilities, like a child
or parent to take care of, or a health concern that might crop
up midtrial. More frequently, jurors were dismissed for cause
because of a personal relationship with someone involved in the
case, for example, knowing one of the defendants, witnesses, lawyers, or police officers involved. Even being distantly related to
an officer not involved in the case could be grounds for dismissal.

Another cause for dismissal was how much jurors already
knew about the case and whether they had already formed an
opinion. This was especially important in the Puopolo case
because the publicity had not let up. Only weeks before the
trial, Mundy had encouraged the Puopolo family to submit
to an interview with a *Herald* reporter. The newspaper ran a
full-page feature story about how difficult it was for them to
adjust to Andy's murder.

Even when the media wasn't reporting on the murder, the
funeral, or the upcoming trial, the Combat Zone was in the
news. Just the month before, the grand jury had begun inves-
tigating ownership records to penetrate fronts that covered

for the mob. Every day, the Boston Licensing Board and the Alcoholic Beverages Control Commission made new headlines as they went after violators, one strip club after another.

The city revoked the licenses of the self-described "world famous" Two O'Clock Lounge and the Silver Slipper and slapped the Naked i with a 100-day suspension—although all would continue to operate while on appeal. The *Boston Globe* ran a piece reporting speculation that the New York Mafia was trying to buy into the embattled Combat Zone porno racket at reduced prices.

Besides the difficulty in finding a potential juror who had somehow missed the onslaught of publicity, there was another major concern in Boston in 1976: racial conflict. Although white working-class communities of Revere, Chelsea, and Winthrop were part of Suffolk County, the majority of the jury pool came from Boston, and most of them were from the same largely white neighborhoods that were still smarting over court-ordered busing. These individuals were angry that their children were being sent to schools torn apart by violence. They were angry that their protests had come to naught. And they were especially angry that the busing violence spotlighted by the media always seemed to be white violence against Blacks.

When they were asked if feelings about race might affect their ability to render a fair hearing, several jurors openly said that it might, the transcript of the jury empanelment showed. A greater number of jurors admitted uncertainty, and several jurors hesitated long enough before answering that Judge Roy decided to dismiss them.

Everyone had heard about the murder, and many acknowledged having followed the developments closely. One woman from Dorchester flat out said that she felt so sorry for the Puopolo family that she couldn't put those feelings aside as she listened to evidence. So many potential jurors admitted to having already formed an opinion about the guilt of the defendants that Easterling's attorney, Wallace Sherwood, begged the judge again to postpone the trial until October when emotions might have cooled. The motion was denied.

Although lawyers for both sides were allowed to ask that the juror be dismissed for cause, it was the judge's decision, and Judge Roy, who dismissed 85 potential jurors for cause, was not particularly receptive to challenges, as indicated by trial transcripts. This may have been because after the judge cleared potential jurors, both prosecution and defense had their own process to eliminate them by use of peremptory challenges.

Peremptory challenges, which go back to Roman times, have always been controversial. They allow a lawyer to dismiss a juror based on a hunch or instinct and weed out the jurors who seem too harsh, too stupid, too intelligent, too whacked out, and, most important, too likely to favor the other side. The key point is that the lawyers don't have to give a reason for dismissal. For example, one young woman used her maiden name even though she was married, which in 1976 was considered progressive. Mundy challenged her. There was no explanation of his reasoning, no discussion: she was out.

In the United States, such challenges led to the creation of jury consultants, who have a supposed expertise in discerning which way potential jurors might lean, raising the cost of trials in both time and money. Because these challenges are often based on intuitive feelings or superficial information, they lend themselves to discriminatory practices by both prosecution and defense.

In Great Britain, where they were long a part of common law, peremptory challenges were abolished in 1988. Only two years prior to the Puopolo trial, Massachusetts unsuccessfully tried to eliminate them as part of a failed jury reform effort.

At a 2011 Boston Bar Association panel discussion organized by law professor Charles E. Walker Jr., who had recently authored a legal analysis of the ongoing controversy about peremptory challenges for the *Boston Bar Journal*, it was clear that neither prosecution nor defense attorneys had any interest whatsoever in giving them up.

One after the other, lawyers on both sides of criminal trials stood to say they needed these challenges to ferret out those jurors who lie about their bias and have already made up their minds about the case. Most considered them a right and essential to counter the absolute power of the judge.

The number of peremptory challenges allotted in Massachusetts depends on the severity of the charges, with murder trials awarded the highest number. In the Puopolo murder jury seating, the three defense attorneys were each given sixteen peremptory challenges—a total of forty-eight chances to remove a remaining juror without having to give a reason why. The prosecution, likewise, was awarded a total of forty-eight opportunities to eliminate a potential juror.

For years, Henry Owens had been frustrated by this jury selection process. In Suffolk County, the jury pool included only a sprinkling of African Americans to start with. If his defendant was Black, he could count on the prosecutors, especially Tom Mundy, using their peremptory challenges to get rid of every last Black juror, he said. All-white juries in Suffolk County had consistently convicted his Black defendants, especially when the victim was white. Owens had just as consistently appealed these convictions to the state's Supreme Judicial Court, arguing that his client's constitutional right to a fair trial had been violated. But no one listened.

The high court was not receptive because of *Swain v. Alabama*, the prevailing federal case law. In 1965, the U.S. Supreme Court had upheld the conviction of a Black man sentenced to death for rape by an all-white jury in Alabama. While acknowledging that the discriminatory use of peremptory challenges could violate a defendant's rights, it set standards that made it almost impossible to prove. This gave prosecutors great leeway.

But Owens felt that change was in the air, at least in Massachusetts. Recent turnover of justices in the state's highest court had made it more liberal and possibly more receptive to a challenge of jury selection practices based on the state constitution. Since Judge Roy had denied Owens's motions to separate his client's trial from the other two, he had decided his best—maybe his only—shot for his client was to angle for an appeal.

From the first day of jury selection, sparks flew, the court transcripts indicate. The eleventh juror interviewed was a thirty-two-year-old Black man from Dorchester recently laid off from a job as a laborer for the Boston Housing Authority. At several points, he either misheard or misunderstood Judge Roy's questions and provided vague and confused answers. Mundy used a peremptory challenge to strike him.

Owens objected to the strike. "If it develops during the course of the selection of the jury that Mr. Mundy systemat-ically challenges Black jurors through the use of peremptory challenges, your Honor, I would like to make an offer of proof at that time. I would take exception to it," he said.

Judge Roy bristled. "Wait a minute. So far as I'm concerned, if I were sitting down there, either on the prosecution or on the defense, I would have challenged that person on the basis of his lack of intelligence."

Owens bristled back. "For the purposes of the record, may I say that that last juror, who was Black, was no smarter nor less intelligent than any other juror we've heard during this examination. I would take exception to the court's statement that this juror was not smart."

"Calm down," Judge Roy told Owens. "That's my estimation of the intelligence of that juror, I don't care whether he's Black or white." Sherwood stood up and joined Allen in objecting. The battle had begun.

Mundy continued to use his peremptory challenges to dis-miss eleven more Black potential jurors—all employed and cogent in their answers. Owens objected, Sherwood joined in, and Judge Roy overruled them.

Owens and Sherwood also challenged the judge himself for excusing one potential Black juror "for cause." This was perhaps the last straw. Judge Roy called Owens into a lobby conference to dress him down.

"I'm not going to have any injection of racial prejudice into this case if I can prevent it, and I want you making no speeches out there. The law is clear in recognizing the purpose of peremptory challenges. You've already got it on the record, and I don't want it being repeated anymore. Now you understand that?" he asked.

The judge also called attention to the defense's pattern of striking all potential jurors who had Italian last names. He told Owens that he could continue to make an exception if a Black juror was struck, but he didn't want an argument every time.

Eventually, a single Black juror succeeded in making it through the peremptory challenges: Woodrow Cureton was a fifty-three-year-old foreman of an electrical company. Judge Roy named him foreman of the jury, reportedly to ensure he sat on the actual jury and didn't wind up as an alternate.

The final jury was made up of six men and six women, with three additional white men serving as alternates. It had taken a jury pool of 185 people to find fifteen people acceptable to the judge, the prosecution, and the defense.

But before that, there were more fireworks, this time from the gallery. On the third day of jury selection, Danny came to court with his father and his uncle, Dr. Anthony Puopolo. The three men arrived during the morning recess to try to find a seat. The eighth-floor courtroom was already packed with spectators and media, but Danny and his father squeezed into two available seats in the front row of the gallery. Anthony found a space several rows behind them.

The courtroom was airless, the wooden bench hard. Danny recalled trying to stay calm. His father had repeatedly told him not to come to court unless he could control himself, warning that he could cause a mistrial.

The three Puopolo men had arrived at the end of a recess. The transcripts showed that the judge and the lawyers were still conferring in the judge's lobby. No juror had yet to be called into the courtroom when guards brought Leon Easterling, Edward Soares, and Richard Allen into the defendants' box.

Danny glared at them. He said the men were only ten feet away, on the other side of the rail, and he wasn't prepared for how close in proximity they would be. As the three began to take their seats in the dock, Eddie and Richie didn't turn to look to see who was in the spectators' gallery, but Leon did. Their eyes met. Danny glowered and later said he saw Easterling smirk.

Danny called Easterling a motherfucker, and before he knew what he was doing, he put his leg over the rail and lunged for Leon. Andrew Sr. caught Danny by the arm, grabbed him hard, and hauled him back. *You stupid bastard. You are going to ruin it for your brother*, Danny recalled him saying.

Immediately, two court officers appeared at his side and led Danny out of the courtroom, according to the *Boston Globe* coverage of the incident. But by then, Uncle Anthony had leapt to his feet. He pushed his way toward the rail, cursing Leon Easterling out. Anthony was six feet one and in shape. It took three court officers to pull him away from the rail. As they hauled him out of the courtroom, he turned back to Easterling and shouted, "Go ahead, look brazen."

Mundy had been out in the judge's lobby when it all happened. Aware of all the Mafia rumors, the prosecutor would later joke to the family that the defendants had mistaken Anthony, who was a doctor, for a hit man. But he also asked that neither Danny nor Anthony return to court for any of the proceedings.

FIGURE 5. WGBH (Boston public television station) artist rendering of the three defendants, *left to right*, Richard Allen, Edward Soares, and Leon Easterling at the 1977 trial. Courtroom sketch by Sonja Benson; From the WGBH 10:00 News, 1977. Courtesy of WGBH Educational Foundation.

CHAPTER ELEVEN
A Noble Act

"THE DOCTORS WILL testify that when the cells go without oxygen, they die, they literally rot. The cells begin to liquefy, and as they liquefy this causes what's known as edema of the brain, or swelling of the brain, and since the brain is housed within the skull cavity, there's no room for expansion," Tom Mundy said, using his opening statement to explain the devastating effects of the stabbing on Andy's brain, according to court transcripts. The prosecutor, known for his gift of cutting through jargon to make a victim's suffering especially vivid, was previewing the damaging medical evidence the doctors would later present. Standing before the jurors, he said, "As the cells die and liquefy, the brain expands. Encased within the skull, which causes further expansion, this in turn causes arteries to be closed shut, causing further failure of blood supply to the cells that are still alive, causing those cells to die. This vicious cycle just keeps repeating itself until the entire organ is destroyed."

Leon Easterling's defense attorney, Wallace Sherwood, jumped to his feet and moved for a mistrial. Henry Owens also rose to object. "The statements made by Mr. Mundy in his opening were just completely inflammatory and will stay in the minds of jurors and carry throughout the course of the trial," he said.

The air in the packed courtroom in Suffolk Superior Court was electric, recalled Susan Wornick, who was then reporting for WBZ radio. The press section was three rows deep, filled with television broadcasters, radio reporters, and journalists from Boston's major metropolitan and suburban newspapers. Spectators, which included family and friends of the Puopolos and the three defendants, spilled out into the hall, waiting for someone to leave so a seat would be available.

Judge Roy denied the motion. He told the defense attorneys to sit down and asked Tom Mundy to proceed.

In giving the prosecution's case, Mundy had thirty exhibits of evidence and twenty-five witnesses to present. In addition to damaging medical evidence from the doctors, and more than a half-dozen Harvard students who would give eyewitness testimony as to how the fight in the Combat Zone unfolded, he also had neutral witnesses. These were observers who had been on the street or in cars, and six police officers who had all been on the scene. His challenge was less about proving that Leon Easterling had stabbed the victim to death and more about convincing the jury that all three men were responsible.

To get a first-degree murder conviction against Leon Easterling, Mundy had to prove the stabbing was premeditated, that Leon had time to think about it first.

To get a first-degree murder conviction against all three defendants, Mundy had to convince the jury that Eddie Soares and Richie Allen followed Leon to the alley knowing full well that he had a knife and would use it.

In addition to Eddie's and Richie's proximity to the stabbing, which by itself could be used to establish joint enterprise, Mundy wanted to prove that the three men were working as protectors for the prostitutes who stole the wallet of one of the football players. This would make them conspirators in a commercial endeavor.

Because it was a combined trial, each of the three defense attorneys could object to testimony as Mundy presented a witness, and they all could cross-examine each prosecution witness, one after the other. Once the prosecution rested its case, each defense lawyer would mount a separate defense with witnesses that Mundy, in turn, could question. Occasionally, lawyers could recross one of their own witnesses to clear up information that came out during a cross-examination. It made for a lengthy back-and-forth.

Sitting in the courtroom, the three defendants had cleaned up, trimmed facial hair, and dressed in conservative clothes. Richie was in dress pants and a button-down shirt under a green down vest. Eddie and Leon wore suits and ties. Eddie carried a red-covered Bible.

It made for a respectable tableau that Mundy wouldn't let stand. Later, putting a police photographer under oath, he pointed out that Leon Easterling, bookish in a pair of glasses, had not been wearing them the night of the stabbing, when he had sported a long black leather jacket and a diamond stud earring. Mundy did so partly because witnesses would identify the defendants by their clothing, but he put enough emphasis on the now-removed earring to emphasize that on November 16, 1976, Easterling looked the part of a pimp.

The courtroom gallery was so crammed that many spectators couldn't get in. Even in the lobby, also packed, emotions ran high. Tim Fitzgerald, a schoolmate and friend of the Puopolo brothers from Boston Latin, was home from college on spring break. He recalled that he and his father arrived too late to get a seat inside the courtroom and stood clustered in the vestibule, trying to watch the trial from the narrow window panes on the double doors.

Glancing over his shoulder, Fitzgerald spotted a couple of the Harvard football players sitting on one of the long benches in the lobby, waiting to testify. Fitzgerald, who was tall and wore his blond hair long, looked like a surfer in those days, but he had been a Golden Glove boxer. He said that he and his Boston friends felt that if they had been there with Andy that night in the Combat Zone, he might still be alive.

Fitzgerald zeroed in on Charlie Kaye, the six-foot-five Harvard lineman whose need to get back his wallet had launched the Combat Zone incident. Kaye was leaning back, legs crossed, reading the *Wall Street Journal*. Seething at what he saw as a cavalier attitude, Fitzgerald headed to the bench, but his father, equally incensed, jumped ahead him.

"What are you doing?" the senior Fitzgerald barked at Kaye, unaware that he wasn't one of the witnesses. "You're reading the newspaper when you're about to testify in court?" He ripped the newspaper out of Charlie's hand.

Meanwhile, inside the courtroom, Andrew Sr. was called to the stand. Wearing a white shirt and a somber suit and tie, he spoke in a quiet, firm voice, mixing simple, old-world expressions into his speech patterns. Responding to Mundy's questions, he told the jury that he'd been born in Italy and come to the United States as a five-year-old. It went without saying that his Italian immigrant family had emigrated to build a better life.

"How old was your son in the fall of 1976?" Mundy asked.

"He made twenty-one years old," Andrew Sr. replied.

"And at that time, back in the fall of '76, was he attending Harvard College, sir?"

"Yes, he was."

Owens, who would later complain that if he heard "Harvard" once during the trial, he heard it fifty times, objected. Judge Roy swiftly overruled him.

Asked to recount his trip to the Tufts New England Medical Center emergency room at a quarter to three in the morning the night of the stabbing, Andrew Sr. remained steady. But as he was about to identify the clothing his son wore the night he was stabbed, his voice cracked, according to the *Herald* story.

Just as the torn and bloody jersey was raised for Andrew Sr. to identify, Wallace Sherwood objected. When Judge Roy overruled his objection, Owens quickly offered to "stipulate" the identity of the clothing, which meant the defense did not challenge this point. He later said that he wanted to get Andrew Sr. off of the stand and out of the jury's mind as soon as possible.

Over the next two days, the Harvard equipment manager and seven football players testified to the night's events. The prosecution's story began to emerge: it wasn't just one street fight but three escalating conflicts at three separate locations. This was important because it gave defendants time to reflect on their actions.

Chester "Chet" Stone, the thirty-four-year-old equipment manager, led off. His testimony established the sequence of the night's events and tried to obliterate any assumptions that the football players had gone to the Combat Zone to get hookers.

As Harvard dean Archie Epps had testified the day before, Stone emphasized that this trip to the Combat Zone was part of a long-standing Harvard team tradition. It was a team ritual that for years followed the annual breakup dinner, not a spontaneous idea. Stone had even driven nine of the students to the Zone in the Harvard team van. The others, some forty in all, came by car or taxis.

Stone testified that when the strip club closed at 2:00 a.m., he agreed to take six of the football players back to campus in the Harvard van. It was an interracial mix of three Black students (Russell Savage, Kwame Olatunji, and Gordon Graham) and three white students (Charlie Kaye, Malcolm DeCamp, and Mitch Witten) who passed the Carnival Lounge heading to the parking lot.

Stone testified that prostitutes hanging outside the Carnival Lounge approached the group as they passed. Two of the young women, later identified as Naomi Axell and Cassandra "Cassie" McIntyre, offered blow jobs and asked the football players if they wanted to get laid. Stone said that the football players tried to discourage the prostitutes, but the young women followed the students back to the parking lot anyway. His testimony implied that the women forced their way into the Harvard equipment van. "I started the truck up and was ready to leave, and all of a sudden the passenger door opened up, and one of the prostitutes jumped into the truck, and she started feeling around," he said.

Under cross-examination by Owens, Stone was forced to admit that money had been discussed between Charlie Kaye and the prostitutes, with the Harvard student bragging that he had fifty dollars to spend. Later, as other witnesses were cross-examined by Sherwood, the jury learned that the prostitutes had been invited to drive back to one of the Harvard men's clubs, called the Pi Eta Club.

Whether only one or both prostitutes got inside the van, and what exactly happened in the front seat, remained unclear. But Stone and three of the students who testified agreed that the women had been inside the van only a matter of minutes before the two women bolted.

When Charlie Kaye discovered his wallet missing, he jumped out of the van to chase the two women. Three others, including Stone, but none of the three Black students, followed him. The prostitutes split up, one running toward the Carnival Lounge. Following her, the students ran into Richie Allen, who was working that night as a bouncer. He stepped out of the Carnival Lounge door and blocked their way to the alley, DeCamp testified.

According to the witnesses, there was a brief shoving match between Richie Allen and Charlie Kaye, which allowed the woman to get away. Several students testified that Richie Allen shouted at them: "Why don't you guys, you whiteys, get out of here. You're looking for nothing but trouble. Why the fuck are you guys down here? All you want to do is look for trouble. Why don't you get out of here?"

After arguing that all they wanted was the stolen wallet, the Harvard group retreated to the van to go home. At this point of the story, Russell Savage, the only Black Harvard student to testify, became a key witness. He testified that when he looked out the van window into the alley behind the Carnival Lounge, "I saw two girls and a dude, and it looked to me that they handed him something."

This implied that the stolen wallet passed from the prostitutes to Richie Allen. Chet Stone went as far as calling Richie Allen "the ringleader" of the night's trouble because he had originally stepped in to protect the women outside the Carnival Lounge.

Henry Owens attacked Stone in his cross-examination of Mundy's redirect. Why had the equipment manager never mentioned Allen's key role as "ringleader" in the report he made to police that evening? he asked. Why had Stone never mentioned it in his testimony before the grand jury? How could he come up with this ringleader characterization when, by his own account, he did not see Richie Allen again until after the stabbing when Stone pointed Allen out to the police and told them to arrest him? Each of Owens's questions grew progressively louder with outrage.

Judge Roy grew annoyed. "Quiet down, Mr. Owens," he said.

One of the most tragic details to emerge from testimony was that the Harvard van and the teammates almost made it out of the Zone unscathed. But as the van exited the parking lot to head back to campus, one of the students in the back seat spotted the prostitutes running up the one-way Boylston Street in the opposite direction. He shouted, "Hey, there she goes!" and Charlie Kaye jumped out of the van while it was still moving to chase the young woman.

Stone told the court that he pulled the van across Boylston into an alley on the other side, and he and two students chased Charlie and the prostitute up the street. Again, the three Black students opted again not to join in. Stone testified that he'd told them to stay behind and keep an eye on the van.

A half-dozen teammates took the stand to describe a chase that grew to involve seven of them running down Boylston Street after a Black woman. It was at this point that Steve Saxon, who was driving home the group including Andy Puopolo and Tommy Lincoln, got involved. He testified that he was standing at the open driver's door of his Chevy Nova when a Black woman wearing a long rust-colored coat and platform shoes ran past him screaming. His teammates were shouting that she had one of their wallets.

Andy Puopolo and another teammate, Jim Boland, were already in the backseat of the two-door Chevy Nova, but Saxon and two other members of their group, Scott Coolidge and Tom Lincoln, joined the chase. Saxon was the first Harvard student to reach the prostitute, who fell on the street. He said he picked her up and asked her if she had the wallet. When she said she didn't, he didn't know what to do so he let her go.

As soon as she took off, he was kicked to the ground by a short, stocky Black man wearing a sheepskin coat and a floppy two-tone blue hat: Edward Soares.

What happened next would be challenged by the defense. The Harvard students testified that Soares backed away from them and crossed Tremont to the MBTA station at the corner of Boston Common. Three of the white football players from the Harvard van and Stone, now joined by Saxon, Tommy Lincoln, and Scott Coolidge, the three who'd been heading home separately in the Chevy, followed Eddie Soares across the street, creating a half circle around him.

Backed up against the brick station building, Eddie Soares, who later would testify that he was very drunk, threw off his jacket, rolled up his sleeves, and got into a crouch position. "Come on. I've been waiting for this. Come on. Let's fight. Let's go!" he shouted.

Tommy Lincoln, who was a premed student in many of the same classes as Andy, was Friday's star witness. Another Harvard student testified that Tommy had laughed at Soares's drunken karate kicks and parodied an air kick back, but no actual kicks or punches were landed by either party. Tommy's testimony focused on the retreat.

Because he had a biology exam the next day, Tom Lincoln would later say, he hadn't been drinking as much as his teammates. He could see this conflict was getting way out of hand. In court, he testified that he told teammates, "Wait a minute. Let's get out of here. This is silly because he doesn't have the wallet," and the football players were about to go back to the van.

Right then Leon Easterling came from behind him and stabbed Tom Lincoln in the abdomen, according to Chet Stone's testimony. The equipment manager shouted, "Run! They've got knives," and they all turned to run back to the Harvard van. Lincoln testified that he heard Easterling shout after them: "We're going to cut you, you white motherfuckers. You're looking for trouble. Here it is."

This threat, which three other eyewitnesses also reported, was key to the prosecution's case. It established that Leon

Easterling had a plan, and the plan was to use his knife again. Prosecution witnesses also placed both Eddie Soares and Richard Allen within earshot of the threat, which meant they likely heard it too.

Several of the Harvard witnesses testified that as they ran away, they looked back up the street and saw Leon, Richie, and Eddie joined by a new man. This new man was big—about six foot three and about 230 pounds by one report. There was confusion about his race, with some identifying him as white, and others as Black or Latino, but all reported he wore a "cranberry-colored" or "maroon" jacket. After a moment—and this moment would become very important to the prosecution's argument that the defendants had time to reflect—the four men headed down the street after the football players.

Chet Stone reached the alley first and jumped behind the wheel of the Harvard van, according to Tommy Lincoln, who would later explain that he was still in enough shock that he didn't feel his stab wound. He climbed into the front passenger seat. Charlie Kaye tried to get in beside him but he was too slow, and the man in the cranberry jacket pulled him out of the van by the tie.

The three Black Harvard students saw the fight erupting and wanted nothing to do with it, according to Russ Savage's testimony. They had fled the van as their teammates returned to the alley. He said that when he, Kwame Olatunji, and Gordon Graham reached Washington Street, about twenty-five yards away, he turned to see what was happening. He saw a Black man in a long leather coat running down Boylston Street with his knife drawn. From evidence already entered, it was clear this was Leon Easterling.

Tommy Lincoln told the jury that the man in the cranberry jacket had Charlie Kaye propped up against the side of the van. He was punching him so hard the van shook from side to side.

This was what Andy saw, according to the testimony of both Steve Saxon and Jim Boland, who would become the seventh teammate to testify. Boland and Andy had gotten out of the back seat of the Chevy to see what was happening up at the intersection. Before they could get very far, their teammates whizzed by them on Boylston Street toward the alley where the van was parked. They were followed by three defendants and the man in the cranberry jacket.

They stood still a few seconds on the street. The students all got inside the van except for Charlie. When Andy saw Charlie out alone taking punches, he charged over to help him.

Tommy testified that he climbed out of the van and pushed the man in the cranberry jacket off of Charlie Kaye. The man tumbled down the sharp incline of the alley and disappeared and Tommy was able to get Charlie back into the van.

Told from the points of view of a total of seven different Harvard students and the equipment manager, some details were inconsistent, especially in regard to Richard Allen's role in the fight, but the basic story was the same. It all lasted less than five minutes.

Eddie Soares raised his fists to block Andy's arrival. They fought their way from the back of the van to the front and around the other side. A couple of the teammates jumped out of the van's tailgate to try to help Andy. One of them, Malcolm DeCamp, testified that a man with a long leather coat and an earring, Leon Easterling, threatened him with the tip of his knife, shouting: "Where are you coming from, motherfucker?"

One of the Harvard students testified that Richie stood at the back of the van and cautioned everyone else to stay out of the fight. "Leave them alone, it's one on one." Others could not place Allen at the scene. Russ Savage was the only one to testify that Richie Allen physically involved himself in the fight. He told the jury he saw Allen attack Andy when he first arrived in the alley, but other witnesses who were closer to the scene, including Eddie himself, testified that it was Eddie Soares who first challenged Andy.

At least four of the Harvard students, as well as an off-duty employee of the city's mass transit system who was sitting in his parked car on the street, pointed to Leon Easterling in the defendants' box, identified him, and said that he lunged over Eddie Soares's back and pushed Andy to the ground and stabbed him. Andy staggered to his feet, and Eddie Soares attacked him again, throwing punches, several witnesses testified.

Scott Coolidge told the jury that he saw that Andy had been stabbed and jumped in to pull him away from the fight. Andy was coherent and said he was fine and wanted to get out of there. As the two left the alleyway, Leon Easterling came at Andy a second time, stabbing with wild motions, thrusting the fatal blow.

Scott testified that he had to hold Andy in his arms. He described his last moments of consciousness to the jury. "Blood came out of his mouth. I was at his feet when I laid him down. His jacket was open. He was covered with blood. His eyes suddenly rolled back in his head."

By all witness accounts, Richie Allen did not run when police first arrived. Two cruisers pulled up just as Andy collapsed, and as one set of cops took him to the emergency room, Richie stayed in the alley as the other two officers chased after Eddie and Leon, who had fled.

When police returned with Eddie Soares in custody, Richie Allen shouted at the cop to leave Soares alone, that he hadn't done anything. Chet Stone pointed to Allen and said: "There's one of them." Police arrested a somewhat baffled Richie Allen and put him in the cruiser with the other two men.

Henry Owens wasn't happy. He felt that the prosecution had a strong case against Leon Easterling and Edward Soares. It was hurting his client. The lackluster defense of the other two defendants wasn't helping matters.

The transcripts show that Walter Hurley, who represented Eddie Soares, rarely objected and kept his cross-examination of prosecution witnesses brief. Intellectual and soft-spoken,

Wallace Sherwood was no legal attack dog—not long after the trial, he would take a job in academia. Throughout the trial the judge repeatedly told Owens to quiet down, but he was forever telling Sherwood to "keep your voice up."

Henry Owens asked the judge to stop the proceedings to make yet another motion that Allen's case be tried separately. Judge Roy denied his request.

Through his cross-examinations of the prosecution's witnesses, Owens established how much alcohol all the Harvard football players drank that night. He hammered each witness about even small discrepancies between testimony and statements made to police and the grand jury. His line of questioning implied that the prosecution's witnesses had gotten together and cooked up a unified version of events.

But his aggressive defense was no more effective than that of the other two defense lawyers, largely because of the tension between him and Judge Roy. The transcripts show that during the seating of the jury, the judge grew angry when Owens and Sherwood challenged his dismissal of the Black juror for cause and at the implication that he was racially biased. Throughout the trial, he seemed to take it out on Henry Owens, shutting down Owens's objections and motions at every turn.

When Owens cross-examined a witness, Judge Roy interrupted him to interject questions of his own, hindering Owens's attempt to establish doubt about whether Richie Allen was even at the scene. Without Mundy making an objection, Judge Roy would step in and cut off Owens midsentence as he tried to break down the prosecution's testimony.

The transcripts recorded little overt conflict between Tom Mundy and Henry Owens in the courtroom, but when Mundy raised his voice during a cross-examination at one point, Owens rose to object. Judge Roy was outraged on Mundy's behalf. "You're the last one who should be complaining about the volume of voices," he told Owens.

Throughout the trial, Owens objected, and Judge Roy overruled—and in most cases, swiftly overruled. In total, the judge overruled objections of the defense attorneys 157 times.

Three times the judge called Henry Owens "Mr. Allen," as if he couldn't tell the lawyer and the defendant apart. Owens called him on it. "Your honor, for purposes of the record, my name is Henry F. Owens—not Allen."

Judge Roy: "It isn't?"

Owens: "My name is Henry F. Owens. The court three times this morning called me Allen. My name is Owens."

Testifying in his own defense, Leon Easterling shocked the courtroom with a confession. He admitted to stabbing both Tom Lincoln and Andy Puopolo. But he also claimed that it was in self-defense and the defense of a friend, Eddie Soares. "I didn't want to see Eddie get hurt."

Leon told the jury that he had no choice but to join the fight in the alley because he saw fifteen students fighting Eddie, who was already sporting a bloody lip from the assault. "I jumped up in the air to hit Mr. Puopolo with my knife and yelled at them to let him alone."

Leon admitted to stabbing Andy, but only once, when he jumped over Eddie's back to defend him. "I thought I was trapped in the alley . . . I thought I was going to the aid of somebody, trying to help," He didn't remember following Scott Coolidge and Andy Puopolo to Boylston Street to administer the second and fatal blow, but he didn't deny it. Doctors had already provided powerful testimony that detailed the two separate and distinct puncture wounds and the damage they had inflicted.

At one point, Leon became emotional. His voice cracked and tears streamed down his face as he apologized. "I'm sorry about Mr. Puopolo. At that particular time, I just didn't realize how serious it was . . . I'm awfully sorry this happened."

Sitting in the gallery, neither Andrew Sr. nor any of the family's friends interpreted this as a sincere plea for forgiveness but, instead, a maneuver of a man cornered. At this point in the trial, more than a half-dozen eyewitnesses had already testified to the stabbing.

Leon Easterling had only a ninth-grade education, but he was intelligent and articulate as he answered his own lawyer's questions. He did not hold up well during Mundy's blistering cross-examination, which was two and a half times longer that the direct testimony itself. The prosecutor challenged the sincerity of Leon Easterling's remorse and suggested it was calculated. "You were sorry about the consequences to yourself, weren't you?" Mundy asked.

Mundy methodically picked away at the arguments of self-defense and defense of a friend. He got Leon to admit that he had not actually seen anyone hit or throw a punch at Soares at the MBTA station before he stabbed Tom Lincoln. Mundy also hammered away on Easterling's claim that he'd been concerned about his own safety.

"And you were concerned about your safety when you left Tremont Street to go down to the alley by the Silver Slipper, weren't you?"

"Yes."

"And you were so concerned with your safety, yet you still went into that alley to see what was going on?"

"Yes,"

Mundy challenged Leon's inability to remember how many times he stabbed Andy, while he remembered so many other details. A few beats later, he added, "But you have a memory lapse concerning how you stabbed Andy Puopolo?"

"Yes."

"But you remember everything else clearly?"

Leon had testified that he didn't know either of the two prostitutes, but Naomi Axell, a hostile witness for the prosecution, had already taken the stand and said that she knew Richie Allen and Leon Easterling well. She had been drinking with them inside the Carnival Lounge the very night of the stabbing.

On the witness stand, Eddie Soares said he worked as a street peddler of jewelry. He had gone down to the Carnival Lounge to play pool and drink enough so that he could sleep comfortably on the 2:30 a.m. bus to New York City to buy inventory. This, he explained, was why police had discovered $700 in his pockets: it was a cash business.

Soares claimed that he knew Richie Allen only by name and only because he was the Carnival Lounge bouncer. He said that he knew Easterling only by sight. Only minutes earlier Easterling had testified that he'd known Soares for five or six years and that Soares had bought him a drink earlier that evening.

Soares, who had only finished the sixth grade, was not as smooth as Easterling, and he could ramble, but he got the better of the exchange with the prosecutor on more than one point. He denied Mundy's accusation that he had been in the Zone working with the "so-called wolf packs of Black prostitutes" who robbed men. Rather, he had come to Naomi Axell's rescue because she was a lone Black woman being chased by white youths.

"You described the girl that ran up as a young lady."

"Yes."

"Is that what she appeared to be?"

"Isn't she a human being because she's a prostitute?"

"The question is: Did you know she was a prostitute?"

"Please. I recognized her as a young lady."

Mundy kept throwing more accusations, reminding the jury that Soares, Easterling, and Allen had all been in the Carnival Lounge with the two women shortly before the wallet theft. "I'm asking you: Were you working with those two whores that night?"

"Of course I wasn't. Why should I be working with them? Doing what?" Soares responded.

"Why did you go up to render them assistance so they could escape?"

"I'm going to answer that question, and I hope you wait to hear the answer. All right? I went up there because I seen a Black woman being pursued by anybody—white persons—and they looked like they was about to attack. Now I'd be a damn fool to turn my back. I was responding in a humane way to a situation that I thought was getting out of hand, that's all," Soares said.

He said that the football players had backed him up against the Tremont MBTA station and that Leon had come to his defense. "He jumped on Tommy Lincoln's back and was scrapping him for me, but in the meantime, they kept attacking me." One of the football players grabbed him around the neck and tried to throw him to the ground, but he wrestled his arm off and got up, he said.

Soares said that he'd followed the football players back to the alley because he was angry and had then challenged several of the Harvard students to a fight. Only Andy was willing to fight him. He said that while he swung his fists at Puopolo, he was so drunk that he never made any contact. "He had some energy," he said of Andy. "He was just swinging so wild; the best I could do was just hold onto him." The one time Soares said that he could throw a punch, "I was missing him by a foot."

Earlier, Scott Coolidge had testified that he'd seen something "shiny" in Soares's hand up at the MBTA stop confrontation, but he wasn't sure if it was a knife. Eddie said, "I never carried a knife, not in my entire life."

He also denied testimony of one of the football players that he had continued to punch Andy in the chest after the stabbing. "Never happened," he insisted.

Because of his extensive criminal record, Richie Allen did not testify in his own defense. Instead, Henry Owens put three coworkers at the Carnival Lounge on the stand who all told the jury that Richie had not left the premises until 2:10 a.m. According to the time line already established, this meant he hadn't been at the first confrontation with students, blocking the alley so that Naomi Axell could first get away, or at the second confrontation outside the MBTA station, where Tom Lincoln had been stabbed.

His manager testified that Richie Allen left his post as bouncer only when he heard the fight erupt at the van, outside in the alley across the street. He said Richie had left the club to break up the fight.

Under cross-examination, Mundy challenged each coworker's recollection but also used his line of questioning to remind the jury about the prevalence of the pickpocket scheme that had plagued the Combat Zone for the last couple of years. He asked each of the Carnival Lounge employees if they were "aware" of the "robber-whore" problem in the Zone, how these women "wandered around the streets ripping off innocent people," and they said they were.

After he got all three employees to say that these "kinds of individuals" would never be permitted inside the Carnival Lounge, Mundy was allowed to put one more prosecution witness on the stand. Her testimony would challenge the credibility of Richie Allen's coworkers.

Cassie McIntyre, the sixteen-year-old prostitute who had jumped out of the Harvard van, would normally have been called to the stand before the defense had its say. But she'd evaded her parole officer and efforts to compel her to court all week, and the police had only caught up with her that morning.

Cassie was thin, small in stature, and aged by the scar running down the side of her face. She was mad about being hauled into court and made it clear she didn't want to be there. But she testified that she and Naomi Axell had been inside the Carnival Lounge all evening.

It was a powerful moment for the prosecution, according to one lawyer familiar with the trial, who described her as "bobbing and weaving" on the stand. She contradicted Leon's testimony that he didn't know the prostitutes. She was young and unsteady, typifying the exploitation of young women in the Zone. When asked how long she had known Leon Easterling, she replied, "Since I can remember."

"And how old are you?" Mundy asked.

"Sixteen."

"You say you're sixteen?"

"I'm still in juvenile court, so I must be," she replied.

Mundy asked her if she remembered what she'd said to the police officer that morning when he'd recognized her by her scar. "Do you recall saying to him, 'I did not stab that white motherfucker, but I'm glad the motherfucker is dead'?"

Sherwin and Owens objected to the question, which the judge overruled, and Cassie was forced to answer. "Nope," she said, but the damage was done.

In closing, Edward Soares's attorney argued that there was no credible evidence that he had a knife. He said the stabbing was a result of a street fight, not a shared enterprise like in a bank heist, planned beforehand. Joint enterprise did not apply, he said.

Walter Hurley told the jury that they couldn't decide the case on sympathy for Mr. Puopolo or on sympathy for the defendants. In a relatively muted and brief closing, he asked the jurors to decide on the evidence, the facts, and the law "as the court gives it to you."

As the trial went on, Wallace Sherwood overcame his reticence. By the closing, he'd grown impassioned. Like Hurley, he argued that the stabbing was the last act of a spontaneous brawl that didn't offer the defendants an opportunity to reflect or premeditate. But he also rebuked what he called the "arrogance of the Harvard football players" and questioned the credibility of their testimony.

"You would think that they were in some monastery praying and people broke in and robbed them. They came from Harvard with their traditional dinner, but they weren't drunk, nor were they affected by alcohol. They had a cocktail hour, two coupons for each person, but they weren't drunk. They had beer afterward, and they only had two beers, but they weren't drunk. They went to the Naked i, a place that one of the witnesses admitted made you drink fast because that's how they make their money, and they only had one or two drinks. But they weren't drunk?"

He emphasized a point that seemed to be otherwise overlooked: that Cassie McIntrye, the prostitute invited back to the fraternity house, was only sixteen years old. He asked the jury to consider whether the diminutive teenager could have forced herself into the van and onto the lap of six-foot-four, 240-pound man without solicitation. "Do you really believe that? Just one swish of the hand would have knocked her out of the car."

He argued that the football players initiated the fight by cornering Soares at the transit station, "plain and simple." He added, "You know it has to take a certain amount of arrogance to get on that stand and say that Mr. Soares—I guess they want people to believe this—just backed up like a crazy man and they, the students, not at all pursuing him, simply followed."

He concluded his closing by praising the victim. He called Andy Puopolo's attempt to rescue his teammate a noble act. "I think that whatever may be said, that Mr. Puopolo must be a fine gentleman to disregard his personal safety to go help his friends." But Sherwood argued that if it was a noble act for Andy to come to the assistance of friends, surely "it's noble for Mr. Easterling."

Henry Owens used his closing argument to tell jurors that they couldn't draw any conclusions from the fact he hadn't put Richard Allen on the stand and that the burden of proof was on the prosecution. He questioned the testimony of Russell Savage, the only Black witness and the one who said he saw Richard Allen punch Andy. He reminded the jury of the testimony of other football players who heard Richie Allen encouraging them all to go home and "get out of the area."

The government, he argued, was stretching to bring his client, Richard Allen, into this joint enterprise case. "Somehow the government's case just doesn't stand up when you look at it as it applies to Richard Allen. Somehow the guy is not involved. The mere presence at the scene of the crime does not make one guilty." He added that Richard Allen was being charged with murder for one reason only: he was a Black man in the vicinity.

The prosecution gets the last word in a criminal trial, and Mundy, who was known for his powerful closings, made good use of it: a seventy-minute closing that disputed all the defense's arguments, one by one.

As Sherwood had inveighed the "arrogance" of Harvard, Mundy invoked the respectability of the Ivy League institution. He also reminded the jury that the victim himself wasn't "a millionaire's son from some suburb in Connecticut." He was a local boy, a product of working-class Boston who had grown up in the North End and gone through the Boston school system.

Mundy challenged defense attorney Sherwood's likening of Easterling's act with Andy Puopolo's defense of his team-mate, pointing out that Easterling had jumped in front of Tom Lincoln and stuck a knife into his belly, without Lincoln having thrown a punch. He pointed out that Easterling slashed Andy, not once but twice—the second time while Puopolo was trying to leave the scene.

"And it was no flick of the knife," he said, reminding the jury of the powerful medical evidence presented. Doctors who had worked to revive Andy in the hospital testified that the two wounds in Andy's heart were deep, "twisted and jerked," Mundy said.

Mundy told the jury that the defendants weren't the only ones who had constitutional rights. They had to think about the victim. "The man we have been talking about is under six feet of dirt in Holy Cross Cemetery . . . He had a right to life, and he was deprived of that right. He had a right to a peaceful death, and he was deprived of that right. He had a right to make his peace with God, and he was deprived of that right."

It was in the jury's hands to dispense justice, not just justice for the defendants, but justice for the six million residents of the Commonwealth of Massachusetts, and justice for the victim's family, Mundy said. "You are the conscience of Suffolk County."

CHAPTER TWELVE
State of Mind

FINDING A VERDICT—or verdicts—would not be easy. The case had three defendants, seven indictments, and a complex legal theory. The jury had to decide what was or wasn't a shared state of mind, what was or wasn't premeditation, and whether the right of self-defense or defending someone else applied.

Besides all that, the jurors had to decide what constituted "the heat of passion" in a street brawl and how much passion was needed to make premeditation unlikely. Doing so became even trickier when the judge told them that according to the U.S. Supreme Court, premeditation only required a few seconds— and time wasn't as important as the sequence or logic of events.

In his closing, Tom Mundy had already gone over how the joint enterprise theory applied to the case. In his instructions, Judge Roy explained it to the jury again. Addressing Henry Owens's argument that his client was being charged for merely being a Black man in the vicinity of a crime, Judge Roy also emphasized that a person's "mere presence" at the scene didn't justify a conviction. The jury had to decide if Edward Soares's and Richard Allen's presence in the alley made them "ready to assist" the stabbing or somehow provided encouragement.

Judge Roy made his own views about Leon Easterling's defense pretty clear in a special conference that he had with all the lawyers before he gave instructions to the jury. "There isn't a single indication that Easterling himself was inflamed by any blow upon himself, and the heat of passion upon adequate provoca-tion, it doesn't seem to me, is in this picture." According to law, the judge told Easterling's attorney, the heat of passion couldn't apply because his client had testified that he'd been responding to the attack on Soares, which made whatever he did intentional. Soares's lawyer, Hurley, concurred with the judge on this.

But the transcripts also show that in the instructions to the jurors themselves, which were almost an hour and a half long,

Judge Roy's language was neutral as he explained the law and possible verdicts. It boiled down to this: If Leon Easterling had intended to kill Andy and premeditated, that was first-degree murder. If he had meant to kill Andy but hadn't premeditated—or thought about it first—it was murder, but in the second degree. If he had no intention to kill but was using the knife recklessly, it was manslaughter. If the jurors believed Leon had been defending himself or Edward Soares, they could find him innocent. But this, the judge noted, was only a valid defense if he hadn't been the aggressor and if he had to stab Andy to save himself and Soares from death or serious harm.

If the jury bought into the joint enterprise theory and believed that Edward Soares and Richard Allen shared Leon Easterling's "intent" as he headed to the alley with a knife, they were as responsible for the murder as he was. For Eddie Soares, who had been in a fistfight with Andy on his own, the jurors could convict him of assault and battery, even if they decided that Easterling had acted alone in the stabbing, the judge said.

The knife itself was a problem. By law, its mere existence in Leon's hand was enough for the jury to infer both malice and an intent to kill—even without any verbal threats, the judge said. Similarly, the medical evidence, which spoke to "the method and number of the stab wounds," was, by itself, enough for the jury to decide that the murder was intentional. If the jury found Leon Easterling had been defending himself or Eddie Soares but used "excessive force," the jury could still find him guilty of manslaughter.

In the stabbing of Tom Lincoln, all three defendants had also been charged with assault and battery with a deadly weapon (the knife). Eddie Soares had an additional charge: assault and battery with a dangerous weapon (a shod foot), for kicking Steve Saxon when he first caught up to him helping Naomi Axell up after her fall on Boylston Street.

Judge Roy reminded jurors that while the defendants were being tried together, they had to weigh the evidence against each of them separately. If they had reasonable doubt that

Richard Allen or Edward Soares did not share Leon Easterling's state of mind, they must find them not guilty of the murder charge. However, if they believed the prosecution's joint enterprise theory, that the two other defendants had shared Easterling's state of mind, they had to convict them all equally.

The jury began deliberating that afternoon.

Andrew Sr. had decided that he didn't want to be in the courtroom when the verdict was read. Hounded by the press from the first day in the emergency room, followed to the funeral parlor where he made arrangements to bury his son, and chased by TV cameras during the trial, he wanted privacy now. He didn't know how he would react, but whether it would be relief or disappointment, he didn't want the world watching. He went back to work at his office in the North End and waited for the news to come by phone from his sister-in-law Janice Puopolo, who had attended the trial.

At home waiting with the rest of the family, Helen Puopolo was in torment, living "a nightmare" that would not end, as she later described to a *Herald* reporter. She struggled with feelings of hatred for the three men who had taken her son and prayed to God each night to lessen her feelings of hate. She also prayed that her son would get justice, that these three men received the maximum sentence. She couldn't sleep for worry that they would be acquitted.

While Helen's means of survival was not to ask too many questions and not know too clearly who had been in the alley or exactly how the knife had plunged into her son, Danny burned to know every detail. On spring break from Boston College, he consumed every newspaper story about the trial and every radio report, and he watched the television footage in the evening. He waited anxiously for the daily updates from his father, his Aunt Janice, and his Boston Latin School friends who attended the trial. How was the trial going? What were their impressions of the jury? Did the prosecution have enough evidence?

With time on his hands, Danny had written a letter to Mayor Kevin White. It had been White's agency, the Boston Redevelopment Authority, that had backed the idea of zoning the Combat Zone as an adult entertainment district. Part of that original plan had been to increase the policing of the area, not neglect it, and Danny asked the mayor why that never happened: Why had District One police been allowed to sit on their hands, and why had they been drinking in the bar instead of stopping prostitutes and their pimps from ripping off people on the streets? Why had the mayor of Boston allowed any part of the city—his city—to become so lawless that in a single week both his brother and the off-duty state trooper had died after fights in the Combat Zone?

The mayor responded, sending a letter back immediately. After a couple of lines expressing his condolences for Andy's death, the letter quoted crime statistics meant to show what a good job the mayor was doing in making the city safer. Danny recalled that it pissed him off. But he was equally angry at the criminal underworld. He felt sure that neither prostitutes nor pimps would be able to run any kind of pickpocket operation in the Combat Zone without the tacit approval of the mob.

For the ten days since the trial began, Danny read every detail about his brother's murder. But now he just wanted it to be over. When the jury didn't reach a verdict the first day, he and his family grew anxious. They had been told that the longer the jury stayed out, the better the chance for the defense.

At his mother's suggestion, Danny had begun saying a rosary for Andy every day when his brother was in the hospital. Danny kept saying a rosary every day even after Andy died, praying his brother got justice. While he awaited the verdict, he prayed that the jury would convict all three defendants of first-degree murder so that they never had a chance to get out of prison. Then, maybe, he would find peace.

Henry Owens was worried. In a private conference with the lawyers, the judge had made it crystal clear that he felt the defendants became aggressors in the fight once they followed the retreating students back to the van. Owens said he thought the judge's opinion was obvious in his phrasing of instructions to the jury and that in a complex case such as this one, when the jurors struggled to understand legal terms and concepts, they relied heavily on the judge's instructions.

And whether the judge offered his opinion or not, the jurors' ears were sharply attuned.

The jury, which had deliberated four and a half hours the first afternoon, resumed the next morning. But after only twenty minutes the foreman announced that they had a verdict.

Early that morning, a large North End crowd had begun to gather anxiously outside in Pemberton Square, Danny recalled. They filed into the courtroom, alongside friends and family of the Puopolos and of the defendants, filling the gallery to capacity by 10:20 a.m. Court clerk Ernest Handy would later tell the press that the air was so tense his knees had been shaking.

More than a dozen deputy sheriffs surrounded the defendants, according to media accounts. Richard Allen and Edward Soares were handcuffed together. Leon Easterling, handcuffed with his hands in front of him, sat in the defendants' box. The jury entered the courtroom, heads bent.

The clerk asked Leon Easterling to stand and Foreman Woodrow Cureton, the sole African American on the jury, began to sort through the seven indictments. He declared Leon Easterling guilty of first-degree murder.

Leon gasped, pursed his lips, but then turned stoic, according to the news reports. Friends and family members gasped and moaned. The jury also found Leon guilty on assault and battery with a deadly weapon for stabbing Tom Lincoln. The judge gave him an additional eight- to ten-year sentence, which he specified be served consecutively.

Leon's lawyer, Wallace Sherwood, thought maybe he hadn't heard the judge correctly. "After a life sentence, on which there is no parole?" he asked. "Yes," the judge insisted.

Soares was next. Foreman Cureton announced: "Guilty of murder in the first degree." Eddie, who had been clutching his Bible and praying, rolled his eyes and turned to his family and friends, who were sitting together on a bench along the wall. His mother, Mary Soares, burst into tears and screamed, "Eddie . . . Oh, God."

The judge sentenced Edward Soares to life without parole on the murder charge and an additional eight to ten years for assault and battery for the Tom Lincoln stabbing. The jury also found Edward Soares guilty of two counts of assault and battery with a deadly weapon (a shod foot) for kicking Lincoln and Saxon, but Judge Roy filed those charges instead of imposing an additional sentence.

As the court officer took Eddie away in handcuffs, Mary Soares reached out and tried to touch her son. She was so distraught that friends and family had to help her out of the courtroom. She kept crying, "He didn't do it, he didn't do it. My God, he didn't do it."

Finally, the jury found Richard Allen guilty of murder in the first degree but not guilty of stabbing Tommy Lincoln, which meant they didn't believe there was enough evidence to either place him at the first fight at the MBTA station or share his half-brother's intent in that stabbing. It didn't matter, though, because he was still getting a mandatory life sentence without parole. Richie was silent after the verdict was read, but when Judge Roy sentenced him to life in prison without parole, he asked, "Do I get to say anything?"

"I don't think anything needs to be said," Judge Roy responded.

Richie Allen ignored him and turned to the jury. "Well, I want to let you know that there was a miscarriage of justice here, and there was a lot of racial prejudice. You know what I mean? There was a lot of bigotry here, and I don't feel that I got due process of this court, and I feel ashamed for the commonwealth, and I feel ashamed for the jury system, and

I hope that someday the Divine Forces will forgive you, and that's the truth," he said, before the officers removed him from the courtroom.

Janice Puopolo had called her brother-in-law with the news from the courtroom lobby phone booth. When reached by the press, Andrew Sr. was quiet and deliberate. "My wife [Helen] and I feel that the verdict was just . . . because now they won't be able to do any further harm to people such as Andy."

Reporters staked out the Puopolo home, and a *Boston Herald* reporter knocked on their door. Helen invited the reporter, Rich Bevilacqua, into the house. She brought him into her sons' shared bedroom, where Andy's pictures, plaques, and trophies honored his athletic achievements. When asked how she felt about Mary Soares's emotional reaction to her son's life sentence, Helen could not pretend sympathy. "Their mothers can at least go into jail and touch their sons . . . but I can't."

Judge Roy had not tried to silence the jury by demanding that they keep quiet after the verdict, but on their own they formed a pact: no one would talk about their deliberations. Descending swiftly from the bus with their collars up against the wind, they pushed past news reporters and the cameras staked out at the entrance to the Hotel Lenox, where they'd been sequestered for almost two weeks.

"No comment," jury foreman Woodrow Cureton offered. Others simply said, "Sorry," and kept walking.

Tom Mundy was naturally pleased with the verdict. He called it a close and hard-fought case that had involved a number of complex legal technicalities. Ironically, he noted that the trial had caused little friction between the attorneys involved. At the time, he didn't know how dramatically that would change.

While Walter Hurley, Eddie's lawyer, declined to comment other than to say that it was a hard case, Henry Owens and Wallace Sherwood filed an appeal almost immediately.

CHAPTER THIRTEEN
The Color of Justice

HENRY OWENS MAINTAINS that his client, Richard Allen, never stood a chance—not when he was tried together with Leon Easterling and Edward Soares. Not when there was so much pretrial publicity lumping the three defendants together and identifying them as pimps. Not when the whole city was in a furor about the Combat Zone.

At the time, he railed against the power of Ivy League prestige, and he suspected that the Harvard name was the reason three heads had to roll for this crime. "If you'd changed the facts," he told the *Boston Globe*, "if it had been a Black kid from Roxbury Community College involved in a fight, I don't think it would have even gone to trial."

But most of Owens's anger was reserved for the judge. He firmly believed that Judge James Roy was appointed to preside on cases when the state had a special interest in winning a conviction. In his mind, that rigged the trial from the start.

Then and later, he called Judge Roy "the thirteenth juror." Jurors tend to take their cues from any judge, who they see as the neutral expert, he said. Judge Roy had transmitted his belief that all three defendants were guilty through his dismissiveness toward the defense—not to mention his inability to get Owens's name straight

After four months of negative publicity for his case, Owens received a groundswell of support after the verdict. Two days after the jury came back, the *Boston Globe* wrote an editorial questioning the fairness in sentencing three men to life for a crime only one of them committed. The verdict was "harsh justice," joint enterprise was a "murky theory," and the jury had taken a leap to find malice and premeditation in a "spontaneous brawl." The editorial partly blamed the verdict on the public's "pervasive" interest in the case and Combat Zone crime—in other words, the publicity that had, in part, been drummed up by the *Globe*'s own news coverage. The rest of the blame was placed on "undertones of race and class," a reference to Harvard prestige and the city's virulent racism.

In a separate column a few days later, the *Boston Globe*'s Robert Jordan blasted "the outrage of the white sympathizers of the victims," which he said went beyond the call of justice. Those who "identified with Puopolo" didn't want an "eye for an eye," he wrote, "but three eyes for an eye."

Boston's biggest names in civil rights law immediately rallied around Owens. The legendary William Homans, the lawyer credited with helping abolish the death penalty in Massachusetts, told the *Boston Globe* that there hadn't been enough evidence that Richard Allen and Edward Soares had shared Easterling's "intent" to justify a conviction for first-degree murder. Attorney Harvey Silverglate, a prolific author as well as a prominent civil rights lawyer, said that the jury hadn't understood the meaning of premeditation. He called the outcome of the trial "a horrible miscarriage of justice."

As if to validate this conclusion, another jury in another racially charged case rejected the prosecution's use of the joint enterprise theory the very next month. Richard Poleet, the white car mechanic who had been pulled from his car and beaten in retaliation for the white assault on Theodore Landsmark with an American flag, had and would continue to linger much longer than Andy in his coma. As a result, the case against his assailants hadn't been rushed. It didn't go to trial until the month after the Puopolo verdicts.

The similarity between the two cases continued to invite comparisons. Both victims were white men who suffered comas, although Poleet was still in a vegetative state when the case finally went to trial. In both cases the prosecution had charged three Black men for the crime. But here the similarities ended.

In the Poleet case, the jury acquitted one of the Black teenagers of all charges, found a second defendant guilty, but of slightly lesser offenses, and convicted only one of the defendants of the maximum charge. (Poleet died the following year, never having come out of his coma, and five years later the conviction against the defendant for the maximum charge, intent to murder, was overturned and never retried.)

The circumstances of the two crimes also differed significantly. There was only a single confrontation in the Poleet case, fewer eyewitnesses who testified, and no confession. And although Poleet was robbed, there was also no allegation of any organized criminal activity like the Combat Zone pickpocket scheme. But coming so quickly on the heels of the Puopolo trial, the verdict seemed to be a clear repudiation of the joint enterprise legal theory that had convicted Edward Soares and Richard Allen of first-degree murder.

For years, Henry Owens had been frustrated in his attempts to appeal the prosecution's use of peremptory challenges to eliminate Black jurors, but now in the spring of 1977, with the turnover of justices in the state's Supreme Judicial Court, he was hopeful. He said he felt that if there was any time his argument might be heard, it was "right here, right now."

At first, his family didn't worry about the appeal, Danny said. Defense lawyers did that with every guilty verdict. Everyone who had gone to the trial had said that the evidence against the defendants was overwhelming and that winning an appeal would be a long shot. But quickly, family members began to feel the shifting sands of public opinion.

Trying to finish his sophomore year at Boston College that spring, Danny began to feel like the headlines would never end, he said. Walking to a class, he'd notice a passing gaze linger on him in the hallway: *He's the guy whose brother was murdered in the Combat Zone,* he imagined at first. But then because of all the media attention on the verdict, he began to imagine an accusation: *You know, the one involved in that racist trial.*

Danny didn't understand what race had to do with it. Andy hadn't been killed in an antibusing demonstration and the defendants hadn't been innocent Black teenagers from Roxbury who found themselves caught up in a street fight. Easterling, Allen, and Soares had been Combat Zone hustlers with long criminal records. Why did wanting them to go to prison for taking his brother's life make him a racist?

"If three Italian white guys from the North End had murdered my brother, I would want them convicted just as much," Danny said. He would spend his life obsessing over the identity of the mysterious man in the cranberry jacket who had pulled Charlie Kaye out of the van and reignited the fight, believing the man was probably Italian and mob connected. To him, this explained why witnesses were confused over whether he was white, Latino, or Black. It would also explain why police couldn't "find" him to arrest him that night, why no one ever turned him in, and why, even decades later, no one could guess his name.

For Boston, the race issue was, as a *New York Times* piece would put it, "The problem that won't go away." While the city was hardly the only one beset by racial violence in the 1970s, it was starting to nail down its reputation as the "most racist." As the *New York Times* piece noted, the sustained level of white violence against Blacks set Boston apart from other troubled cities—and it was what kept capturing national attention. The city was known for its elite academia, brilliant technological advances, and liberal politics, yet its white residential neighborhoods were dangerous for Blacks. There were large portions of the city where it wasn't safe for Blacks to work, play, or even drive through.

As tension in the schools began to subside in 1977, it escalated in the neighborhoods. Massachusetts Bay Transportation Authority buses were stoned, racial graffiti was painted on homes, car windows were smashed, and buildings were firebombed. The violence went both ways, but white violence was at a peak. White gangs threw liquor bottles and beer cans at the homes of Black families that had the audacity to move into their Dorchester neighborhood. A Black homeowner in Hyde Park had to hold off white teenagers trying to attack him with a shotgun.

Blacks in Boston had to be wary of baseball games in Fenway Park, where fights regularly broke out in the bleachers, or at the

Boston Garden, where fans might hurl the N-word at their own Celtic stars on the floor. Even in upscale white neighborhoods such as Beacon Hill and Back Bay, where the white residents claimed racial enlightenment, Blacks felt no more welcome.

Carson Beach was the perennial problem, so volatile each summer it became a symbol of the city's racial intolerance. Located between white South Boston and the predominantly Black and Hispanic housing project in Dorchester's Columbia Point, the public beach was in the news throughout the summer of 1977. One day police had to break up a band of white teenage girls who encircled a couple of Black mothers with their babies and carved the N-word into the sand. Another day, police in riot helmets were called out to stop a gang of white male teens trying to prevent Black teenagers from swimming in the water.

After a single day of fighting between Black and whites led to eleven arrests, Governor Michael Dukakis called a press conference, and the state attorney general announced that the Special Violent Crime Commission would be reconvened to speed up prosecution of racial incidents. But it didn't matter how many arrests police made, how outraged the governor became, or how disappointed the mayor, if Black victims received no justice from the courts and the white perpetrators got off easy.

One of the most glaring cases of racial injustice was the murder of eighteen-year-old Brian Nelson in Medford, a suburb just north of Boston. In an incident of road rage following a traffic dispute, a van filled with nine young white males chased a car full of three Blacks. The car fishtailed on the ice and came to a stop. In the fight that erupted, one of the Black teenagers was stabbed to death with a knife and a broken bottle and apparently beaten with a tire iron. In a particularly tragic twist for the family, he was killed only three blocks from the West Medford city square named in honor of his older brother, a corporal who had died in the Vietnam War.

The media gave the incident little coverage. Police who investigated the crime wouldn't even acknowledge that the attack was racial. The court not only reduced the original murder charge on nineteen-year-old Robert Colangeli, a U.S. Marine, to manslaughter and assault and battery with a dangerous weapon but also dismissed the assault charges against the other whites involved in the fight.

Like Andy, Brian Nelson was stabbed several times with a knife, but also assaulted with a broken bottle and possibly a tire iron. Three witnesses, two Black and one white, provided testimony in court that linked Colangeli to the knife. And yet in the July 1977 trial, an all-white jury acquitted him of all charges.

Coming just four months after the Puopolo verdict, the contrast was hard to ignore. As the *Boston Globe*'s Robert Jordan noted in his column, in one case there was "harsh justice," in another "no justice."

At Boston City Hall, Clarence J. Jones, the first Black deputy mayor in the city's history, was so enraged he wrote a letter to the *Boston Globe* comparing the two verdicts, in part complaining about the lack of media attention. In the Puopolo case, he wrote, a man everyone agreed had nothing to do with the physical attack was in jail with a life sentence for murder; while in the Nelson case, the man who was accused of the murder went free. The difference, he said, was the race of the victim.

Boston might have been, as the *New York Times* described it, a city where "angry and bitter whites feel that they, too, are the victims of race, not its exploiters," but by the fall of 1977, white voters were growing weary of the anger and bitterness.

They rejected the most vociferous of the antibusing activists and voted Louise Day Hicks and John Kerrigan off the Boston City Council. Pixie Palladino, the feisty antibusing School Committee member from East Boston, lost her seat, and for the first time in nearly a century, a Black candidate, John O'Bryant, was elected to the School Committee. Mayor Kevin White went as far as saying that busing "is no longer an issue in the city."

Busing *was* becoming less of an issue now that it was in its fourth year, but largely because whites, in droves, fled to the suburbs or put their children in parochial schools, making white students a minority—less than 42 percent—of enrollment in the Boston Public Schools. But intense racial battles raged incessantly in other arenas, especially in neighborhoods like Hyde Park and sections of Dorchester, which were being slowly integrated.

In fact, the U.S. Justice Department's Community Relations office announced that it received more reports of racial violence in Boston in 1978 than any other office in the nation—including those in the South. The city decided to start keeping its own data on racial crime. It was not flattering data.

Boston had more than six hundred incidents of reported racial violence in 1978, according to its own police statistics. The data confirmed that while the violence did go both ways, 64 percent of the reported cases were white attacks against Blacks in 1978, increasing to 71 percent in 1979.

The worst of all these attacks would expose and deeply humiliate a city that liked to think of itself as the cradle of American liberty. At the tail end of 1977, twelve African American boys and girls from a private religious school in Pennsylvania came to Boston to visit the historic Bunker Hill Monument with two chaperones. On their walk back to the bus stop, a group of white young men attacked the tourists with baseball bats and hockey sticks. Four Black male teenagers and one of the chaperones were rushed to the hospital, according to the *Boston Globe*.

These were innocent, out-of-state schoolchildren on a field trip who just wanted to see Bunker Hill. They hadn't understood that in the segregated city of Boston, it wasn't safe for Blacks to venture into all-white Charlestown.

Three white men were swiftly arrested, perhaps too swiftly, and Garrett Byrne, the Suffolk County district attorney, promised to expedite their prosecution through the Major Violators Division. An outraged Mayor Kevin White visited the wounded visitors in the hospital and was quoted in the *Globe* as promising that "this lawless act of inhumanity will be punished to the full extent of the law."

The problem was that the "full extent of the law" would prove extremely limited. When the three men accused of the attack were tried in Suffolk Superior Court in November 1978 on forty-two criminal charges, fourteen various assault charges each, an all-white jury acquitted them.

One problem was that there was a credible issue of mistaken identity at the trial. A witness aboard the bus told the grand jury that the attackers were years younger than the defendants who were charged, and two of the victims who testified at the trial could not identify the attackers. Criticism about this verdict focused less on the jury than the shoddy police work that had gone into capturing the wrong culprits in the first place. But the acquittals in this high-profile case underscored, once again, that Black victims could not get justice.

The director of Boston's Human Rights Office, Buford Kaigler, called a press conference at City Hall Plaza after the acquittals. "You don't want to second guess a jury, but if these aren't the people, where are they?" he asked.

He railed against "Mississippi justice" where there was one set of rules for whites and another for minorities. The acquittals were starting to add up, with the exoneration of the white Marine for the stabbing of Brian Nelson and now this. Other Black community leaders, from state representatives to officials at the Massachusetts Commission against Discrimination and the newly formed state Human Rights Council, began to question whether Black victims in Boston could get justice.

At a press conference called on Beacon Hill at the end of 1978, the chairman of the Human Rights Council, John O. Boone, announced that according to his statistics, there had been nine hundred incidents of racial violence statewide in a six-month period, "and hardly any convictions except against Black people."

He promised to petition the U.S. Justice Department to investigate the attack on the Black tourists in Charlestown and bring the perpetrators to justice. But no whites would ever again be tried or punished for the crime.

*

Meanwhile, a new twenty-five-member interracial coalition had formed that September to demand fairer treatment for Blacks in the criminal justice system. In what was just the beginning of a trend that would escalate over the next few decades, Blacks nationwide were serving time in prison at a rate 8.5 times higher than whites. In Massachusetts, it was worse: data collected by counsel to the U.S. House Subcommittee on Crime showed that Blacks were serving time in the state's prison at a rate seventeen times higher than whites.

The interracial coalition included the Legislative Black Caucus; the same John Boone who headed the state's Human Rights Council; the renowned activist Erna Bryant, who was director of the Black Ecumenical Council; several Black ministers; the Citywide Coalition for Justice and Equality; Boston University professor Howard Zinn; and Harvard professors George Wald and Ruth Hubbard. Its first mission was to demand that the state overturn the convictions of Leon Easterling, Richard Allen, and Edward Soares.

On the day before the attorneys for the defendants began appeal arguments before the Massachusetts Supreme Judicial Court, the Citywide Coalition for Justice and Equality held a press conference across the street from the statehouse. Activists argued that the racial hysteria created by the city's hatred and prejudicial pretrial publicity had made it impossible for the defendants to get a fair trial.

Inside the stately John Adams Courthouse the next day, defense attorneys made a similar claim to the high court: the jury had been poisoned by the publicity and the city's racism. Specifically, on legal points, the defense argued that there hadn't been enough proof of premeditation or of joint venture to justify the first-degree murder convictions.

As protesters picketed outside in Pemberton Square, carrying a banner that read "Free Soares, Allen, and Easterling," Wallace Sherwood told the high court judges that while he was reluctant to bring up racism, he had no other choice. He pointed to the prosecution's use of peremptory challenges, which had prevented 92 percent of the potential Black jurors from sitting on the Puopolo case. "The present system does not provide a mechanism by which a Black man can get a fair trial in Massachusetts."

In the fall of 1978, the Citywide Coalition for Justice and Equality produced a leaflet entitled *What the Boston Media Never Told You: Puopolo Defendants—Victims of Racist Injustice*, which argued that the three defendants convicted of first-degree murder had only been "defending themselves and others" against a racist attack. A comparison was made to the Brian Nelson case in Medford, where the white teenagers involved in the attack had their charges reduced or dropped and the white Marine who witnesses said stabbed Nelson to death had been acquitted. The leaflet, which urged its members to write the Massachusetts Superior Judicial Court justices to support the defendants, called the first Puopolo trial "an appallingly racist double standard of justice."

In a coalition that was full of heavy-hitting activists, Edward Soares's mother was, perhaps, the most effective spokesperson. Mary Soares, who now went by Mary Harris, was a religious woman in her midfifties and emanated motherly devotion. Tireless in her efforts to free her son from a life sentence, she attended protests and made appearances on network television. She held her own with the famed lawyer Alan Dershowitz when they were both featured on *Say Brother*, a public affairs program about African American issues produced by Boston's public television station, WGBH.

For viewers, Dershowitz explained the legal definition of "joint enterprise." His tone suggested that its requirement of "prior agreement" between the parties meant it didn't apply to the defendants in the Puopolo murder, because the murder was an outcome of a spontaneous brawl, which was the defense's argument. Without specifically referencing it, Mary Harris sought to prove her son wasn't a part of any robber-whore operation. Not only wasn't he a part of any "joint enterprise," she said on the television program, but he had only recently returned from living in New York and had not seen Richard Allen and Leon Easterling for five years prior to the night of the stabbing.

Eddie Soares wrote a letter from prison, dated September 21, 1978, telling his side of the story, intending to lay out "the facts of the matter, as I personally viewed them." At the trial, he'd testified eloquently that he'd come to help the Black woman on the street because she was a human being in need, but in this letter, he said that he hadn't come to the aid of the Black woman at all, that Richie Allen had. He had been walking up the street when the Harvard football players cornered him at the MBTA station and assaulted him. But his major point was that Tom Mundy had been trying to pin the entire stabbing on him at the original bail hearing and switched tactics to joint enterprise only after Leon Easterling announced that he wanted to confess.

In keeping with his trial testimony, Soares said in his letter that he had followed the football players back to the alley alone and challenged everyone to a fistfight, but only Andy accepted. He had not even known that Leon Easterling followed him until the man jumped on his back and into the fight. Soares said he learned that Andy had been stabbed when he looked at his own knuckles and saw his skin bleeding after police had arrested him.

Later, in a separate statement included in the Coalition's May 26, 1979, press release, Soares pointed out that he wasn't a "major violator," or hardened criminal—the designation that had pushed the case to an early trial amid fresh publicity. "I was charged with unarmed robbery when I was 17 years old and sent to Walpole for five years," he was quoted as saying. "I am now 35. I made a mistake when I was young, and I paid for it. This is the extent of my so-called extensive record."

He sold jewelry for a living. "People may remember me on Washington or Tremont Street. I had a table with a black velvet cloth on it. I always wore a blue denim hat. I used to yell: Everything for a dollar, no need to holler. Everything's a buck, everyone's in luck." In the same statement, he asked anyone who remembered him as a jewelry peddler to contact the Citywide Coalition for Justice and Equality.

Soares's September 21, 1978, letter from prison played up the class differences that he said had worked against him receiving a fair trial. "I assume that Puopolo being from Harvard, and these witnesses, made it an easy task for the jury to believe them, instead of my testimony—the truth. I never attended Harvard. I made it only to sixth grade in school. But, I am aware that my very life has been taken from me because of lies and not validated by my actions. I am sure that Harvard and the Puopolo families are powerful enough to cause my end."

As the criticism about the verdict mounted, the Puopolo family tried not to pay attention, Danny said. It was the first year after Andy's death, and they all struggled with their grief. If the public support had turned against them, they still had overwhelming support from their friends, the Harvard and Boston Latin School communities, and their neighborhoods.

Much of that support came in the form of tributes to Andy: memorial basketball games and road races, a special Hasting Pudding show dedication the year he would have graduated, and, eventually, a touch football tournament between former teammates of Harvard and Yale before the end-of-season matchup that would become a tradition for years to come. All these events helped raise money for scholarships in Andy's name.

The biggest tribute of all came at the end of October 1977. Danny's older cousin Daniel Puopolo and friends of the family spent the summer collecting signatures to petition the city's Park and Recreation Commission to rename a park in Andy's honor. The Boston City Council approved the ordinance.

The waterfront park, on Commercial Avenue at the foot of Foster Street, was where Andy had begun his athletic career playing baseball on the dusty diamond and working on his jump shot in the basketball court directly behind the field. The park also had a public pool almost at the harbor's edge and, along the northern side, several bocce courts where the old Italian men from the neighborhood played for hours.

The park had been designed by Olmsted and Eliot, the firm responsible for New York's Central Park and Boston's Emerald Necklace system, but the city had neglected it for years. On a sunny and crisp day in late October, however, the park was dressed up in wreaths of carnations and laurel, with a new sign on a ten-foot post that proudly read "Andrew P. Puopolo Jr. Park." For the dedication ceremony, a grandstand was centered just beyond the pitcher's mound in the baseball diamond facing the street, with rows of folding chairs in the outfield. A crowd began to gather: extended family, including both of Andy's Italian grandmothers, in their eighties and wearing black, sitting in the front row, photos show; Andy's former roommates at Harvard, friends, teammates, former coaches, Boston Latin School's current football cocaptains wearing the school's purple and white colors; and the Harvard dean of students, Archie Epps, all attended.

Danny, in a suit and tie, stood on the grandstand beside his father. He recalled taking the microphone later to say a few short words, mostly thanking everyone for coming and the committee for organizing, and to say how much this would have meant to his brother. He and Andy had played a lot of baseball together on the patchy baseball field, and Andy would have been touched by the turnout, Danny said. All the seats were taken, and people, trying to get a view of the grandstand, pressed up behind the last row and along the sides. Danny saw neighbors they hardly knew, faces he only recognized from the street. The crowd had grown to about three hundred.

Governor Michael Dukakis took the microphone to say how Andy's hard work and dedication was a model for all youth. Next, the state representatives and senators gave short speeches about how important Andy had been to the community and how fitting it was that the park where he played baseball should be named for him.

Boston City Council members were there in force, including Louise Day Hicks and John Kerrigan, the antibusing activists who were, at the time, up for reelection; the flamboyant

Albert "Dapper" O'Neil; and Frederick Langone. All praised Andy's character.

With so many politicians in attendance, it was impossible for Danny not to notice a glaring absence. Boston's mayor Kevin White, who was known to be cautious about his image as the mediator of Boston's racial storm, had not shown up.

It was one of the early signs that Andy's murder was becoming politicized. The city was dividing into two camps roughly aligned with antibusing and pro-busing forces: those who believed justice had been served at his murder trial, and those who believed the verdicts were racist. Andy Puopolo had somehow come to represent both Harvard privilege and the city's beleaguered white neighborhoods.

CHAPTER FOURTEEN
Death Grants No Appeals

ONLY MONTHS AFTER the trial was over, the Puopolo murder was being talked about as the "turning point" of the Combat Zone. Perhaps "tipping point" would have been better words. It was actually a trio of events that began with the outgoing police commissioner's secret report exposing mob influence and rampant police corruption, followed by the Puopolo murder and the death of the off-duty state trooper. Together, these three events had unleashed enough outrage to focus the city on cleaning up the Zone. The new police commissioner, Joseph Jordan, had quickly begun to prove that with a little political capital, the job could be done.

In addition to the initial "saturation" enforcement strategy that flooded the Combat Zone with police, Jordan also cleaned house. Two months after Andy was murdered, he'd installed a new command staff in District One with carte blanche to select thirty-seven new uniformed officers and twenty-four detectives from anywhere in the city. Changing leadership and ridding the department of corrupt cops had an instant effect. Robberies, assaults, theft, and pickpocketing declined by 33 to 55 percent in the first four months of the year.

Police kept up the pressure on nightclubs and bars, doubling the amount of complaints filed. Arrests for robberies shot up 89 percent. Car thefts were down 27 percent, and arrests for car theft rose 107 percent. Neighborhood and citizen activists commended the improved professionalism of the police.

By June, the Alcoholic Beverages Control Commission had revoked the license of the Zone's largest strip club, the Two O'Clock Lounge, and two nude bars. It suspended the license of the Piccadilly Lounge, the Naked i, and ten others—on prostitution charges—although all would appeal.

With more cops than prostitutes walking the streets, the world's oldest profession had taken a hit. For a brief moment, efforts by the prostitutes' union to decriminalize their trade, supported by the American Civil Liberties Union, appeared to have a fighting chance that spring: the Massachusetts Supreme Judicial Court agreed to hear arguments that the existing state law was sexist because female prostitutes were persecuted while the male clientele were let off. But the high court responded by issuing an advisory to law enforcement: arrest more male clients. That couldn't have been good for business.

Former U.S. congressman Barney Frank, then a state representative but formerly in Mayor Kevin White's office, had filed a bill on Beacon Hill to legalize prostitution in specially zoned areas like the Combat Zone, but he was swimming upstream. There would be no new leniencies in the Zone.

The Boston Redevelopment Authority (BRA), the prime mover behind the original concept of a zoned Adult Entertainment District, had done an about-face. After briefly considering moving the Zone to one of the harbor islands and other options, the BRA announced a plan to "shrink" it out of existence. And while this would take longer than anyone imagined, the mission was unalterable.

District One police continued to aggressively patrol the bars and clubs for violations that the Alcoholic Beverages Control Commission and Boston Licensing Board used to issue suspensions and closures. At the same time, the Suffolk County District Attorney's office dug deeper into the true ownership of the nightclubs, X-rated theaters, and bookstores used by the mob to launder illegal profits. The secretary of state hauled a half dozen of the bar owners into court for failing to file the adequate corporate paperwork, and the FBI probed the mob distribution of pornographic materials in Boston as well as nationwide. While most of the strip clubs with suspended and violated licenses remained open on appeal, the Combat Zone in the summer of 1977 was a ghost town.

At the Two O'Clock Lounge, the *Boston Globe's* Jerry Taylor found the place so empty one June evening at 10:00 p.m. that two stage bars were closed and the main salon only half full. Over at the Naked i, which had been a goldmine, dozens of bar stools and booths were empty. Owner Ray Comezo estimated that business was off 50 percent. "Adverse publicity has hurt us a lot," he said. "I think a lot of people in the metropolitan area think the Combat Zone is closed."

Was the Boston mob pissed off that profits in the Combat Zone were down? At the time, Danny desperately wanted to believe they were.

That October, in a cellblock at Walpole state prison, an inmate who had mob ties went after Richard Allen and stabbed him with an ice pick. It was bad enough that he was rushed to Norwood Hospital.

As it turned out, he'd escaped serious harm by curling up into a ball and protecting his chest—but Danny recalled being heartened by the attack. Walpole state prison was always a violent place, overcrowded with the state's worst offenders, but the state police had also recently unearthed the existence of "assassination squads" that executed fellow inmates on orders from the outside.

In 1977, when the Angiulo brothers ran their headquarters in the North End, many people in the neighborhood had a connection inside Walpole state prison—a brother, a cousin, or a friend of a friend who was an inmate—Danny said. He and Andy had several childhood playmates who'd wound up doing time. When Danny returned to the old neighborhood to visit his grandmothers, he'd look up old friends and ask everyone the same question: Did anyone know if the attack on Richie Allen had been in retaliation for his brother's murder?

No one knew for sure, but everyone had a theory, Danny said. Some were sure the attack was revenge for Richie Allen's role in the stabbing. Others said it was payback for all the money the mob-owned strip clubs had lost because of the police crackdown. But it was all speculation.

Years later, outside Polcari's storefront on the corner of Parmenter and Salem Streets in the North End, Danny recalled approaching the most credible source of all: a mob boss recently released from prison. This mob boss, who Danny didn't want to name, told him that they were being "watched" as they spoke, and he was careful with his words. The attack had been partly in retaliation for Andy's murder, he said, and partly because Richie Allen had shot off his mouth to an inmate who was affiliated with the mob. Danny said he wasn't sure whether to believe it.

Andrew Sr. recalled receiving an offer for street justice for his son about six months after the Walpole state prison incident. He said he was at the Fernwood in Revere, a classic Italian restaurant with heavy woodwork and dim lighting. Even in midafternoon, it was dark and cloistered. The restaurant was owned by one of his clients. In the late 1970s, the economy was beginning to rebound, and J. Gandolfo and Sons, which sold specialty items like olive oil and cheeses to restaurants, was flourishing.

Having grown up with many of the transplanted North Enders who were opening Italian restaurants in the suburbs, Andrew Sr. had certain advantages as a salesman. For one thing, he still spoke fluent Italian; for another, he was willing to work hard. Work had become a welcome distraction from grief, and he made frequent visits to client restaurants to build his accounts.

He and many of these restaurant owners often shared stories about their youth in Boston. More than a few locations were frequented by mobsters, some they had gone to school with as kids. Bookies liked to hang out at the Fernwood. As he sat with the owner at one of the tables near the kitchen, concluding business over coffee, the front door opened. A man approached them with a message for Mr. Puopolo: some "friends" wanted to help him.

Decades later, in 2017, Andrew Sr. recalled the conversation this way: The man said that nothing had been done about his son, and the way his friends saw it, something should have been. The going price for an in-house execution at Walpole state prison was five thousand dollars, but in this instance, certain contacts wanted to provide this service as a gesture of sympathy and respect. The inmate who had made an attempt on Richie Allen could get rid of all three of the defendants, but the main target would be Leon Easterling. There would be no cost to the family.

"All you have to do," the man said, "is give your okay."

Andrew Sr. recalled that his friend, the restaurant owner, didn't seem surprised by this offer. Everyone at the time knew about the "execution squads" at Walpole, which had made headlines. Andrew Sr. was sure the offer was genuine.

He thanked the man and said he would get back to him. To his very core, Andrew Sr. wanted to avenge his son, cut down in his prime. It was an instinctual urge, he knew that. This form of justice would be final. Over once and for all. He wouldn't have to think about taking the stand again. Death grants no appeals.

At home, he found Helen in the kitchen. Danny had been on his way downstairs from his bedroom. He recalled hearing his parents talking in hushed tones. He halted midway on the stairway and listened to every word.

He said his mother wasn't shocked or horrified. She'd had an uncle who had been an enforcer in the early twentieth-century Mafia. It was instinct, wanting revenge. In her own way, she wanted these men to suffer for taking her son from her and had taken to writing letters to all three of the defendants in prison, detailing what they had done to her family so they would know the extent of the misery they had caused.

Danny recalled that his emotions leapt when he heard about the offer. He imagined the shiv, sharpened glass, or razor blade attached to a pencil or toothbrush plunged into Leon Easterling's heart. He saw Soares and Allen pummeled until their brains shut down. The three men who ended his brother's life deserved nothing less.

We are Christians, Andrew. We can't give way to hatred, he heard his mother say.

No. No, thought Danny. Don't listen to her. His father had to agree to the justice that Andy deserved, he had to accept the offer and let the North End avenge its own.

Although they remained devout Catholics, Helen's grief had been so unyielding, so relentless since Andy's death, that the weekly ritual of Mass couldn't touch the pain. She and his father had turned to new religious programming on television—something she'd never considered before—listening to preachers who weren't Catholic. But Pentecostal evangelist Jim Bakker and his wife with the trademark fake eyelashes, Tammy Faye, brought his mother some solace. The televangelists and their PTL (Praise the Lord) Club would go down in scandal in the next decade, but in the short term, their emphatic promise of an afterlife made mourning more bearable.

You will never see Andy again, Helen said to her husband, meaning in the next life, Danny recalled. If Andrew Sr. agreed to this and killed those men, he would be damned to hell. She reminded him that he had two sons, and he had to think about what would be best for the other son who still lived.

Standing on the stairway, that other son heard his father agreeing with her. Danny said that he realized in that instant that his father would not have asked his mother for her opinion on this particular matter unless he wanted this kind of advice.

In Danny's bedroom, *The Godfather* poster was still taped to the wall. He tried to console himself with the thought that he didn't *want* Easterling or Soares or Allen to get off easy with death—that death would be an easy way out. The *real* justice—the *real* revenge—would be for them to suffer long, miserable lives, rotting away in prison. But it was no good. No amount of rosary prayers could change his thinking or touch the fury that had come to live just beneath his skin.

CHAPTER FIFTEEN
Landmark Decision

IN THE SMALL living room in the back of the Puopolos' house, off of the formal dining area, the television was left on, droning at a low level when no one was watching. Danny said that since the stabbing, his family had developed a habit of always listening from the kitchen, with half an ear.

In March 1979, Danny was a senior at Boston College. He said he never regained his ability to concentrate on his business major and still fantasized about becoming a cop, armed and trained to clean the city scum off the streets. Cop killing was at its peak in Boston as crime and homicide rates continued to rise sharply in the seventies and eighties. Most days, Danny didn't really care if he got caught in cross fire, which might be a relief. But he knew his mother still struggled daily and felt he couldn't make it worse for her. If she worried every day about him, she might not survive. So, Danny muddled though his accounting classes as if he could care about a balance sheet. He just had to make it to graduation—this was as far ahead as he could see.

One day, in late afternoon, he was in the kitchen, trying to get up the energy to study, while his mother was at the stove, starting dinner. They both heard the familiar promo music for the five o'clock news from the next room. And then their last name.

He recalled both of them rushing into the family room to watch the broadcast. The court had found a systematic rejection of potential Black jurors. Danny started shouting at the television, asking what the hell was going on, although he knew. They both knew: the verdicts had been overturned.

To them, it meant justice had been taken away from Andy, snatched away as life had been. His mother retreated to the kitchen, not wanting to hear anymore. Better to shut it all out than suffer one more indignity.

But Danny could not shut it out. He understood this meant the family would have to go through a trial all over again. They'd have to deal with the reporters, the stories, the questions in everyone's eyes about what Andy had been doing in the Combat Zone again. And if the prosecution won another conviction, he wondered, could some new high court take that away, too? Did it ever end?

He couldn't understand how the courts could do this to his brother. Had all the evidence, all the people who'd been right there and seen Leon Easterling stab Andy to death, meant nothing? Had Easterling's own confession meant nothing? Danny thought of his brother collapsing on the street, all the surgeries he went through—his heart fighting like hell to beat again. He thought of all those days in the hospital when Andy had been helpless—one organ shutting down after the other. Did his brother's suffering mean nothing?

The state's highest court didn't "give a shit"—that's what it felt like to Danny. The court cared more about the rights of three Combat Zone hustlers. Men he saw as criminals who had spent their entire lives high, stealing cars and ripping people off. Lowlifes. Their rights were more important than Andy's?

The Suffolk County District Attorney's Office promised to appeal the state decision to the federal court, but Danny couldn't take any solace in that. If the state court didn't care about how much his family suffered, he doubted a federal court would.

He couldn't believe that the verdict had been overturned, even though he'd known it was a possibility: Mundy had said as much last fall after a high court in California overturned a murder conviction because of the jury makeup. But at the time, Danny didn't understand why something that happened in a California court ruling should affect what happened in Massachusetts.

To Danny's mind, the only thing that had kept his family going—justice for Andy—had been ripped from their hands. He wished more than anything that his father had agreed to have the defendants whacked in prison.

On the television newscast, a reporter was interviewing a defense lawyer who called the high court's decision

groundbreaking—a much-needed reform. Danny snapped
off the television set. The phone in the kitchen began to ring
and would ring all night with friends and family who had
heard the news.

Danny didn't want to hear their shock or their sympathy.
When he was upset or needed distraction, he tended to go the
gym, where he boxed to blow off steam. He couldn't remember
exactly but said this was likely one of instances when he might
have needed to punch something. Hard.

The Massachusetts Supreme Judicial Court's eleven-page
decision rejected all the defense's arguments that there had
not been sufficient evidence for premeditation or joint enterprise to warrant the convictions of all three defendants for
first-degree murder.

The justices determined that there had been "ample" evidence submitted at trial that Easterling stabbed the victim with
deliberate premeditation. The decision noted that according
to testimony, Easterling brought a dangerous weapon into a
brawl, used it twice before the fatal blow, pursued the fleeing
football players two hundred and twenty-five feet from the first
fight at Tremont Street to the van, made verbal threats that he
was going to "cut" people, and stabbed the victim "with great
force," while the victim "attempted to disengage from combat."

Despite the opinion of all the high-profile defense attorneys
who had weighed in on the misapplication of "joint enterprise"
to a street brawl, the high court ruling stated that the facts of
the case also supported the conviction of both Soares and Allen
for first-degree murder. Both men had been within five or six
feet when Easterling stabbed Tom Lincoln, close enough to see
the knife and hear his threats to "cut the whiteys." All three
defendants had charged down toward the van after the retreating football players—and after a pause for reflection. According
to the legal standards, this made the two men accomplices.

The high court's written decision had even stated that in
Soares's case, "there is little question that the jury could deem

Soares an abettor in the murder of Puopolo because he had fought Puopolo up to the moment Easterling did the stabbing." While noting that Allen took no part in the physical fight, the high court pointed out that he was the first of the defendants to confront the students to prevent them from chasing the women believed to have stolen the wallet. Even "if he does not participate in the actual perpetration of the crime," his presence at the scene helped "encourage and embolden the perpetrator," because he was available to give assistance if needed, the high court wrote.

In a landmark decision, however, the high court ruled that Tom Mundy's challenge of twelve of the thirteen Black potential jurors showed a "pattern of conduct" that suggested a likelihood that the jurors had been excluded because of their race. In what would become known as the *Soares* decision, the high court said that it didn't matter that the Puopolo jury had not been exclusively white. The percentage of Black potential jurors the prosecution had rejected—92 percent compared with 34 percent of white jurors—was proof that that defendants' rights to a fair trial had been violated.

The Massachusetts decision came on the heels of a decision by California's Supreme Court known as *People v. Wheeler,* just six months earlier in September 1978, the first state court to reject the lenient standards of the prevailing federal case law, *Swain v. Alabama.* The California high court had overturned the murder and robbery convictions of two Blacks by an all-white jury because the prosecution's use of peremptory challenges had denied the defendants their right to an "impartial jury" that was representative of a cross section of the community.

The decisions of the California and Massachusetts high courts would become known as the "*Wheeler-Soares* approach" to the use of peremptory challenges. It would be adopted by several other states and eventually, although it would take seven years, influence federal law.

The high court's remedy also addressed the prosecution's complaint that the defense had used its peremptory challenges in exactly the same way to eliminate seventeen potential jurors with Italian last names. The new legal standards applied equally to defense and prosecution and prohibited a pattern of peremptory challenges that were exclusively based not only on race but also on sex, color, creed, or national origin.

No one was happier than Henry Owens, but the larger Black community in Boston also rejoiced. In an editorial for the *Bay State Banner*, the state's newspaper for the African American community, founder and editor Melvin B. Miller called the new protections essential to Blacks. The issue was the fundamental unfairness for Blacks in the criminal justice system itself. Noting the Brian Nelson and Bunker Hill cases, he wrote, "When whites are victims of violent crime, Black defendants bear the full weight of the law, but when the victim is Black, white defendants often are charged with a less serious offense and can hope to be acquitted by an all-white jury."

Miller noted that Blacks "were never sympathetic to the three men convicted of this brutal killing," but he criticized Tom Mundy who "saw to it that he had as white a jury as he dared to make it." He added, "Understandably, the Puopolo family is upset. We sympathize with them. Unfortunately, the process of creating a new law is sometimes awkward. It opens wounds and renews grief."

Andrew Sr. said he'd done everything the court had asked of him. He put his faith in the court system and turned his back on mob justice and now he felt betrayed. But not by Tom Mundy. From the start, the prosecutor had been compassionate and sincere. He was the one person in the system who truly cared about justice for Andy, and he was the one person Andrew Sr. continued to trust.

When Tom Mundy arrived at the Puopolo home later that week, Andrew Sr. welcomed him inside. Mundy made his way through the living room to the familiar kitchen, where Helen was likely already heating coffee. It was after work for both men, Andrew Sr. recalled, in the evening.

Mundy didn't talk about was what the Massachusetts Supreme Judicial Court's decision meant for him personally. Andrew Sr. did not know that Mundy was in line for a judgeship or that the high court's sharp rebuke of his use of peremptory challenges was the first taint on the prosecutor's otherwise stellar legal career. This could and ultimately did negatively affect his chances for a seat on the bench, but it didn't lessen his dedication to the case. The prosecutor committed himself completely.

The fact that the high court's decision specifically said that the evidence in the first trial fully supported the jury's guilty verdicts made the decision harder for Andrew Sr. to understand. If the justices knew these men were guilty, why were they still letting them off? It didn't seem to matter to them that Tom Mundy's juror challenges had been legal at the time or that the defense had used their challenges the same way to strike Italian jurors. No one seemed to care about that. Sitting in the kitchen with Andrew Sr. and Helen, Mundy explained that the high court was simply saying that they had to make their arguments all over again—with a new jury. He understood that it was painful for the family to go through, but he was going to work hard to win.

He told Andrew Sr. he was important to the case, a sympathetic witness, and asked if he would be willing to get back on the stand. Andrew Sr. wasn't eager to go through it all over again, which would involve putting on his most somber suit and telling the world what it's like to rush to the hospital in the middle of the night and learn that your son had technically arrived dead on arrival. What it was like to realize that the emergency room rescue, the miracle, was for nothing. To accept that no amount of praying could bring his son to life.

Helen typically stayed quiet at these meetings with the prosecutor. But Andrew Sr. knew how much she had suffered and how much more she would suffer when new headlines in the daily paper, on the radio, and on television made it impossible for her to avoid the details of her son's murder.

He didn't want to look at the blood-crusted shirt and pants again, didn't want to think about how carefree his son had been when he'd put on those clothes to go to his team banquet. He didn't want to stand up in the front of the courtroom with those three human beings who had killed Andy in his line of sight. He recalled asking the prosecutor: how were their chances?

Over the last two and a half years, Tom Mundy had been to the Puopolo home many times—twice with his wife for dinner—and he was usually comfortable sitting in the sunny kitchen with its spotless counters and Italian countryside mural painted on the wall. But not on this day. He didn't try to ease the conversation with a pleasant joke. He wasn't grim, necessarily, but he didn't attempt to create false hope.

Mundy said that the justices' decision proved that the prosecution had enough evidence to support both premeditation and joint enterprise. That was as close to an objective opinion as they could get. But, no matter how strong the case, the prosecution was always at a disadvantage at a second trial.

The case wouldn't be tried until the fall so as to give the federal court a chance to review Mundy's appeal of the state's decision, which was a long shot, he acknowledged. But the fall of 1979 was a full three years after the murder. Not all witnesses would be readily available to testify, and memories naturally faded. Eyewitness testimony tended to be less fresh, less specific, and less believable to the jury after so much time had passed.

Defense attorneys also had more time to prepare. They would review the transcripts and hunt for any slight inconsistencies between testimony at trial and testimony given at the grand jury proceedings and on the police reports. They would exaggerate those inconsistencies. The attorneys would also challenge anything said at the second trial that deviated even fractionally from the first trial testimony, with the aim of impeaching the credibility of each and every prosecution witness. It might make sense to offer a plea bargain of second-degree murder, Mundy said.

Of course, this was incomprehensible to a man who had lost his son. *They murdered him in cold blood*, Andrew Sr. said he had responded.

Mundy explained that a conviction for second-degree murder carried almost the same penalty—life imprisonment—and the defense might not accept it anyway. The only difference was that there was a possibility for parole after the convict had served fifteen years.

Andrew Sr. had sat through the trial and heard Scott Coolidge explain how Andy had limped away from the fight with his abdomen bleeding. How he'd made it to the street when Leon Easterling came after him a second time. Andrew Sr. had listened as the doctors described the fatal wound and how it was caused by a knife thrust not just into the abdomen, but up until it reached the heart.

That knife killed the dreams and hard work that had fueled his son's young life, crushed many of the dreams Andrew Sr. and his wife had had, and left them all wounded in a way that would truly never heal. He couldn't stomach the idea that these three men might one day be back on the street. Andrew Sr. would not drag himself to court again and listen to every gory detail or look into the eyes of murderers for anything less than full justice for Andy. You have to honor my son, he remembered telling the prosecutor. These three men had to be charged with first-degree murder.

Mundy promised to do his best.

At a pretrial conference at the end of April 1979, Tom Mundy announced that the Suffolk County District Attorney's office would again seek first-degree murder charges against Leon Easterling, Richard Allen, and Edward Soares in the retrial.

The Citywide Coalition for Justice and Equality, which wanted all charges against the defendants dropped and the men set free, went on the attack. In a press release issued on

April 30, the organization condemned the "racial prejudice" of both Tom Mundy and Judge James Roy, as well as the commonwealth's decision to retry the three defendants. "In the first trial, the defendants were convicted of conspiracy to commit first-degree murder even though their act was to come to the defense of two Black young women who were being pursued and attacked by the Harvard football team and were themselves attacked and outnumbered at all points in the incident," the press release stated. "It was only by continuously slandering the defendants with lies falsely characterizing them as 'pimps' and the women they were defending as 'whores,' that Mundy obtained his conviction in the first trial," the press release said. The coalition was outraged that Tom Mundy had repeated these same slanders at the pretrial hearing.

To add emphasis to the cause, the press release also referenced a *Boston Globe* exposé that had run earlier that month on racism in prison sentencing. The *Boston Globe* Spotlight team investigated nearly forty-five hundred court cases over a two-year period and found that Black defendants served longer terms for the same crimes as whites. The judges also regularly sent Black inmates to the prisons with the worst conditions, which at the time were Deer Island, Walpole, and Norfolk, and shipped white offenders to the more humane Billerica and Concord state prisons. An added benefit of Concord state prison was that inmates were eligible for parole much earlier than they were at Walpole state.

As more attention focused on the racial inequities in the criminal justice system, Danny felt increasingly nervous. He said he kept wondering why no one was talking anymore about the injustice done to the man who had been murdered. It all seemed to be exclusively about the rights of the murderers.

Danny kept thinking about the family's lost opportunity to have the three defendants killed in prison. It was too late now. As they awaited a new trial, the three defendants were transferred to Charles Street Jail, away from the execution squads of Walpole state prison. The only way anyone could ever get to them, it seemed, was if the family's worst nightmares came to fruition and they were freed.

The sixth year of court-ordered desegregation in Boston began so peacefully it almost justified Mayor Kevin White's proclamation that the busing crisis was over. But midway through September, all hell broke loose.

As the school buses rolled into South Boston High School one morning, fifteen masked teenagers waited in ambush. From the street, they launched rocks, bottles, paint, and two-inch metal bolts at the glass windows, forcing the Black students inside to dive for cover. The attack, which injured two students, was retaliation: Blacks had stoned a bus full of white students leaving the McCormack School at Colombia Point the previous week, and Southie was furious it had received so little media attention.

The students' use of ski masks and other signs of sophistication led police to speculate that adult antibusing advocates had been involved in planning the assault. One community leader actually defended the bus stoning: "The kids were frustrated—this was just their way of showing that they were not going to be pushed around," a spokesman for the South Boston Marshalls, an antibusing organization, told the *Boston Globe*.

As Pope John Paul II prepared for a ten-day trip for peace that would honor Boston as its first U.S. stop, and as city officials rerouted traffic for the motorcade, spruced up the Boston Common, and double-checked the papal sound system, racial violence in the city took the ugliest of its many ugly turns.

It was a Friday afternoon football game at Charlestown High, and the away team, Jamaica Plain High, was up six to zero. Darryl Williams, a Black sophomore from Roxbury, had just played a great first half for Jamaica Plain. A talented wide receiver who had his sights set on winning a football scholarship to college, he must have felt like he was on his way. Not only had he been given a starting position at only fifteen years old, he'd just caught a pass that had led to the team's touchdown.

September 28 was a warm, sunny day, and the Black coach took his primarily Black team to the end zone instead of the locker room for a pep talk. There, on the field, which afforded a view of the nearby Bunker Hill Monument, the students formed a huddle. As the coach concluded and the players began to rise, a shot rang out.

Fifteen-year-old Darryl Williams dropped to the ground. Oddly, there were no signs of blood or a wound, but the coach asked him if he was all right. He didn't answer. In the era of busing, four Boston police officers and four private security guards were on hand securing the football field. As Darryl was loaded into the city ambulance, a police cruiser chased after a red car that had been seen careening past the field but found no suspects, the *Globe*'s Dan Shaughnessy wrote.

A slog of Friday afternoon rush-hour traffic slowed the ambulance on its way to Boston City Hospital. When Darryl Williams finally arrived at the emergency room, surgeons discovered a .22-caliber bullet wedged in his spinal column. The bullet had found its way through the small amount of skin exposed between the bottom of his helmet and the top of the shoulder pads. Darryl Williams showed no signs of nerve or brain reaction. Doctors put him on life support, but they didn't expect him to make it.

The shooting of a fifteen-year-old on a high school football field repulsed everyone, not just city officials, politicians, and civil rights activists. Neighborhood residents, people who protested against Blacks coming to their schools, and the angry student fans who rooted against Jamaica Plain were appalled. White violence had finally gone too far.

As the city held its breath waiting to see if the fifteen-year old would regain consciousness, high school students all over the city began to raise money for the Williams family. In white Charlestown, which was normally fanatically protective of its own, the community organized to help police catch the culprits. Two Charlestown priests made their way to a Roxbury Church.

Darryl Williams awoke from his coma the day after the shooting. He could respond to questions by blinking his eyes, but he still needed a respirator to breathe. The bullet could not be removed, and he would be paralyzed from the neck down for the rest of life.

Mayor Kevin White told the press that he knew in his gut that the shooting had been racially motivated, and he called in the FBI to help find the attackers. United States senator Paul Tsongas, speaking at the state's largest antipoverty agency downtown, told a crowd of fourteen hundred that the attack was "propelled by the festering of prejudice." State representative Mel King, an influential Black activist who would make a competitive but unsuccessful run for mayor, said the world should be made aware that this event wasn't an isolated case but a pattern of white violence against Blacks.

Three days after the shooting, police arrested two teenagers who were high school dropouts with criminal records, as well as one juvenile. The three youths had been on the rooftop of one of the buildings at the *Bunker Hill* housing project across the street from the football field. They claimed to have been drunk and shooting at pigeons.

The shooting put Boston's racism back in the national spotlight just as all eyes were on the city for the upcoming arrival of Pope John Paul II. Protesters threatened to stage a "walk" at the Boston Common where the Pope, who was one year into his papacy and at the peak of his popularity, was to say Mass to a crowd expected to be in the hundreds of thousands. The city decided to change the venue, citing the need for increased security.

Mayor White's approval rating dropped ten points in the city's neighborhoods after he called the shooting a racial crime, just before he was up for reelection in November. A police investigation determined that the .22-caliber handgun had been shot from 100 yards away, and the mayor backed off on his original assessment of the crime. "With a pistol? Not even the most skilled military marksman could have deliberately picked off a target at that range and hit it," he told the *Boston Globe*.

Whatever the true motivation of the sniper attack, the mayor's change of heart came too late. Few believed him, least of all Darryl Williams or his family. Fifty of the city's political, business, church, and community leaders gathered to denounce racial violence.

The day the Pope conducted a service at the Holy Cross Cathedral in the South End, eighteen hundred protesters chanted "Justice for Darryl" and carried a sign that said "Holy Father, please stop racism in Boston," all of which appeared on network television. Two days later, hundreds of students in Madison High School in Roxbury, Boston Technical School, and Boston English High School boycotted classes and staged a protest at City Hall Plaza.

As *Boston Globe* reporter Richard Stewart explained in his coverage of the events, "One of the tragedies of Boston's divisions may prove to be that even the truth is not acceptable if it does not sustain the preconceptions." In other words, whether the three drunk teenagers on a rooftop meant to or could have pinpointed and shot a Black football player on the football field at one hundred yards was irrelevant. It was the kind of repugnant white-on-Black violence that happened in Boston.

For security reasons, Charlestown High School would not be allowed to host another home game for nine years. Darryl Williams was quadriplegic for the rest of his life. His family eventually sued the city for his medical care costs, lost, and received no compensation. The youngest of the three suspects was tried as a juvenile and found not guilty. The two older teenagers on the roof pled guilty and were sentenced to only ten years—and at the preferred Concord state prison, where that sentence could make them eligible for parole in as little as two years. They received longer concurrent sentences for a previous crime: an armed robbery of a Little Peach variety store where no one was injured.

CHAPTER SIXTEEN
The Edge

THREE DAYS AFTER Darryl Williams was shot, the U.S. Supreme Court rejected Mundy's appeal of the state's decision to overturn the Puopolo trial verdicts. The judge began hearing pretrial motions for the new trial the next day.

Henry Owens's opinion of the case hadn't changed. He said he still believed that the prosecution had a very strong case against Leon Easterling and Edward Soares. He wanted his client, Richie Allen, tried separately. Edward Soares had a new lawyer, and he, too, wanted his client's case tried separately.

Andrew Good was a tall, thin, white defense attorney just setting out on his own. Originally from New York, he had graduated from Boston University Law School and earlier in his career had worked for Henry Owens. Like many young lawyers who had gone to college in the sixties, he viewed the law as a means of advancing civil liberties and civil rights. He was as frustrated as Owens was about a jury selection process that managed to always produce all-white juries to decide the fate of Black defendants. "It was maddening," he said.

Good privately raged at Tom Mundy. He said it infuriated him that the prosecutor presumed that the three defendants were pimps just because they were Black men in the Combat Zone at night. Good had gotten to know his client pretty well and said Eddie Soares was deeply religious and hardly fit the macho, tough-guy image of the 1970s street pimp. "He was just a guy trying to make a go of life, selling trinkets on the street," Good said. He was determined to give Eddie Soares better representation than he had received in the first trial and began preparing for the case almost a full year before the jury was seated.

While the judge was deciding on pretrial motions, news coverage of Darryl Williams's medical condition and the lifelong struggles he would face as a quadriplegic ran almost daily. This would continue throughout the trial, with the story sometimes running on the same page as the trial coverage. Darryl's mother, Shirley Simmons, was the same kind of sympathetic media figure Andrew Sr. had been. A religious and gracious woman, she called for prayer instead of protest.

Just as the stabbing of Andy Puopolo galvanized the city to clean up the lawlessness of the Combat Zone, the shooting of a fifteen-year-old Black student who was just trying to play football on a high school field was another tipping point. It forced a reckoning.

The city's racial conflict became a central issue in the mayoral race. Challenger Joseph Timilty, a Boston city councilor who had nearly beaten Kevin White in the previous mayoral election, repeatedly attacked White for "pretending" the city's racial problems didn't exist. White countered by attending just about every community meeting held across the city, especially the highly publicized "neighborhood summits" that brought people together to address Boston's racial hostilities.

Norman Zalkind, who was Leon Easterling's new lawyer, considered all this publicity a boon to the defense. "What kind of press you get before a trial begins is very, very important," he said, in an interview decades later. "And even afterward, when the jurors are sequestered and aren't supposed to be reading the newspapers, sometimes they do."

The judge denied all motions to separate the cases, and jury selection for the single trial began October 16, 1979.

Protesters marched for racial justice at the Park Street subway station, and Channel Five televised the demonstrations. Members of the Citywide Coalition for Justice and Equality issued another press release condemning Tom Mundy for his "illegal and unconstitutional" actions. They also picketed outside the courthouse in Pemberton Square.

Upstairs on the ninth floor, Judge James McGuire presided. White-haired and professorial, he'd been called out of retirement for this delicate assignment. He was known for thoroughness and an even temperament under duress, but

FIGURE 6. Defense Attorney Norman Zalkind, taken around 1979. Courtesy of Norman Zalkind.

he had boxed as an undergrad at Catholic University and was no pushover. He was considered equally hard on defense and prosecution attorneys. "He's the kind of judge I'd like to have in any case where there are emotional issues that a lawyer might be concerned would sway a judge," the legendary defense lawyer William P. Homans told the *Herald*.

Judge McGuire was determined that there would be no question afterward that this Puopolo trial was fair. The court transcripts show that he questioned potential jurors so methodically and exhaustively about their exposure to publicity and their racial bias that jury selection took twice as long as it did in the first trial.

But it wasn't the only reason. The high court decision that overturned the verdicts had included limits on the way both the prosecution and the defense could use peremptory challenges. These were being implemented for the first time in the seating of the second Puopolo jury. There was a sense among the lawyers that everyone was watching. The new standards themselves became a kind of weapon.

Although Andrew Good was the least openly combative of the three defense attorneys, the transcripts show that one of the three objected each time Mundy used a peremptory challenge to strike a juror who was Black. The defense kept a running tally of the percentage and kept the judge apprised of the number. Under constant criticism, Mundy took to explaining his reasoning for striking a juror even if no one challenged it.

Mundy went on the offensive with countercharges. "The defense struck thirteen out of fourteen potential jurors with Irish last names and 83 percent of those with Italian last names," he told the judge. The charge was picked up in a news story, and the next day Zalkind complained in court that people were coming up to him on the street and asking why he didn't like Irish or Italian people, he recalled.

But Zalkind, who was born, bred, and schooled entirely in Boston, was actually the only one of the defense attorneys who liked Tom Mundy. A tall man with untamed hair, Zalkind was an unconventional lawyer who cut his legal teeth representing voter rights protesters in Mississippi in the 1960s and later went on to represent the counterculture, including the Black Panthers, the Weathermen, and Students for a Democratic Society.

Zalkind was fond of saying that to win a case, a good defense attorney went "right up to the edge" of what was allowable in the courtroom. He said he saw Tom Mundy as doing the exact same thing, just from the prosecutor's side. In his view, the jury selection practices that had so infuriated Henry Owens and Andrew Good were less about racism and more about the prosecutor's competitive spirit. In his view, Mundy's error had been a miscalculation in determining that "edge."

Although Mundy and Zalkind sparred from time to time, the real rancor in the courtroom was between Mundy and Owens. Their conflict had become intensely personal. Mundy had been passed over for the judgeship, and he blamed Owens. It went beyond the fact that Owens's successful appeal had put Mundy's jury selection procedures, which up until that point had been legal, under a new light. Owens said that a judicial review committee member had also asked his opinion about Tom Mundy's trial practices; he had been "candid" in his opinion, and Mundy knew it. In 1977, judges recommended by the governor's Judicial Nominating Commission were further vetted by the Joint Bar Committee of Judicial Appointments, a joint committee of the Boston and Massachusetts Bar Association that made extensive investigations to determine which candidates were best qualified to become judges.

Halfway through jury selection, the defense filed a motion asking for a special hearing as to whether Mundy was systematically striking potential Black jurors once again. Judge McGuire ruled against the motion, finding there was no such pattern. But Mundy saw it as a deliberate tactic by Owens and was frustrated that the judge didn't take action to stop it.

"He is talking to the press and making me out to be a racist," Mundy complained to the judge in one of many lobby conferences recorded in the court transcripts. "It was either stand up and make wild accusations or end up in a fistfight with the man, and I was helpless and unprotected by this court."

Mundy worried aloud that Owens would use "this tactic" before the jury throughout the trial. Judge McGuire essentially told Mundy to buck up and stop complaining, but Mundy was right to worry: race would come up again and again.

Outside the courtroom, there was a carnival air. A dozen activists rode the elevators to the ninth floor. According to one of the assistant prosecutors, these protesters were almost exclusively white and looked like "old hippies." They chanted slogans and called Mundy a "racist" as they made their way into the courtroom. A couple of them veered into rooms that were closed to the public and were intercepted by court officers and sent back outside. They wrote letters to the clerk protesting their treatment. Mundy complained that protestors talked to and tried to influence the potential jurors on their way inside. The judge took one of the jurors aside and quizzed her about the conversation with protestors and its influence.

Jury selection was a nonstop battle for fifteen days. The transcripts show that the lawyers argued in open court. They argued in lobby conferences. They argued so much that the even-keeled Judge McGuire lost his patience. With a fair Irish complexion, he grew ruddy with anger as he ordered Mundy, Owens, and Zalkind to knock off their "acrimonious remarks."

This occurred midway through jury selection. If the trial had been a basketball game, all the attorneys—except for Good, whom McGuire pointedly excluded from his criticism—would have fouled out before the jury heard the first piece of evidence.

After two weeks, Judge McGuire, like Judge Roy before him, gave up trying to seat a complete jury. He settled for fifteen jurors: eight men and seven women. There were two Black men and one Black woman among the twelve regular jurors and one Black woman among the three alternates.

The trial began on a cool, overcast morning, the day before Halloween. As the jurors made the required tour of the seedy Combat Zone, the courthouse began to fill. The press section, while fully occupied, was smaller than last time. Again, spectators crowded the gallery leaving few free seats, but with no overflow into the lobby.

Among the spectators were three older men, retirees who sat in the back row, one of the assistant prosecutors recalled. They attended every murder trial in the courthouse and were called "the regulars" by the bailiff, clerk, courthouse guards, and attorneys. Defense and prosecution lawyers had taken to seeking their opinion about how the trial was going: the regulars were known to be highly accurate.

Henry Owens led the defense in the first trial, but now Norman Zalkind was at the helm. He'd insisted on this, which caused early skirmishing with Owens, but the lawyers had come to terms. They agreed that Zalkind, as he put it, was representing the defendant with "the worst case," which meant he needed to be out front.

Norman Zalkind liked his client. He said Leon Easterling at forty-four years old was more mature than many of the other people he represented and seemed "clear-headed." Easterling kept himself in shape while in prison, working out in the gym, and seemed devoted to his new wife, Mary, a twenty-year-old white woman who attended the trial every day with Easterling's sister and other supporters.

While Zalkind thought first-degree murder charges should never have been brought against either Soares or Allen, he couldn't say the same thing for his own client. Leon had stabbed a young man, "a kind of hero," not once but "twice," according to multiple witnesses and medical testimony: the prosecution had a strong case.

But Zalkind was known for seeking out hard cases. And he was known, as Thomas Dwyer, the former prosecutor, put it, "as the kind of lawyer who put $50,000 worth of effort into every $10,000 fee" that the state paid him for defending indigent clients. In the courtroom, Zalkind might have looked like an antiwar protestor in an occasionally rumpled suit, but he was well prepared and extremely aggressive. He needed to be to take on Tom Mundy.

The prosecutor had not forgotten his promise to Andrew Sr., and he planned to put his all into round two, said the newly minted lawyer working for him, Jack Dawley, who would go on to become the top assistant district attorney in Essex County. Dawley was assigned to round up the witnesses who had testified in the first trial. It wasn't easy, he recalled. The Harvard football players had graduated and scattered across the country. Several were in medical school, and others badly wanted to put the tragedy behind them.

Dawley was in search of new evidence as well. He hunted for the man in the cranberry jacket, interviewing at least eight different people who had tips about his identity, but none panned out. He found numerous informants who verified information they already had and talked to several "crackpots" with stories that led nowhere. But in the end, he got lucky in the hardest of the assignments—locating the prostitutes three years after the fact and rounding up significant testimony that corroborated the "robber-whore" pickpocket scheme.

On the first day, Andrew Sr. again took the witness stand to identify the bloodstained clothes his son had been wearing the night of the stabbing, but he couldn't bear to attend the trial all day, every day. Instead, his daughter would go, accompanied by her aunt, to represent the family.

Sitting in the defendants' box, Leon Easterling was well groomed and well tailored in an expensive three-piece suit, looking, some said, more lawyerly than his lawyer. Eddie Soares also wore a suit and again carried a Bible throughout the trial. His mother, who came to court every day, carried a rosary. In contrast, Richie Allen looked more intimidating than the other two defendants. He now had his head shaved and a tooth missing. He wore dungaree overalls, a hooded sweatshirt, and socks and sandals, as if, perhaps, he'd already conceded defeat.

Leon Easterling's young wife, Mary, and several other family members and friends attended, as did friends of Andy and of the Puopolo family. Former coaches, law school students, and random spectators vied for seats further back in the courtroom.

With only a few exceptions, the prosecution witnesses all returned. According to the transcripts, the Harvard equipment manager Chet Stone and the football players took the stand again, and their testimony was nearly identical to the first trial, although the passage of three years faded details. For example, Russ Savage, who had moved back to New York, couldn't remember that Boylston Street was one way and, when reminded, couldn't say which way the traffic flowed.

One after the other, the three defense lawyers cross-examined the witnesses. Just as Tom Mundy had predicted, everything the former football players said was compared against transcripts of the first trial, grand jury testimony, and the statements they had all made to the police in the early morning hours after the stabbing. For example, a key part of the football players' testimony was the threat Leon Easterling shouted before chasing them back to the alley—that he was going to "cut the whiteys." Chet Stone was one of the first witnesses, and Zalkind attacked his credibility by asking the Harvard equipment manager to read from the report he'd made to the police the morning of the stabbing.

"And you didn't tell them about this yelling about cutting people up, you didn't tell them about that, did you?" Zalkind asked. With the report in his hand, Stone had to admit he hadn't originally mentioned the threat to police.

Zalkind next asked Stone to read from the transcript of his testimony to the grand jury. "And you never mentioned anything about cutting—the statement about cutting people up, here either, did you?" Zalkind asked.

Later in his redirect, Mundy pointed out that Stone's testimony at the last trial ran to 105 pages of transcript and was likely to include more details than his four-and-a-half-page report to police the morning of the stabbing or his three-and-a-half-page grand jury testimony.

Zalkind also asked the equipment manager how many times he and the Harvard football players had spoken with each other about the stabbing before they came to court to testify at the first trial. In his cross-examination, Andrew Good asked Stone the same question, if he'd discussed the night's events with the Harvard students before the first trial, and he'd answered, "No I didn't."

Zalkind had noticed that this answer conflicted with Stone's testimony in the first trial. Pulling out the transcript, Zalkind had Stone read his testimony aloud to the jury. Stone had originally said he didn't know how many times he talked to students about the night in question. When asked "more than once," he'd said yes. When asked "less than a dozen," he'd replied, "Right around there." Zalkind's implication was clear: the football players had gotten together and "hatched" their story about Easterling threatening to cut them so the prosecutor could prove premeditation.

Owens had complained that during the first trial, the prosecution mentioned "Black" whenever the prostitutes were discussed. It was never prostitutes, but "Black prostitutes." In the second trial, the defense lawyers repeatedly added the adjective "white" whenever mentioning the football players. It was never the Harvard students, but the "white Harvard students." To underscore that they were privileged white Harvard students, Zalkind noted the late-model cars the young men had driven to the Combat Zone that night and that others could afford to come by taxi.

Jack Dawley, the young lawyer assisting Mundy, called it the "undercurrent" that ran throughout the trial, with the defense shifting the focus away from the crime itself. The defense attorneys also emphasized a racial divide within the van. The white equipment manager and the three white football players ran out after the Black prostitute to retrieve the wallet in two separate instances, and both times the three Black football players in the van chose not to follow them.

ZALKIND: "So, in fact, those were all the Black students that were [remaining] in the van, is that right?"

STONE: "That's right."

ZALKIND: "And all the white students and yourself ran up after—toward this Black lady. Is that correct?"

STONE: "That's right."

A little later Zalkind noted, "And, in fact, at the half-moon circle [the conflict at the MBTA station], those were all the white ballplayers, is that correct?"

Mundy objected to the insertion of race, and Judge McGuire sustained his objection. But Good brought it up again in his cross-examination, which while establishing the physical location of witnesses inside the van, also subtly illuminated that the whites had been sitting in front of the van and the Black football players were in the very back. Good continued: "And up until that time, is it correct to say that the white students that were in the rear of the van had jumped out [the tailgate] by going right past Black students, isn't that true?" And a few moments later: "And the Black students were seated in the rearmost section of the van before anybody left, is that right?" Stone agreed that Good was correct.

Parts of Stone's testimony in the first trial had made it sound as if the two prostitutes practically fought their way into the Harvard van. Henry Owens and Wallace Sherwood had both challenged this characterization in their cross-examination of football player Russ Savage in the first trial. Sherwood also brought it up again in closing, but it hadn't gained much traction with the jury.

Now Good turned up the heat on exactly how the two prostitutes got into the van in the first place. He repeatedly asked Chet Stone if he heard any talk about bringing the prostitutes back to the Pi Eta Club at Harvard. Stone responded he hadn't heard this discussion in the van.

> GOOD: "Now do you recall testifying in 1977 in this court?"
>
> STONE: "Yes, sir."
>
> GOOD: "And you recall saying at that time that there was some discussion at some point during the evening about fifty dollars between a football player and a girl?"
>
> STONE: "That was in front of the Carnival Lounge, right."
>
> GOOD: "There was some discussion about fifty dollars, wasn't there?" Stone acknowledged this.
>
> GOOD: "And did you testify in March 1977 that Charlie Kaye had a discussion with one of these women about fifty dollars?"
>
> STONE: "I believe, like I said, he made the statement."

His annoyance at Good's belaboring of this point might have sounded to the jury like he was trying to cover up the football players' sexual transactions, given a later interview jurors gave to the *Herald*. It may have made them wonder what else he was covering up, which was clearly Good's objective.

Malcolm DeCamp, the sophomore in the van who was now in medical school in Kentucky, was taken to task for the language in the report he made to police the night of the stabbing. To both police and the grand jury, DeCamp had said that the football players "backed" Soares up against the MBTA building. He also said that Andy had "jumped" on Eddie Soares. He hadn't used either of those characterizations in his testimony at trial.

In the first trial, Henry Owens and Wallace Sherwood had pointed out that DeCamp's earlier terminology suggested aggression by the students, but DeCamp had replied that he had been exhausted and still in shock immediately after the stabbing when he gave the police the report in the early hours of the morning. He called it "a poor choice of words." Now, in the second trial, all three defense attorneys challenged DeCamp about these statements. They implied, with varying levels of sarcasm, that "a poor choice of words" was the "Harvard" expression for covering up a lie. Decades later, DeCamp would recall the experience as "humiliating" and say the nitpicking by lawyers pulled his words out of context, adding that he would never again have faith in the criminal justice system to discern the truth.

Throughout their cross-examinations, Zalkind, Good, and Owens repeatedly asked for the witnesses to state and restate the height and weight of each white football player. This, presumably, was to establish the magnitude and threat they posed running down the street after the Black woman and gathering around Soares. Finally, Judge McGuire cut it off, noting that the jury had already heard these statistics at least three times.

While his voice still reverberated through the courtroom, Henry Owens's focus was narrowed on his own client, in proving that Richard Allen had no physical contact with any of the Harvard students that night. He questioned some witnesses to make them confirm that they had not seen Allen in the alley around the van and others to confirm that they had not seen Richard Allen touch Andy Puopolo.

While the defense was substantially more aggressive in the second trial, it was a strong match up. Tom Mundy's demeanor in the courtroom was less theatric than that of Owens, but his oratory style was calculated to conclude in a well-timed crescendo. He was a master strategist who had thought through nearly all the contingencies, Jack Dawley said. "There was a Plan B and a Plan C."

While Dawley was often out of the courtroom locating witnesses, Gerard Burke, a former teacher who had just graduated
from law school but not yet passed the bar, sat by Mundy's side
through the trial acting as a paralegal investigator. Burke, who
later worked years as a prosecutor before moving on to become
a lobbyist in the Massachusetts State House, described Mundy
as a smart and tough prosecutor who fervently believed in his
case. He said Mundy had a lot of evidence about Easterling and
the pickpocket robbery scheme that had been ruled inadmis-
sible in court. That evidence had convinced Mundy that the
three defendants were guilty. Even forty years after the trial,
Burke remained impressed by Mundy's passion, the "heart and
soul" he put into his prosecution of the case in the second trial.

The case was at its peak when Scott Coolidge, one of the
last Harvard students called to the stand, testified. He'd come
back from Maine, where he was working for GTE Sylvania, and
was extremely nervous, he said in an interview years later. He
knew that his testimony had been crucial to the first trial and
was afraid that three years after the stabbing he might not
remember all the details. He might botch the job and Andy
would not get justice.

But once he began testifying, his nervousness disappeared.
At key points, his memory, instead of fading, intensified, he said.
He told the jury he'd followed teammates Saxon and Lincoln
to the MBTA station, where they surrounded Eddie Soares. He
recalled clearly how not a single one of the football players had
thrown a punch or even made a threat. The mistake they made
was laughing at Eddie Soares in his crouch position with his
Kung fu kicks, as if he was going to take them all on. He vividly
recalled that as he headed down the street, he looked back and
saw three Black guys and "this white guy" (the man in the cranberry jacket) having a discussion before they came after them.

Scott Coolidge's testimony also worked against the defense's
implication that the students were fashioning their testimony to
suit the prosecutor. In his statement to police the night of the
stabbing, he said he thought that Eddie Soares carried a knife
because he'd seen something "shiny" in his hands. When Mundy

asked him about this on the stand, Coolidge said he couldn't be sure. In retrospect, he thought he might have imagined the knife after Chet Stone had shouted, "These men have knives."

But he had no doubts about the tragic end to the evening, which remained painfully vivid three years after the event. The transcripts show that Coolidge did not waver about any of the details as he described the fight that killed Andy Puopolo. He told the jury that he'd witnessed both Edward Soares and Leon Easterling punch Andy in the head and chest and that when he'd grabbed Andy away from that fray, Andy's stomach was bleeding.

"I walked over to him and we started out to the mouth of the alley," he testified. They were halfway across Boylston Street, when "the next thing I knew, the man with the brown leather jacket came up and grabbed hold of him, and he turned around and I saw the knife again and Andy and he started fighting. He was taking, you know, sideways punches with the knife into Andy's chest."

As the intensity of the memory heightened, Coolidge stopped to regain his composure. Then, he explained how he had struggled to hold Andy up as they ran across the street, looking for help. How Andy crumpled to the ground. At this point in his testimony, Coolidge choked up again, according to press accounts. His eyes filled with tears, as he struggled to continue. "I laid Andy down, and he started to bleed from the mouth and his eyes rolled back," he told the jury.

A hush fell over the entire courtroom. The silence was broken by Fran. Crying, she ran from the courtroom in tears.

In cross-examination, the defense attorneys tried to break down Coolidge's testimony, but to no avail. Zalkind asked if he really wanted the jury to believe that he saw Andy on the ground and didn't jump into the fight himself. Owens asked Coolidge to confirm that his client, Richie Allen, hadn't laid a hand on anyone. Good tried to establish that Coolidge had testified that Andy "looked physically okay" after his last exchange with Edward Soares.

"No I wouldn't say he was okay," Coolidge replied. "He had blood on the bottom half of his chest and he was holding his chest. His jacket was open and he was holding his chest or stomach."

Good reminded him that he had testified at the first trial that "he looked pretty good at that point in time."

"Yes, compared to how he looked a couple of minutes later," Coolidge retorted.

Medical testimony from the doctors backed up Coolidge's story. Dr. Joseph Amato told the jury that Andy had not one wound but two. The first had punctured the lung, but not fatally. The second had come from a blade, plunged upward into Andy's body, deep enough to penetrate a thick wall of chest muscle and pierce his heart in two places. The neutral, scientific delivery of the doctor enhanced the power of the testimony.

One of Mundy's biggest challenges was to remind the jury that the robber-whore schemes, once such a well-known problem in the Combat Zone, had even existed. During the first trial, the pickpocketing scheme was a widely reported problem still fresh in everyone's mind, but in the last three years, police had substantially reduced street crime in the Combat Zone. The headlines had faded, and the scheme was a thing of the past.

The media had speculated that because the cleanup of the Zone had caused so many prostitutes to scatter, the prosecutor would have a hard time finding the two prostitutes who had testified in the first trial. But Tom Mundy had a surprise. In addition to locating Naomi Axell and Cassie McIntyre, Jack Dawley had found the third prostitute who had been standing with the other two women outside the Carnival Lounge that night: Helen Thompson. She told Dawley that she knew of prostitutes who had worked for Leon Easterling and that he tried to get her to work for him.

Dawley found twenty-four-year-old Naomi Axell at Rikers Island Prison in New York, he said. She was nearing the end of a sentence for prostitution and larceny convictions. Because she had so little time left in prison, Dawley said, he couldn't offer her any kind of deal, but unlike the first trial, when she was a hostile witness, she was now willing to come back to Massachusetts to testify.

Axell intended to tell the jury that Leon Easterling worked as a pimp and that Richie Allen had worked protecting prostitutes in the robber-whore operation before the 1976 stabbing, Dawley said. The transcripts show that the defense attorneys objected, arguing that her testimony would be tantamount to giving the jury the defendants' past criminal records, which were excluded. Judge McGuire considered their objections. He allowed her to testify to the jury, but in a serious setback for the prosecution, the judge limited Axell's testimony.

Axell was able to tell the jury only that that she and Cassie McIntyre had followed the students back to the van expressly to pick their pockets. She could not identify Leon Easterling as a pimp, but she told the jury that she knew both Leon Easterling and Richie Allen very well during her four years of hanging around the Combat Zone and saw them every night. She also explained that if a pickpocket victim caused a commotion over a stolen wallet, some of the men who regularly hung around the Zone would step in to allow the female pickpockets to escape. There was a glitch in her testimony: she quickly identified Leon Easterling and Richie Allen, but she could not identify Edward Soares.

Next, Mundy put Detective Edward Miller on the stand. He described "a system of larceny" that was common in the Zone in 1976. He detailed how the robbery worked, saying that these women typically distracted their marks—men—by "running their hands over his body." He explained how these women were protected by men in the Zone who would start a "scuffle" if a victim began to complain and that the women would later pay these men, known as "gaffers," for their help.

Cassandra McIntyre and Helen Thompson were called to a lawyers' conference with the judge. Helen Thompson had given written statements to Jack Dawley identifying Leon Easterling as a pimp in the Combat Zone and implicating Easterling and Allen in the robber-whore scheme. But the transcripts showed that both women, who were serving time in prison, balked at testifying when it was explained to them that they could be incriminating themselves.

Tom Mundy asked the judge for an immunity order that would protect the women from prosecution so they could not claim self-incrimination in refusing to answer questions. This would compel them to testify. In an emergency session before a justice of the Supreme Judicial Court, Andrew Good, who would later become known for his appellate work, argued that because of the timing of the request, the state could not grant immunity. He won.

Neither woman would agree to take the stand. After much back and forth about its admissibility, Judge McGuire ultimately allowed Mundy to read McIntyre's testimony from the first trial to the jury. She had said that she had known Easterling "all her life," which contradicted his claim that he hadn't known her before the stabbing in 1976.

Reading testimony in the courtroom was not as compelling as hearing direct testimony. Burke said that the jury received only a "sanitized version" of the evidence the prosecution had that established that the defendants' involvement in the robber-whore scheme. Nonetheless, Mundy had put on an exceptionally strong case. When the prosecution rested, the three older retirees, the "regulars" who attended every murder trial in Suffolk Superior Court, gave Mundy an enthusiastic thumbs-up.

Zalkind said that at this point of the court proceedings, he had a heavy feeling that the prosecution was winning.

Leon Easterling again testified in his own defense, only this time there were no tears or apology. He admitted to stabbing both Tom Lincoln and Andy Puopolo but said both times were in defense of Eddie Soares, who was outnumbered. Leon said that he followed the others to the alley out of concern for his brother, contradicting Allen's alibi witnesses who said that Allen was in the Carnival Lounge at that time. Leon also testified that he later jumped into the fight in the alley because he saw Eddie, his mouth bloodied, fighting "three or four" of the football players. Eddie contradicted this assertion minutes later.

Leon first identified Soares as someone he knew only by name but then began referring to him as his "buddy." Initially

smooth and composed, he lost his cool when Tom Mundy
cross-examined him. He reluctantly took the seven-inch pen
the prosecutor gave as a stand-in for the knife he'd carried the
night of the murder, then reenacted the wild stabbing gesture
he had used on Andy Puopolo with apparent gusto. He grew
increasingly argumentative and repeatedly ignored the judge's
instructions to answer Mundy's questions instead of making
his own unrelated statements. In essence, he made an excellent
witness for the prosecution.

With all the pins now set up, Mundy simply had to knock
them down. Zalkind recalled that it was then that the prosecutor made his first misstep. Perhaps frustrated by how the judge
curtailed the prostitute's testimony, Mundy sought another
way to make clear to the jury that Leon Easterling was a known
pimp in the Combat Zone. He deviated from details of the night
of the stabbing and questioned Easterling about his lifestyle.
He asked Easterling how he could afford those expensive suits,
where and how he lived in the Combat Zone from 1972 to 1976,
and how he had the money for a gym membership, a foreign
car, a motorcycle, and a diamond earring.

At the defense table, Zalkind listened attentively, about to
object. Mundy's questions, harsh and sarcastic, were aimed at
revealing that Leon had the kind of expensive lifestyle that only
an illegal income could buy. Then Zalkind glanced at the jury.

He wondered if the jury was hearing Mundy's questioning
the way he was hearing it: as if Mundy were saying there was
no other way a Black man could afford a nice car or a gym
membership *unless* he were a pimp. The defense attorney saw
a cool look in a few of the juror's eyes. He decided to let Mundy
go on, uninterrupted.

Did Leon Easterling's (then) seventeen-year-old girlfriend
give him money to spend on overpriced drinks in the Combat
Zone that cost a buck and a half a drink? Mundy wanted to
know. He didn't say *white girlfriend*, but his meaning became
clear as he gestured toward the spectator's gallery to the white
woman sitting with the defendants' families, Mary Easterling,
who was now Leon's twenty-year-old wife.

Zalkind said he could feel the impact of that gesture. Again, he could see it in the jury members' eyes. Mundy seemed to be saying, How else could a Black man get a white woman unless he was a pimp? This was an insult not just to the defendant but also to his wife. Zalkind let Mundy twist on his own rope a bit before he finally rose to object.

Eddie Soares took the stand next, and he contradicted himself and a key part of Easterling's testimony. At first, Soares told the jury he was "petrified" when surrounded by the football players at the MBTA station but later said that he'd run down to the alley looking for a fight.

Contradicting Leon Easterling's testimony, Eddie denied that he'd had a fat lip or bloody mouth from the fight. Under cross-examination, he said he didn't know how his knuckles got bloodied when under direct testimony he had just said that Easterling's knife bloodied his knuckles.

In direct conflict with Leon Easterling's claim that his buddy had been fighting four or five football players when he arrived to save him, Eddie said he hadn't been fighting anyone, that he had challenged fifteen football players but all turned him down. Andy was the only one to take his challenge, he testified. His main point was that he hadn't landed a single punch on the football player. When he left him, Andy was "all right, he was standing."

Andrew Good called a jewelry wholesaler from New York City to the stand. He testified that Soares had been buying cheap jewelry from him in Manhattan and selling it on the Boston streets for years. This information hurt the prosecution's argument that the three defendants were all pimps or protectors, working together and helped support Soares's claim that he became involved in the brawl simply because he saw a young Black woman chased by a group of drunk white men.

As in the first trial, Owens didn't put Richard Allen on the stand. The same coworkers from the Carnival Lounge came to his defense, testifying that the bouncer had been working inside the club all night. His manager again testified that Richie didn't leave the premises until 2:10 a.m., when the fight erupted around the van directly across the street. He said that Richie only went to the alley to tell everyone to break it up, that the police were coming.

As Mundy's cross-examination would point out, this testimony contradicted the eyewitness testimony of nine other witnesses, including Richie Allen's two codefendants. Easterling and Soares both testified that they saw Allen up at the intersection of Boylston and Tremont trying to help Axell when she fell in the street. In fact, the testimony was so contradictory that the *Boston Globe* headlined its story "Conflicts in Defense Testimony at Puopolo Trial."

In Mundy's closing statement, he returned to his theme: Leon Easterling was a pimp. He asked the jury members to use their "common sense" as to how he made his money. Do you believe he makes his money by doing the cooking and shopping with an apron or cleaning the house?" he asked, sarcastically.

He also tried to focus the jury on the victim's suffering with a graphic account of how Andy passed from life into a comatose state "gurgling and choking on his own blood in the gutter of the Combat Zone."

Owens objected.

Judge McGuire told him to sit down and said the jury should disregard Owens's objection "completely."

Mundy, impassioned now, urged the jury to remember that while defendants had "rights," so did the victim and so did society. "Andrew Puopolo had a right to a peaceful death," he insisted. "It wasn't quick and clean. His death was slow and obscene."

Zalkind objected. Judge McGuire overruled.

In his closing argument, Mundy told the jury, "If you decide these cases on the theory of giving someone a break, if you don't decide this case on the basis of the evidence, you would, by such a verdict, endorse lawlessness."

As he continued, the defense attorneys interrupted Mundy so frequently with objections that Judge McGuire started banging his notebook on the bench, Good recalled. He urged the jury to ignore the acrimony of the lawyers. And for the final time in what had been a long, heated trial, his face turned ruddy red.

CHAPTER SEVENTEEN
Behind Locked Doors

AFTER THREE HOURS of final instructions from the judge, the jury met on the eighth-floor mezzanine. In a *Boston Globe* feature story, "Searching for Justice behind Locked Doors," reporter Anson Smith described this room as pale blue with two windows overlooking Pemberton Square. Jurors sat around a long wooden table that became littered with crumpled papers and overflowing ashtrays as deliberations continued in the smoke-filled room. They had their own bathroom, a clothes closet, and an ancient wall clock to remind them how much time was passing. No one, not even their guard, was allowed to listen in.

Determining even one verdict for a single defendant requires many back-and-forth arguments. Jurors object, compromise, take votes, tabulate, and retabulate as they argue. One of the jurors would later tell the *Herald* that the only thing they initially agreed on when they first entered that jury room was that they would have to convict Leon Easterling of *something*. They weren't sure of exactly what.

The jurors had to reach unanimous agreement in a case with three defendants, multiple charges, and the thorny legal concept of joint enterprise. In his instructions, Judge McGuire spent three hours outlining the law surrounding joint enterprise and the differences between first-degree murder, second-degree murder, and manslaughter, but it was still confusing. The transcripts show that the jury twice sent a court officer with messages to the judge asking for clarifications. Each time, the judge discussed it with all the lawyers before sending a reply.

Today, jury sequestration has fallen into disfavor because it pressures jurors to reach a decision so that they can return home. The jurors in the second Puopolo trial were under additional pressure: they had already been cooped up in a hotel for eighteen days, deliberations began on Tuesday, and Thanksgiving was Thursday.

According to Andrew Good, the Puopolo jury had another problem that made this period exceptionally uncomfortable for a few of them. One of the jurors was an active alcoholic who smelled terrible. No one wanted to share a hotel room with him or sit next to him. Several jurors asked the judge to discharge the smelly juror in favor of an alternate, but the judge had ruled against it.

After five hours of deliberations Tuesday and eight more on Wednesday, the jury announced just before 3:00 p.m. that it had reached a verdict. Everyone rushed back into the courthouse—except for Fran and her father. They had waited in the lobby the first day of deliberations but afterward had been instructed by the prosecutor's office to stay at home, for their own safety, in case of a victory.

The press returned. The jury filed into the courtroom and took their seats on the elevated box. Leon's young wife, Mary, sat with Eddie's family in the front row, according to Alan Sheehan's coverage in the *Boston Globe*. Defendants were led back into the courtroom individually to receive their verdicts, still in handcuffs.

Easterling, looking short and slight in a three-piece suit, was first. The court clerk rose. "Have you reached a verdict on the first-degree murder indictment?" he asked.

"We have," said the jury foreman. "We find him guilty of manslaughter." On the charge of assault and battery with a dangerous weapon for the stabbing of Tom Lincoln, Easterling was found not guilty.

Leon stood for a moment, stunned. Then he sighed with relief, according to the *Herald*. His eyes began to tear as he sank into his seat, dazed. Norman Zalkind threw his arms around him. In the first row of the spectator's gallery, Mary Easterling slid across the bench and kissed Soares's mother.

It was an incredible victory for Zalkind. The verdict meant that despite the medical evidence and eyewitness testimony, the jury believed that Leon Easterling stabbed the Harvard student to protect Eddie Soares. Mary Easterling met reporters with tears of joy in her eyes. "It's going to be a real happy

Thanksgiving. Our lawyer had hoped for a second-degree verdict. This was better than expected."

Eddie was led into the courtroom next. He appeared to have
heard the Easterling verdict and expected the same. "Have you
reached a verdict on the first-degree murder indictment?" the
court clerk asked the jury.

"Not guilty," the foreman said.

Eddie closed his eyes and mouthed a prayer. He raised his
red, cloth-covered Bible heavenward, exclaiming, "Thank-you,
Jesus!" His attorney, Andrew Good, whooped with joy. Appearing
as shocked as his client, Good reached to shake Soares's hand.

As he walked out of the dock a free man, Eddie was swarmed
by family members and friends who huddled around him
and held newspapers over his head to block reporters from
approaching. His mother, Mary Harris, was ecstatic, so happy
it appeared she might collapse. "It's beautiful. I'm so happy,
thank God," she told reporters.

Led into the courtroom next, Richie Allen, still wearing
his dungaree overalls, had overheard the cheers inside the
courtroom and was prepared for good news. When the foreman
announced the verdict—not guilty—Richie shouted, "Justice
is served!" and bear-hugged his lawyer. Aggressive in battle,
Henry Owens was subdued in victory. "It's what my client was
looking for all the time. A fair trial."

Tom Mundy, well accustomed to the stress of high-profile
cases, had been hospitalized for an undisclosed ailment earlier
that day. He wasn't in the courthouse when the verdicts were
read. But the Suffolk County district attorney himself was on
hand. Newman Flanagan, who had replaced Garrett Byrne,
declined to speculate on why this jury reversed the earlier
decision. He also refused to answer the media question that
was on everyone's mind: Had the racial makeup of the jury
changed the outcome of the verdict?

"We present the evidence in the light most favorable to the
Commonwealth. We don't determine the guilt or innocence.
Neither does the defense counsel. The jury decides that," was
all that he would say.

*

Lawyers on both sides of the case had their theories about the reversal, and most of it had to do with jury selection. At the time, Owens told the *Herald* that he didn't think the addition of three Black jurors swayed the outcome of the second trial, but when looking back on the trial years later, he said he knew from the moment the jury was selected that he was going to win.

Decades after the trial, both he and Zalkind remembered that one juror—a young Black man—had been wearing an earring when he first appeared in the jury pool, but he took the trouble to remove the earring before he was interviewed in the voir dire session. They presumed he did this so he would look more conservative to the prosecution. Mundy did not challenge him, and the man was seated on the jury. To Zalkind and Owens, the man's removal of his earring was significant. It meant that he wanted to serve on the jury, and they suspected that it was because he was sympathetic to the defense.

Zalkind recalled another juror, a young Black woman. She had young children at home, which was sufficient grounds for the judge to offer to excuse her. Because she declined the opportunity to withdraw from the case, Zalkind guessed this meant she already sided with the defense.

Tom Mundy was convinced that the jury selection worked against him. More than a month after the verdict, the *Herald* published an analysis piece by Laura White, who had covered parts of the trial. Afterward, she interviewed the prosecution and defense attorneys was well as the jurors, trying to make sense of the wildly different verdict. Mundy complained, "Every middle-aged person with a pretty good job who we felt would make a good juror had read about the case and felt a retrial was redundant. The judge excused them for cause," he said.

But the biggest factors in Mundy's defeat may have come from outside the courtroom. He went on to tell White that the jury may have been unduly influenced by the *Boston Globe* Spotlight series on racial disparities in the criminal justice system. While that series, which reported that Blacks received harsher sentences than whites, was first published six months before the trial, it was in the news that fall as the judiciary conducted its own study. The *Globe* and its readership awaited that report.

Easterling's lawyer, Norman Zalkind, also believed that what was going on in the city at the time played a role in the verdict. When asked by the *Herald* reporter if the publicity surrounding the Darryl Williams shooting had helped his case, he said, "Let's say it didn't hurt."

In a matter of two and half years, two different juries that had reviewed the same evidence, listened to the same witnesses, and decided the fates of the same three men reached wildly divergent conclusions. If justice was blind, it certainly wasn't deaf. It operated with its ear to the ground, responding to subtle shifts in societal norms and events that had little to do with the crime itself.

In the heat of white outrage at federally imposed busing and an out-of-control Combat Zone, the first jury found three Black men equally culpable of murder, although one had no physical contact with the victim. Two and a half years later, a new jury, while likely also affected by the change in judges presiding over the case, were impaneled shortly after a new set of outrages: white kids who shot a Black youth trying to play high school football; two high-profile court cases in which Black victims of white violence did not receive justice; and a *Boston Globe* Spotlight series with data showing that Black defendants typically received harsher sentences.

Inside the courtroom, the jury this time was less impressed with the Harvard influence that Henry Owens had complained about. In the *Herald*'s posttrial analysis piece, Good said he thought the most damaging testimony came from the Harvard witnesses—particularly Chet Stone, the equipment manager, who tried to make it sound as if the students had been "victimized" by the women who followed the men to the van. Good

said that when the cross-examination revealed that Charles
Kaye had been trying to get the prostitutes to come back to the
Harvard campus, the jury stopped believing Stone's testimony.

In the same analysis piece, the jurors spoke anonymously.
But several of their comments confirmed Good's position. One
said, "To begin with, no one on the jury believed Chet Stone.
This guy changed his testimony again and again." Another juror
was equally skeptical: "The case presented seemed too pat. It was
as if the defendants all seemed to know just exactly what they
had to do, and did it, so they could be tried for first degree."

But a close review of the second trial transcripts found
no pattern of Chet Stone changing his testimony "again and
again." In fact, aside from a clear reluctance to admit that the
two women had been invited into the van and encouraged to
come back to the campus, his testimony was remarkably con-
sistent. The second Puopolo jury also discarded compelling
eyewitness testimony, clear and damning medical evidence,
and conflicting stories among the defendants themselves to
decide that Leon Easterling was acting defensively.

A number of witnesses, including an outside observer with
no ties to Harvard or the students, had provided testimony that
the Harvard football players had fled from the first confrontation, running down Boylston Street and into the alley, chased by
several Black men. Medical evidence conclusively proved that
Easterling stabbed Andy not once but twice, thrusting a knife six
to seven inches into his chest. And a sympathetic and credible
eyewitness testified that the second stabbing occurred after Andy
was already wounded and in retreat, which was corroborated by a
police officer who testified that he saw Easterling chase and stab
Andy Puopolo as his teammate was trying to get him away from
the scene. In fact, the prosecution's case was so strong that the
verdicts came as a surprise to "the participants in the trial, their
families and the media," Alan Sheehan of the *Boston Globe* wrote.

As in the Poleet case—when Black teenagers pulled a
white mechanic from the car and beat him into a coma with
rocks—the jury rejected the prosecution's application of joint
enterprise. Although witnesses testified that Leon Easterling

had stabbed Tom Lincoln in full view of Eddie and Richie in the first altercation, the jury didn't believe that the two men expected him to use the knife a second time. Despite several reports that the football players were chased back to the alley as they tried to flee, the jury chose to believe that the stabbing resulted from a single, spontaneous brawl and rejected the argument that Eddie's and Richie's presence in the alley played a role in the fight's escalation to murder.

This may be an understandable conclusion in Richie Allen's case, but as the state high court had pointed out in its decision on the first trial, Eddie Soares had been fighting Andy up until the last minute. This alone gave the jury evidence to convict him of murder. And according to one witness, Soares was still punching Andy after Leon stabbed him in the lung.

Richard Allen had simply been standing nearby and—according to his defense attorney—urging the football players to go home. There was little evidence he struck a single blow, and he believed himself innocent to the point where he didn't bother to run away when the cops first arrived. But acquitting him also meant the jury either disregarded or didn't believe Naomi Axell's testimony that Richie Allen had previously provided protection for the female pickpockets who worked the Zone. Or perhaps the jury didn't put much credence in the existence of a robber-whore scheme that had since vanished from city streets.

In addition to rejecting joint enterprise, the jury also declined to convict Eddie Soares, who had been fighting Andy on his own, of manslaughter or even assault and battery. Instead, the jury chose to believe self-defense arguments that were so riddled with contradictions that they headlined the *Boston Globe* coverage that day: "Conflicts in Defense Testimony at Puopolo Trial."

To this day, Andrew Good remains passionate that his client was innocent of the charges. He said Tom Mundy's case fell apart because of the prosecutor's insistence that all three defendants were involved in a robber-whore scheme. He said that Eddie Soares, a stocky, short, slightly effeminate man who clutched his Bible, didn't fit the pimp stereotype of the time, and that threw Mundy. The defendant was, as the evidence proved, a jewelry vendor, and his jewelry supplier from New York City had testified to that. When Naomi Axell, the prosecution's own witness, couldn't identify Eddie Soares as one of the "protectors," Tom Mundy and his case lost credibility, the defense attorney said.

Several jurors who spoke anonymously to the *Herald* said that they were impressed with Soares's honesty. Others believed that Leon Easterling had needed to defend his friend.

Tom Mundy's biggest mistake was putting so much focus on the robber-whore scheme, which overly complicated his case, Norman Zalkind said, looking back on the trial decades later. "He was obsessed with getting all three of them, and that was an advantage for me." The prosecution had strong evidence against Leon Easterling. Mundy erred in not sticking to that evidence, Zalkind added.

Joint enterprise asks jurors to try to decide what is going on in defendants' minds to establish "shared intent" and then convict or acquit based on that mind-reading experience. Another problem with joint enterprise is that it clearly wasn't applied equally in all cases. Nine whites in a Volkswagen van had chased down Brian Nelson's vehicle, causing it to spin out in the snow. Nine whites had jumped into the street, either fighting Nelson, on hand to "provide assistance," or actively fighting off Nelson's two Black friends when Nelson was stabbed to death. Yet the judge had immediately dropped charges against all but one of the whites—and at trial, the single defendant was acquitted of all charges.

As Harvard Law professor Nancy Gertner, a retired federal district court judge, pointed out, joint enterprise is a legal theory that can "enable" racial stereotypes. "If you are a white person standing nearby when the crime is committed, you may be assumed to be aghast. If you are Black and nearby, you're complicit," she said.

Just as in the months prior to the first trial the intense publicity had focused on crime in the Combat Zone, in the year prior to the second trial the media focus had been on a criminal justice system that was unfair to Black victims and defendants. The Darryl Williams shooting only weeks before the trial was a sharp reminder of the city's racism. It engaged sympathy citywide.

Jack Dawley, the young lawyer assisting Tom Mundy, believed the defense attorneys successfully exploited the racial angst that was dominating the headlines. Defense lawyers combed through transcripts of the first trial and grand jury proceedings as well as the police reports with a strategy. "Any little inconsistency was exploited," said Dawley. "Every little thing was harped on as racially motivated. Every little thing had a racial spin on it."

Judge McGuire would not comment on the jury's decision to the press, but he made his opinion known when he sentenced Easterling in December.

The Victim Bill of Rights was not passed until 1983 in Massachusetts, and the Puopolo family was not given the opportunity to make an impact statement before the sentencing hearing, but Danny said his sister wrote a three-page letter to Judge McGuire telling him how much their family had suffered from this crime.

At the hearing, Tom Mundy asked the judge to give Leon Easterling the maximum sentence: eighteen to twenty years. He reiterated his belief that Easterling was "a known pimp" who had worked the Combat Zone for "at least ten years" before the stabbing, according to the *Boston Globe* coverage.

Speaking in defense of his client, Zalkind denied those allegations. He said Easterling was "scared" and "sorry" and asked for mercy, but Judge McGuire swiftly cut off the debate.

"I have the advantage of the arguments of both counsel[s], but more than that I have listened for many, many days to the testimony of witnesses, and the testimony of the defendant, Easterling, that testimony being more eloquent as to what happened than any of the arguments," the judge said.

He sentenced Easterling to the maximum the law allowed, eighteen to twenty years, to be served at Walpole state prison.

*

It would be twenty years before the O. J. Simpson trial brought the term *jury nullification* to the lay audience. Mundy didn't use that term in his analysis to the press, but several of his complaints and his private comment to the Puopolo family hinted at it.

Jury nullification is the controversial action of a jury to find a defendant "not guilty" for reasons not directly related to the case. Since a not-guilty verdict cannot be reversed, the action is said to "nullify" law. This power of the jury, which goes back to English common law, has also made itself known throughout U.S. history, particularly at key moments of social change. For example, northern juries often refused to convict violators of the much-hated Fugitive Slave Law, despite strong evidence the defendant had protected or hidden runaways. Similarly, many juries were known to go light on liquor smugglers because of the unpopularity of Prohibition laws.

Jury nullification has been defined differently among legal scholars and tolerated differently by federal and state courts at various times in history. In most modern instances, the term has been applied when juries simply grant leniency in criminal cases where the penalties might be deemed too harsh. In the broadest definition, jury nullification doesn't have to be a conscious act of the jury or even a unanimous vote; a hung jury can be considered a "nullification" of the law.

In the O. J. Simpson case, when the term gained popularity in the media, many believe the jury wasn't so much "nullifying" an unjust law as righting a past injustice. The jury was reacting less to the actual murder and more to years of unfair treatment of Blacks by the Los Angeles Police Department and the acquittal of police for brutally beating a Black man, Rodney King.

The transcripts of the second Puopolo trial, held in the Social Law Library of the Massachusetts Supreme Judicial Court, are incomplete. Only one thousand of four thousand transcript pages were preserved on microfiche, and the jury roster is missing. The only four jurors mentioned by name in the media accounts were either deceased, impossible to locate, or did not respond from a last-known address. Except for their answers to questions in a *Boston Herald* article, where they were quoted anonymously, there is no way to know what was in their heads. But in some ways, their conscious arguments don't matter.

For example, it's unlikely jury members discussed Rodney King in deliberations of O. J. Simpson's guilt or innocence. Instead, the knowledge of the Rodney King beating—and that police got away with it—may have affected their lack of faith in the L.A. Police Department and whether they trusted the police evidence.

Charles Walker, former chairman of the Massachusetts Commission against Discrimination, who organized the Boston Bar Association's panel discussion on peremptory challenges and taught "the Andrew Puopolo trials" for many years at the New England School of Law, considered the case crucial to legal history because it stopped prosecutors from using peremptory challenges to keep Blacks and other minorities off juries. He disagreed that the decision was jury nullification. He viewed the verdict reversal this way: "The times, the era, the press, the fervor, and the hemorrhaging of racial discord—that all put pressure on the jurors to be fair." He said the jury struck a balance, punishing the man who committed the murder, but letting innocent men go free.

Tom Mundy had a vastly different take on it.

When the prosecutor was released from the hospital, he went to the Puopolo home to discuss the verdict in person, Andrew Sr. recalled. The prosecutor looked a bit haggard as he stood in the Jamaica Plain kitchen. He had, as his young prosecutor Dawley said, "put his all" into the trial.

The family members were devastated, Danny said. They had watched the nightly news footage of Edward Soares and Richard Allen walking out of the court as free men. They'd seen the *Herald* photograph with Richie Allen and Leon Easterling smiling as the guards guided Leon back to many fewer years in prison.

For part of the trial, Andrew Sr. had slipped into the courtroom and listened to Tom Mundy put on his case. Like the three retirees, the courtroom regulars who had predicted a prosecution victory, Andrew Sr. had been utterly convinced that Mundy had "nailed it." He was shocked by the jury's verdict.

But the rest of the family had been anxious, reading the news stories that condemned the first verdict as overly harsh. And they knew about the pamphlets distributed by the Citywide Coalition for Justice and Equality. But while Helen and Danny had been worried about the outcome, they had never seen this coming. Danny said they'd been losing sleep about the likelihood of lighter sentences for Richie Allen and Eddie Soares, but no one imagined complete acquittals.

Yet what stung most was Leon Easterling's conviction for manslaughter. Even if the jury believed not a single prosecution witness, the medical evidence alone—two separate knife wounds, one thrust deep enough to pierce the inner chambers of his heart—was sufficient to convict him of murder, they believed. To the family, the verdict said that the jury thought Leon Easterling had every right to "defend himself" by following Andy out of the alley to murder him. To them, the jury's verdict implied that Andy somehow got what he deserved.

Even sentenced to the maximum by Judge McGuire, Leon Easterling would, with the time already served since his original arrest, be eligible for parole and back out on the street in little more than eight years. To make matters worse, his defense attorney had announced an appeal.

Mundy had taken his usual seat at the kitchen table. Andrew Sr. remembered asking the prosecutor: How could the jury do this? How could the jury put people who kill back on the street?

Mundy didn't discuss the illness that had sent him to the hospital the day the verdict was read. But Andrew Sr. recalled that he looked pale and his expression was grim. Juries, he said, were unpredictable.

Mundy would continue to prosecute the state's most difficult and controversial cases; he was a professional who knew you could not win them all. But he would tell his friend attorney Tom Carey, the Boston College law professor, that the hardest call he ever had to make was to Andrew Puopolo Sr. that day. Mundy had developed a close relationship with the family and wanted justice for them.

Carey had written the appellate brief Mundy argued before the state Supreme Judicial Court and said that it was an emotional case for everyone. For many years, in November, the anniversary of both the shooting and the second trial, he would ask himself if there was something else he could have done better or written better that might have impacted the high court's decision.

Mundy never mentioned "jury nullification" that day in the Puopolo kitchen, but before he got up to leave, he said something that Andrew Sr. would remember for the rest of his life. *Your son was sacrificed to calm racial relations*, Mundy had told him. *This verdict was about keeping the city quiet.*

CHAPTER EIGHTEEN
A Brother's Responsibility

MOVING ON FROM the jury's verdict was difficult for the entire Puopolo family, but Danny, especially, couldn't get past it. The rest of his senior year at Boston College was a blur. All he could think about was the duty he owed his brother.

As he approached his graduation, he kept thinking about Richie Allen and Eddie Soares returning to their lives in the Combat Zone while his brother lay in the ground. The injustice of it galled him. He tried to funnel his fury into boxing workouts at the South Side gym, he said, going about four times a week, swinging at the heavy bags, hour after hour.

At twenty-two, Danny was solid muscle. He'd been boxing since high school, and although he didn't compete, not even at the amateur level, he was known for intensity and power. A friend and occasional sparring partner, Tim Fitzgerald, a New England Golden Gloves champion, described Danny as "a ferocious fighter, who never took a step back."

His difficulty in moving on was made worse by geography. After graduation, Danny took a job working as a quality assurance agent for the state's Department of Public Welfare, which at the time had its offices at the corner of Washington and Essex Streets—the edge of the Combat Zone. From his desk, Danny could look out the window and see the mouth of the alley where his brother was murdered, he said. When he played basketball with friends after work, they walked past the alley to the gym at the Boston Young Men's Christian Union—a stone's throw from where Naomi Axell had fallen on Boylston Street. He kept his eyes averted and tried not to think about the details of the murder he'd memorized or the violence to his brother that now lived under his own skin.

While he awaited the outcome of the trial, Danny had been able to ignore all the comments he heard in the North End about revenge, how if his Sicilian grand-uncle had still been alive, there never would have been a trial, and how his father could have had the murderers' throats cut in prison. But after the jury had let two of these men go free, it was all he could think about. It seemed clear to him that it was now his responsibility, his duty, to make sure these men paid.

Since the night of the stabbing, Danny had had trouble sleeping. He recalled one night he threw off the covers of his twin bed and hunted through the bedroom closet for a baseball bat. Tossing it in the back seat, he drove the Cutlass to the Combat Zone just after midnight.

By 1980, the Combat Zone had proved itself resilient. Although some buildings were boarded up and the Two O'Clock Lounge and Good Time Charlie's were gone for good, several new clubs had come in to take their place. The area was slowly getting spruced up, and eventually rents would rise. Crime, while not completely vanquished, thrummed more discretely. Hookers no longer created traffic jams by leaning into the cars to fondle men, but you could still find them in the alleys. People still got drunk and gambled. Drugs were bought and sold.

Danny recalled how that night he drove around Tremont and Boylston several times and finally ended up on Beach Street, a quieter street in Chinatown that intersected Washington in the heart of the Zone. He found a space a couple of car lengths from the corner and sat in the dark, watching the pedestrians, mostly men pouring in and out of the bars.

Quickly, Danny recognized Richie Allen among them—his size and shaved head made him hard to miss. Richie weaved erratically up to the take-out counter of the hot dog stand at the corner of Washington and LaGrange Streets and leaned his enormous frame on the counter.

Seeing Allen's carefree stance—as if he owned the Combat Zone—and the jovial way he made conversation with the cashier, set Danny off. He reached for the baseball bat in the back seat. He wanted to shut Richie up, beat him and leave him crumpled on the sidewalk.

Bat in hand, Danny opened the car door. Just then a clump of pedestrians appeared and crossed in front of the hot dog stand, blocking his view of Richie. Two other people walking up LaGrange Street turned the corner onto Washington. Danny halted with one hand on the door handle. He waited for the pedestrians to turn the corner. He saw Richie lift himself off the counter, readying to go.

If Richie Allen had crossed Washington and turned in Danny's direction, away from the bright neon marquees and toward the lower-lit isolation of Beach Street, Danny thought and still thinks he would have attacked him. But more and more people were starting to leave the bars. Richie turned onto LaGrange, where bouncers stood outside the club door-ways looking up and down the street. Danny let the bat dangle from his hand. He decided that it wasn't the right moment but remembers feeling dejected watching Richie get away. A few days later, he called a friend in East Boston and asked him how he could get a handgun.

Estimates vary, but about a quarter to a third of all family members of homicide victims are believed to suffer from symptoms of post-traumatic stress disorder (PTSD) at some point. These include the loss of concentration, insomnia, constant mental replaying of events, and the obsession with revenge that Danny was experiencing.

Danny was only nineteen at the time of the murder, and he idolized his older brother, who had always looked out for him—had always been his role model and his protector. Studies have shown that adolescents and young adult survivors of homicide victims are particularly vulnerable. "It's the most extreme form of loss at a pivotal age," explained Dr. Stephanic Hartwell, the medical sociologist. The brain is still developing until about age twenty-two or twenty-three in the transition from adolescence to adulthood.

This is one of the reasons gang warfare is so intense in the inner cities—many gang members are adolescents who watched a sibling or close friend get murdered on the street. When they retaliate, they are acting on that survivor's urge for revenge, says Dr. Hartwell, who worked closely with the Louis D. Brown Peace Institute in Dorchester for several years. The institute was founded in 1994 following the murder of a fifteen-year-old in the crossfire of a gang shootout to try to interrupt this cycle of revenge.

In an article titled "Life Sentence: Co-victims of Homicide," which was published in *Annals of the American Psychotherapy Association* in the fall of 2007, Bruce Gross, director of the University of Southern California Institute of Psychiatry, Law, and Behavioral Science, wrote that losing a loved one to an intentional act of violence gives rise "to a sort of primal fear and horror" that can overwhelm the survivors. These victims often suffer from "intense and often paralyzing feelings of fear, as well as near-consuming thoughts of revenge."

Danny was still living at home with his parents. He was sleeping in the bedroom he had shared with his brother, with Andy's trophies on the dresser and their posters still on the wall. Every workday, Danny inadvertently made his grief worse by taking the Orange Line from Jamaica Plain to the exact block where his brother was murdered.

He was consumed with the injustice of the court decision, and any sense of injustice could trigger his anger, he said. One day on a crowded MBTA train on his way to work, he accidentally stepped on a Black guy's foot, and the guy kept swearing at him, even after he apologized. Danny said he fumed the entire day, not only at the man on the train. It was the city itself he hated, with all its tensions and injustice. And that night he drove back to the Combat Zone again looking for Richie Allen and Edward Soares.

After much consideration, he hadn't bought the illegal handgun. His Eastie friend had illuminated the risks. He'd noted the tough gun laws in Massachusetts and explained that even if Danny got pulled over for speeding, he could go to jail if the cops found the illegal gun in his car. As obsessed as he was with revenge, Danny was also cognizant of not making his parent's suffering any worse by becoming another Puopolo headline in the news.

His solution was to start carrying a high-powered air gun under the car seat. It was a pistol that resembled a Luger, but it didn't require licensing under state laws. It shot pellets, not bullets. Powered by carbon dioxide gas, the early round of shots could tear through tissue at close range. Danny had hunted and done a lot of target practice as a teenager. He was an accurate shot and felt he could inflict serious injury on an organ with this kind of gun.

He had it under his car seat as he began circling the Combat Zone: Tremont to Boylston to Washington to LaGrange and around again, searching the sidewalks and club doorways for Richie Allen or Eddie Soares. Once or twice, he braked the car to get a better look at someone. On about his fourth or fifth pass, a Ford Crown Victoria pulled up in front of him, hemming him in so that he had to stop the car. A Black man jumped out of the Crown Vic and made straight for him.

Danny said he was about to reach for the air gun but halted, mostly because he could see that he didn't have enough time to fumble with the cartridge that powered the pistol. He wanted to scare the guy off, but if the guy was armed, Danny knew he would lose the battle.

The Black guy came to his window. Instead of a gun, he pulled a badge. He was an undercover cop. He'd seen Danny driving slowly around the blocks and thought he was looking for a hooker. He told to him to "clear out," get the hell out of the Combat Zone, and go home.

Danny said he felt relief at first, happy he hadn't pulled the gun. If he had, the cop might have fired at him. Later his relief was tainted by embarrassment at the thought that he could have died brandishing a BB gun.

But the absurdity of the experience, which eventually he could laugh about, taught him something important, he said. He realized that while he was city born and bred, all his experience fighting had been with his fists. He was out of his league with any kind of weapon.

Yet that awareness didn't alter his sense of duty, his certainty that he owed it to Andy to seek revenge. He decided that he'd just have to find another way.

*

In Boston, white flight from the schools continued at a rapid pace. Much of the already small Black middle class also fled, and by 1980, the school system had lost 35 percent of its student body. There were now only 57,000 students in the school system, and of that, only 19,000 were white. Blacks and minorities now made up 65 percent of enrollment. Although by 1981 Judge Garrity had ended his day-to-day monitoring of Boston Schools and busing protests dwindled, it was hardly a victory for busing.

As the *Boston Globe*'s David B. Wilson put it, "With inconsiderable exceptions, those who left were those most able to leave. Those who stayed were those who had to. The remnants, not the émigrés, are busing's true victims."

In 1983, Boston elected a new mayor, Ray Flynn, the former state representative for South Boston and city councilor who had led the crusade to force the city to clean up the Combat Zone. While he strongly opposed busing, he was one of the few Southie politicians who also strongly came out against the white violence. He ran for mayor on the platform of racial harmony and the need to provide more economic opportunity for Blacks.

This emphasis was made politically necessary by the city's rapidly changing demographics and the fact that Flynn was running against the first viable Black mayoral candidate: long-time civil rights leader Mel King. Still, Ray Flynn was a religious man, a devout Catholic who would go on to become the ambassador to Rome, and was deemed by most voters as sincere.

As a young basketball player, Flynn regularly played basketball with Black athletes and had once played on an otherwise all-Black team. As mayor, he visited Black churches, developed strategic relationships with ministers, and played basketball with Black teenagers. Under his leadership, more Blacks were hired as city employees than in any previous administration. More Blacks moved into top positions in city agencies, and more Black companies were awarded city government contracts. Although detractors would call him a publicity hound with a knack for getting himself on camera, he'd eventually become more popular in Black Roxbury than in his home base of white Southie.

Flynn appointed Mickey Roache as police commissioner. Roache, who was white, had previously led the city's first-ever Community Disorders Unit, which investigated hate crimes, and he had a good track record with the Black community. It would later be renamed the Civil Rights Unit. Under Roache, who would later go onto become a City Council member, relations between the police and all of Boston's neighborhoods improved. A federal consent decree had mandated an increase in minority hiring in the police and fire departments in the early seventies, but turnover had been slow. In Flynn's administration, the number of minority police officers increased from 15 to 25 percent in eight and a half years.

Neither police corruption nor Boston's racial troubles would be eradicated, and in fact, a special commission called to investigate management of the police department issued a scathing report in 1992 and called for an overhaul. Among the most highly publicized failure was the department's handling of Stuart murder in 1989. Charles Stuart's elaborate hoax blaming a Black assailant for his own brutal murder of his white pregnant wife played on and underscored the city's racists fears and stereotypes. It led to a police manhunt and two separate wrongful arrests of Black men. But the mayor still gets credit for making progress in the early years of his administration. The crime rate in Boston, which had been the highest per capita among the thirty largest cities in 1980, continued to rise throughout the decade with a homicide rate peaking in 1990. In that same period, racial crimes began a sharp decline. Over the decade, the number of racial crimes dropped from the 607 incidents in 1978 to 152 reported in 1986.

In late summer of 1986, Tom Lincoln, now an emergency room doctor, was returning with his wife from a trip to his in-laws in Cincinnati, he recalled years later. They were taking a bus from Logan Airport to South Station about midafternoon. As he and his wife climbed into the bus and grabbed two seats, Lincoln noticed a forty-year-old Black man, neat and casually dressed, sitting on the bench seat that was directly across the aisle. Their eyes met.

The man was short and stocky, with intense, piercing eyes. It was Eddie Soares. Tom decided that he couldn't let this weird encounter just go by. I remember you, he told him, and haven't forgotten. He said that Eddie looked at him with no defensiveness. No threatening glare. Instead, he told Tom that he was sorry.

Tom understood that Eddie Soares meant it, he was sincere in his apology, but he couldn't respond. He couldn't forgive the man. The jewelry peddler hadn't done anything to him except feigning a few karate kicks, and he had no anger about the acquittals for stabbing him. But Andy was dead, and that he couldn't forgive.

Tom said that he and his wife rode in silence the rest of the trip with Edward Soares sitting across the aisle not ten feet away. After several stops, he got off. He didn't look back. Tom never saw or heard from him again.

Edward Soares sold jewelry from a cart downtown near Filene's Basement, on Summer Street, throughout the 1980s. Andrew Puopolo Sr. spotted him several times when he was in the retail area. Wisely, he didn't tell Danny this for many years.

The new decade had ushered in the "Massachusetts Miracle," a period of growth so remarkable that it would carry the state governor, Michael Dukakis, to the Democratic nomination for president in 1988. The boom of the high-tech and the financial services industries had begun in the mid-1970s, but its cumulative effects became most pronounced in the 1980s, when the success of the microcomputer and computer peripheral industries rippled throughout the economy. Unemployment, at 11 to 12 percent in the 1970s, dropped below 3 percent, the lowest of any industrial state.

The economy was hot. And so was the restaurant trade. Danny left the job with the state welfare office but still hadn't

figured out a career path. He took a job working in a New Bed-
ford fish processing plant. When he contracted a bacterial
infection that almost cost him his arm, his father decided to
intervene. Andrew Sr. left J. Gandolfo and started his own
restaurant provisioning company, with Danny as a partner.

The newly created APCO Purveyors provided specialty Italian ingredients like roasted red peppers, fresh mozzarella, and
Italian pastas to the growing number of Italian restaurants in
Boston and nearby suburbs. Andrew Sr. handled the sales. Danny
did the bookkeeping and drove the truck making deliveries.

After one year, they doubled their service area from a fifty-
to a hundred-mile radius around the city and picked up new
clients all the way to Cape Cod, Danny said. The new company
was so successful that by the mid-1980s, Danny, who was getting married, was able to buy a house in Westwood, one of the
western suburbs known for its quality schools and where his
sister, Fran, and her family lived.

The night of his bachelor party, Danny dragged one of his
friends through the Combat Zone strip clubs—but it wasn't
the usual bachelor's club ritual. The friend was an expert in the
martial arts, and Danny wanted him at his side as he searched
for Richie Allen or Eddie Soares in the barrooms. To no avail.
Before his first child, a daughter, was born, Danny vowed to
himself and to his wife to give up his quest for revenge.

He succeeded for months at a time, focusing his energies on
other things he could still do for his brother. He helped organize
and attended the annual road races, golf tournaments, and touch
football games that raised money for scholarships in Andy's
name at Boston Latin and Harvard. He kept every letter of
thanks from a scholarship recipient who took the time to write.

But Danny remained in turmoil. He sought no therapy
and didn't even know about the existence of homicide victim
support groups, which at the time were just emerging. Danny
wasn't inclined to think about himself as having suffered from
a trauma; rather, he was frustrated by what he called "his weak-
ness" in executing his duty. But even as he fantasized about
murdering Allen, Soares, and Easterling, he also fantasized

about forgiving them. He closely followed news stories of other murder victim survivors who said they had forgiven the murderers. He felt envy.

He said he wanted to forgive, but he wanted an apology first. His cousin Daniel (Boonie) Puopolo had been friendly with Richie Allen when they were young, years before the stabbing, and they had known some of the same people.

Through his cousin, Danny tried to find out if any of these connections had ever heard Richie Allen express remorse for murdering his brother. He got nowhere.

Decades later, Danny would say that he wished he was the kind of person who could forgive without an apology. But he wasn't.

Friends and family members uniformly describe Danny as easygoing, but he often experienced dark periods in the fall, around the anniversary of the murder. Any little injustice could set him off.

The Combat Zone struggled on. By mid-1986, four adult bookstores, two strip clubs, and the King of Pizza had been evicted from the building adjacent to the alley where Andy had died. Rising rents had forced the more unprofitable adult bookstores out of business. The vacant upper stories of buildings were shuttered, as "gentlemen's clubs" in the suburbs and porno films on home video lured away the market.

In the late eighties, Danny's revenge fantasy focused almost entirely on Richie Allen, mostly because of proximity. The Massachusetts Supreme Judicial Court had unanimously rejected Zalkind's appeal of Leon Easterling's conviction, leaving him in prison and inaccessible. Someone had also told Danny, erroneously, that Eddie Soares had moved to New York. Although Richie was the only one who hadn't touched his brother, Danny believed he was the one strongly tied to the pickpocket scheme that had started the fight. Allen was also the only who Danny ever saw hanging around the Combat Zone.

Danny recalled one afternoon when he and an employee, Fred Rihbany, had to make a delivery to a client restaurant on the corner of Beach and Washington, a block and a half from the murder scene. Danny pulled the twenty-foot truck parallel to the restaurant's basement back door and parked, when Fred, unloading cases of pizza sauce onto the dolly, spotted Richie Allen.

Fred was an old friend from Boston Latin who had also known Andy. Over long delivery drives, he'd listened to Danny about the many ways he'd like to inflict pain on Richie Allen. He immediately offered to help Danny go over and beat Allen up.

Danny recalled seeing Richie, in a black leather jacket and blue jeans, wheeling away from his hangout at the hot dog stand, about to cross Washington Street. He was coming toward them not twenty yards away. Richie looked directly at Danny but hadn't recognized him. His eyes were wild. He looked high. Vulnerable.

Fred, a high school football star, was an athletic guy, six foot, two inches tall and weighing about 280 pounds. He wore his hair in a Mohawk and looked tough too. He was a good person to have at his side, Danny thought. Plus, they had a tire iron in the truck. Danny knew he was never going to get this chance again, not with Fred beside him. Not with so few people on the sidewalks.

Danny knew that if anyone stepped out of one of the LaGrange strip clubs, they would witness the attack, but he thought it would be worth the risk. To execute his duty. Get this over with. To never see Richie Allen, the hulk of his body, the bald head, the missing tooth, in the Combat Zone again.

But caution again intervened. Danny said that out of the corner of his eye, he saw a police cruiser parked a block up on Washington Street. He put a restraining arm on Fred. He had another idea.

A couple of days later, Danny and Freddy were making another delivery, this time to the old Francesco's Restaurant on North Washington Street in the North End, where the mob kingpin Gennaro Angiulo was known to have a regular table. Danny spotted a guy in the kitchen, a former neighbor who worked as an enforcer for Angiulo collecting debts. Danny asked if he could speak to the debt collector in private. The two men went out to the street.

North Washington Street was at the ugly edge of the North End, next to the then-elevated expressway. Rush hour traffic roared overhead. As the two men stood, shoulders bent toward the brick building, Danny asked how he could go about hiring someone to break someone's legs.

The debt collector, a man in his late forties, didn't ask whose legs needed to be broken or why. He either didn't want to know or knew the family's story well enough to guess. Danny recalled that the guy looked at him as if Danny had picked up the "breaking legs" idea from watching too much TV.

You don't hire someone to break someone's legs, he informed Danny. Breaking someone's legs left him alive and available as a witness. If Danny wanted to settle this beef, it could only be done one way. Danny got the message. If he wanted to hurt Richie Allen, he'd have to contract for a murder.

CHAPTER NINETEEN
Furloughs and Escapes

BY 1986 LEON Easterling had served ten years and, considered a model prisoner, would be eligible for parole in less than two more. He was known for being unusually well groomed, with a trimmed Clark Gable mustache and perfect hair, according to one of the corrections officers. At the time, inmates weren't required to wear the prison-issued jeans, and Easterling was among the best dressed, favoring pleated black pants. When expecting visitors, which was multiple times a week, he wore 1960s-style Cuban shirts and well-brushed shoes.

The corrections officer, who asked that his name not be used, said he worked Leon's cell block for seven years and supervised him closely in his work as janitor. He described Easterling as "a pleasant enough guy, not well educated, but well read and well spoken." He said Easterling was the kind of person whom you could have an easy bar conversation with and that he could "talk the cats off a fish cart and sell ice to an Eskimo." But he said that while Leon was "an interesting guy, he wasn't a nice guy. If you knew him at all, you knew there was a sense of evil in him—a meanness."

The guard said that Leon spoke openly about being a pimp, but he always insisted that the women who stole the wallet in the Combat Zone hadn't been working for him. From time to time, Leon discussed the murder and was "cold and casual" about it, insisting that he'd no choice but to defend himself against a much bigger man. There was no remorse, said the guard, but that wasn't unusual. Few expressed remorse in prison.

Leon didn't talk much about his half-brother Richie Allen, only to say he was "crazy," according to the guard, and he never mentioned Eddie Soares. He talked a lot about what he was going to do when he got paroled—he planned to move out of state, possibly New Jersey or further south. He worried a lot about his safety when he got out, although he never specifically referenced the mob. "He was more concerned about the racial tension in Boston," the guard recalled, "and the notoriety of the trial."

But with a young wife and his family waiting for him, Leon wanted out early. He had no conflicts with other prisoners and no disciplinary reports, and as of 1986, he was transferred to the Boston Pre-Release Center in Mattapan. As part of the work release program, he was allowed to leave the center to work as a parks maintenance man for the city. One October day on the job, he disappeared.

The news of his prison escape shocked everyone. With his sentence reduced for good behavior, Easterling had only seventeen months before he was eligible for parole. Mundy was unavailable for comment, but prosecutor Paul Leary told the *Boston Globe*'s Kevin Cullen that it was "unlikely he (Easterling) would take off after serving 90 percent of his sentence," although he added that sometimes "it happens."

By the time the *Boston Globe* published its story about the escape in January, Leon had already been missing almost two months. His nephew Darryll Rogers was quoted saying that the family had checked with Richie Allen and Eddie Soares, and no one had heard from his uncle. "I can't see him taking off without any money, without any contacts in the outside world. My family was all he had," Rogers said.

Leon Easterling had lived in prison "always looking over his shoulder," in fear of someone coming after him because of the "circumstances of Puopolo's death," Rogers, who was the son of Leon's sister, told the *Globe*. Rogers was convinced his uncle was dead. Leon had been regularly visiting the family on his weekend furlough. "If he had escaped, just taken off, he would have contacted us by now."

While Rogers said that he wasn't accusing anyone of anything, the family nonetheless suspected "foul play" and had been checking the morgues. "My uncle did ten years in Walpole state prison, the hardest part of his sentence. Why would he run now, when he had such little time left?" he asked.

*

The Corrections Department hadn't notified the Puopolo family that Easterling had been transferred out of maximum security or into a work release program that put him back on Boston streets. They only learned of his escape by reading it in the newspaper.

Andrew Sr., Helen, and Fran were irate that they hadn't been notified about Easterling's escape, furious at yet another slap in the face from the criminal justice system, but Danny was elated, he said. He felt relief. He was convinced that it was a mob hit and that finally, after all this time, someone had gotten to Leon Easterling.

At the time, the state never told the survivors of murder victims that they had work release programs, which were used as an incentive for prisoners to help control behavior inside the walls. The state didn't advertise that even when convicted murderers were sentenced to "life without parole," they could still earn the right to leave prison on furlough. There was another secret: Even first-degree murderers could have sentences commuted. This was especially true if they had been convicted under the state's joint enterprise law, as Richard Allen and Edward Soares had been in the first trial. This suggested that parole boards, too, considered joint enterprise sentences, if not overly harsh, at least worth reducing.

Massachusetts was not alone in these practices. The state's work release and furlough programs were common in more than thirty states at the time and considered successful in providing incentives to prisoners and reintegrating them back into society. But less than half a year after Leon Easterling escaped, a much more famous convict would put an end to the program and shake up the entire nation.

Willie Horton, a convicted murderer, became the anti–poster boy for the Massachusetts prison release program when he fled the state and made his way to a Washington, D.C., suburb. There, he went on a crime spree, broke into a young couple's home, raped the woman and bound and gagged

her husband. The furlough program in Massachusetts was
first brought to light by Al Gore during a Democratic primary
debate, then exploited sensationally by the Republicans in
the 1988 presidential election between Republican vice president George H. W. Bush and the former Democratic governor
Michael Dukakis. The Willie Horton campaign advertisements
played to racial fears and painted the Democratic candidate
as soft on crime. The ad was widely credited for Dukakis's
subsequent nosedive in the election.

As part of its Pulitzer Prize–winning coverage of the furlough issue in Massachusetts, the *Lawrence Eagle-Tribune* publicized that even criminals convicted of first-degree murder, a
life sentence without parole, were eligible for furloughs and that
survivors of murder victims had no clue about these programs.
Survivors of victims had been under the impression that life
imprisonment actually meant life imprisonment. The public
outrage forced Massachusetts and other states to abandon these
practices and ushered in a national tough-on-crime political
era that would lead to longer sentences, mass incarceration,
and an abandonment of significant prison reform nationwide.

But none of this affected Leon Easterling. After the *Boston
Globe* story ran, he decided to turn himself in, saying he hadn't
realized he had worried his family so much. His nephew said
his uncle had told them where he had been for the six missing
weeks but wouldn't explain to the media. The family was angry
about the escape, but what was the point? Rogers said they
were happy that his uncle was safe.

It almost read like a feel-good story, Danny thought. He
said he felt played—by Leon Easterling, by the criminal justice
system, and by the mobsters who hadn't murdered Leon on
the street.

Leon could face an additional five months to five years for
his escape, but once again, either luck or charm was on his
side. Despite letters of outrage from the Puopolo family and a
request that Leon Easterling be given the "maximum sentence"
as a punishment, he received the minimum. Five months were
added to the original parole date. In October 1988, twelve years

after Andy Puopolo had been murdered, Leon Easterling was officially released from prison.

Sometime after that, Danny finally learned from his father that Edward Soares had not moved to New York but had been selling jewelry in downtown Boston ever since his acquittal. Andrew Sr. mentioned that he'd walked past Soares selling jewelry from a sidewalk cart on Washington Street near the old Filene's Basement and that he'd seen him a number of times.

Danny said he searched Downtown Crossing for Soares but couldn't find him. By then, he wasn't sure what he would do if he did. Easterling's release from prison shifted his thinking about the other two men. Although he still believed Allen and Soares were guilty, they were both less guilty. It was Easterling who had stabbed his brother.

But for months at a time, he could make himself forget that Easterling was out of prison and living somewhere in Boston. APCO Purveyors was booming, and he was busy making deliveries during the day and on weekends and doing the accounting at night.

Danny and Karen's family was growing, and he was making enough money that they could afford a new five-bedroom, 3,800-square-foot contemporary colonial with vaulted ceilings. The house was directly across the street from Fran and her husband, Paul, in a leafy neighborhood in a MetroWest community, within easy driving distance of both sets of grandparents.

Danny and Fran each had three children, two daughters and a son named Andrew, apiece. Danny was a gregarious guy who drove in to the North End every Saturday morning so he could play basketball with old neighbors and had also joined a softball league to get to know the new suburb. He remained in close contact with his Boston Latin School friends too—especially those who had been friends with Andy. But he never slept well again, and his guilt never diminished. He worried anxiously about his children, insisting they go to the doctor for cuts and minor fevers, as if something lurked around the corner, ready to take them away. And every fall the dark periods inevitably returned.

Newly paroled, Leon Easterling stopped at the Silver Slipper strip club, relocated on LaGrange Street and renamed the Glass Slipper, according to Ray Molphy, the bartender who poured his drink. Ray, the friend of Leon's who had regularly played board games with him before the night of the murder, said that Leon seemed surprised to see him still behind the bar—and clearly didn't want to be recognized. It was an afternoon and the club wasn't crowded, but he kept looking around to make sure no one else he knew was there. He never relaxed, and before he left the club, Leon asked Ray not to tell anyone that he'd seen him. The bartender, who worked in the Combat Zone at various bars until the mid-1990s, said he never saw Leon again.

Despite the moral outrage, the police scrutiny, and the Boston Redevelopment Authority's best efforts, the Combat Zone continued to grind its way into the nineties. A few of the nightclubs changed their names or their concepts. For a while, all-night juice bars managed to temporarily evade the city's tighter liquor license requirements. The Club Baths on the second floor of LaGrange Street attracted the gay crowd, as did the X-rated Pilgrim Theatre and State Theater, which became cruising spots. The Naked i, as always, raked in the cash.

By the mideighties, the AIDS epidemic led to concerns of the disease being spread by prostitutes and intravenous drug use in the Zone. The surge of crack cocaine that followed intensified scrutiny of the still-rampant drug dealing.

Burdened by the crime, drugs, and used condoms on the streets for more than a decade, the Chinese community had gained strength since it was originally sold "a bill of goods," to accept an adult entertainment district next door. Now, with greater grassroots organization, leaders began to apply pressure on the city to eliminate it.

Mayor Flynn, who served until 1993, remained the most determined of Combat Zone opponents, and the city redoubled its efforts to rid itself of the adult entertainment industry. Under Flynn's administration, the Boston Redevelopment Authority played an even heavier hand, leaning on existing property owners not to renew leases for these businesses. Bolstered by an improving economy, the city attracted high-priced development nearby in Park Square, which helped raise rental prices in the Combat Zone, making it unaffordable for smaller businesses.

The X-rated Publix Theatre on the corner of Washington and LaGrange Streets closed in the mid-1980s and was earmarked for luxury apartment development, and the old Combat Zone was being remarketed as the "cultural district," or "center city." In the first three years of the Flynn administration, the number of strip clubs, which was twenty-two in 1977, diminished to five.

The mayor's goal of curtailing the Combat Zone was aided by changing technology, which held the winning hand. The proliferation of the videocassette recorder (VCR) in the 1980s accelerated the slow, steady demise of the Combat Zone. By 1989, VCRs were in sixty-two million American households, according to the Washington Post, and hard-core porn was easily available in local video stores. The internet eventually eliminated the inconvenience of picking up a tape or DVD in person and would soon make it easy to find a prostitute without having to trawl an adult entertainment district.

Ray Flynn left office to become the American ambassador to the Vatican. The new mayor, Tom Menino, approved the closing of the Naked i and Pilgrim Theatre on Washington Street and demolition of the building in 1995. The Naked i sold its license to Centerfolds, which opened on LaGrange Street, alongside the relocated Silver Slipper, reinvented as the Glass Slipper. These would be the last and only two sex establishments to survive.

The Combat Zone became the subject of some nostalgia. A photography exhibit at the Howard Yezerski Gallery, entitled Boston Combat Zone, 1967–1978, included powerful images of the human face of its neon glamour, its poverty, erotica, and exploitation, captured by such artists as Roswell Angier, Jerry Berndt, and John Goodman.

At the Boston news site Universal Hub, a thread about the Combat Zone has attracted a flood of remembrances and searches for lost contacts among the former dancers, bartenders, waitresses, musicians, clerks, customers, and people who lived above the storefronts. *Inside the Combat Zone: The Stripped Down Story of Boston's Most Notorious Neighborhood*, by Stephanie Schorow, chronicled the colorful rise, heyday, and fall of an adult entertainment district that burned brightly in the last half of the 20th century and—for all its flaws— remains a particularly vivid memory within the city's increasingly sanitized consciousness.

"As the swinging sixties began to change American attitudes about sex and gender relations, the Combat Zone became a haven for people and places pushing the limits of adult entertainment. It was a hub of counter-culture defiance that many people remember fondly," said Schorow, in an interview. "But the Combat Zone was a product of its time—an experiment that couldn't survive. The Puopolo murder and the city's declared war on its adult entertainment surely played an important role, but changing social norms, real estate pressures, and other factors like the VCR and internet in the eighties and nineties destined the Zone for its eventual demise."

CHAPTER TWENTY
Hitman for Hire

IN THE EARLY 1990s, Danny found out from one of his cousins who took a law class at Bunker Hill Community College that the subject of the Puopolo murder trial had come up. The cousin mentioned to the instructor that he was related to the victim. One of the other students, who identified himself as a cousin of one of the defendants, stood up and called him a racist.

Without ever knowing for sure, Danny assumed that the cousin of the defendant was related to Leon Easterling. He took it as a sharp reminder that Leon Easterling, released from prison, was living his life as though he hadn't murdered his brother, Danny said. "And spreading his bullshit—his racist bullshit."

Danny likened the urge for revenge to gasoline "that keeps burning away at you." One thought seared a circular, relentless pathway in his brain: that Leon Easterling had never got the punishment he deserved." It demanded action from him. A payment due. "I kept saying, it's never been resolved. I've got to resolve this. I can't let him get away with it," he said.

Danny hadn't been willing to hire a hit man to murder Richie Allen, but Leon Easterling was a different story. For days, he wrestled with the practicalities. A part of him felt that it was his duty to kill Easterling himself, with his own hands. Since it was his obligation to his brother, it should be on his soul, and his soul only. But the other part of him knew that he had a wife and children to think about and that he didn't have the skills to secure an untraceable handgun, plan the murder, or even shoot accurately without getting caught. He finally decided that a professional killer was the smarter option.

Danny didn't know any professional killers personally, but he knew plenty of people in the North End and through the restaurant business who, with a few phone calls, could help him make contact. He also knew that whomever he talked to would have something on him for the rest of his life. He had to think carefully about how he made this connection.

A state trooper friend had once told Danny that if anything ever happened to Leon Easterling, he would be the first suspect: "the number one guy." But that was right after Andy had died, now fifteen years ago. Danny figured that enough time had passed for a lot of other people to have reason to kill Leon Easterling.

No matter what the outcome, Danny felt that he couldn't let Leon Easterling remain alive. He owed it to his brother. Danny decided that he'd just have to be sure that he hired the very best, someone with a lot of experience, not some low-level thug looking to make five hundred dollars. He didn't care how much it cost. Finally, he decided on a friend who, while not from the North End, had multiple mob connections through his business. Danny said that he knew not to call him on the phone and instead dropped by his house.

It was a warm Saturday afternoon in spring, Danny recalled. The guy lived in a big home in the suburbs, and the two men went out to the backyard to talk. The pool was still covered. They sat by the barbeque grill.

Danny told the friend that he'd made a decision that something "had to be done" about Easterling and asked the friend if he could make contact with someone who could "take care of the situation."

The friend knew the story and that Danny had been wrestling with his conscience for years. He asked if Danny was absolutely sure that's what he wanted to do. Danny said he had no hesitation.

The friend offered to make inquiries and get back to him in a couple of days. He explained that if he found someone trustworthy for the job, Danny would have to first meet the man in person. The next step would be setting up that date.

While Danny waited to hear back, he tried not to think about the plan he'd set in motion. He said he also tried not think about what would happen if any part of the plan backfired or what his kids would think if they ever found out that their father had hired a hit man. He was also worried that Karen would divorce him, but felt he'd already equivocated for too many years: *You either wanted to do something like this or didn't. It was time for him to stop fucking around*, he recalled thinking.

But as the days went by, he grew more agitated. Danny knew he needed advice about how to proceed, and he needed it from someone who would not be shocked about his intentions.

One of the North End friends that Danny had stayed close to over the years was Francis "Dash" Tirella. Ten years older than Danny, Dash had coached Andy in youth baseball. Another Boston Latin alumni, he had followed Andy's high school football career and then, later, attended his Harvard games. Dash had also been on the committee that collected signatures to dedicate the North End Park in Andy's honor and was so affected by Andy's death that he named one of his sons after him.

Like Andy and Danny, Dash was a North End guy who'd gone to Boston Latin. North End guys who had gone to Boston Latin formed a fairly small club. Dash, who passed away in 2009, was philosophical and deeply spiritual. Sometimes after one of their Saturday morning basketball games, he and Danny would just sit and talk, Danny remembered. Sometimes it was for hours—and often it was about Andy.

One evening after dinner, Danny waited until Karen went upstairs to give the children baths. Taking the cordless with him, he found a corner of the living room where he could hear when the water stopped running. He called Dash.

The living room was large, with vaulted ceilings, leather furniture, a television, and children's toys all to remind him what he had at stake if anything went wrong. In a low voice, Danny told Dash what he'd done.

Dash asked if he was determined to move forward. Danny said having asked his friend to go out on a limb and make the connection to a paid assassin, he was now honor bound to take the meeting—it was too late to back out.

Dash asked him to try to imagine how he would feel after the hit was executed. Would he actually feel any better? Danny remembered saying that he couldn't feel worse.

Dash walked Danny through all the possible outcomes. What would his next action be if the hit man tried to blackmail him? What would happen to Danny's wife and children if he got caught? What would it do to his parents? And, finally, could he live with himself as a murderer?

Danny kept insisting that he needed resolution. He told Dash something he repeatedly told himself: that if the situation had been reversed, Andy wouldn't have let Danny down. Andy wouldn't have rested until he had avenged his brother's murder.

Dash didn't let that stand. He reminded him that Andy had made the decision to become a doctor, which meant he planned to dedicate his life to healing. This didn't gibe with murder. He should honor his brother's memory, not avenge it.

At that moment, Danny wasn't ready to hear that. Mostly, he was angry at himself, frustrated by the other times he'd backed down. He felt like he had failed his brother. He told Dash that he couldn't back down again.

Danny's contact with the mob got back to him two days later. He'd found someone right for the job, but he also had new information. An employee who handled security for his business was a former cop who had done some preliminary investigation to find out where Leon Easterling was living. The address was in New Jersey. And there was one more thing: The former cop had heard that Easterling had AIDS. Did Danny want to think it over one more time before he arranged a meeting with the hit man?

In 1991, an AIDS diagnosis was pretty much a death warrant. Danny remembered feeling lightheaded with relief. There was no point risking his family, his values, his soul to murder a man who in all likelihood would die a slow, painful death. He thanked his friend and told him to forget about the meeting.

Later, the tip proved to be false—Leon Easterling was not suffering from AIDS. Nor was he living in New Jersey. He was alive and well and living in Dorchester. But Danny wouldn't learn this for another decade.

After twenty-five years of busing, the Boston School Committee voted in 1991 to put an end to race-based student assignments and return the city to the neighborhood school concept. Although proponents would continue to argue that the busing order by Judge Arthur Garrity was necessary to desegregate the school system and bring the city's racist attitudes to light, most viewed the court order as a harsh solution that only exacerbated a very real problem. It was a failed attempt at engineering racial justice with consequences that would affect the city for decades. Nationally, Boston became "a potent, nearly universal symbol of what not to do."

And in one ironic twist to the busing story, Ted Landsmark, the African American businessman who was attacked by white antibusing protestors with the flag in City Hall—was one of the critics who urged Boston to abandon busing. Landsmark, who became president of Boston Architectural College, wrote in a *Boston Globe* editorial that the money the city spent transporting students from one underperforming school to another should be invested in improving the quality of education instead. Busing, he noted, "does nothing to change the racial, cultural, and caste demographics of the classrooms."

Meanwhile, the state's high court *Soares* decision that overturned the convictions of the first Puopolo trial had a small but lasting role in criminal justice. It would forever change the way juries were chosen in Massachusetts and, later, in the nation.

The new standards limiting peremptory challenges couldn't prevent the existence of all-white juries if the jury pool was overwhelmingly white. But along with other court reforms that swiftly followed, the *Soares* decision was an important first step in providing Blacks and any defined minority group a fairer trial from the criminal justice system.

In Boston, it changed the way cases were prosecuted, according to Jake Wark, then press secretary for the Suffolk County District Attorney's office. "Race-based jury selection was a lazy rule of thumb. It presumed a person would not be able to sit in judgment of a person who shared their ethnicity or didn't share their ethnicity."

The *Soares* decision wasn't a perfect remedy, in part because of the nature of a peremptory challenge, which is to give the lawyers a chance to strike a juror based solely on a "gut instinct." Even with the new *Soares* standards, the prosecution and the defense could still try to strike jurors they didn't think would vote their way because they were the "wrong" color, ethnicity, gender, or religion. The difference now was that everyone, and especially the judge, was paying close attention.

If the peremptory challenges revealed any kind of pattern, they were immediately called into account—even if there were only one Black person in the jury pool, that single challenge could constitute a "pattern," according to Jonathan Shapiro, one of the Boston's preeminent defense attorneys. Although lawyers could—and did—come up with other excuses to get rid of an unwanted juror, those excuses had to hold up under scrutiny. The burden of proof was on the challenger. Challenges could be appealed to the judge first, then the high court. Trial verdicts could be reversed.

Reform in the late seventies and early eighties also significantly improved the jury pool itself. Instead of drawing from the list of registered voters, where minorities were underrepresented, resident lists were used. The system was reorganized so that jury duty was limited to one day or one trial. Because service no longer imposed a month-long time and financial burden on jurors, no one was excused, neither the highest-paid bank president nor the lowest-paid clerk. The result was a more diverse jury pool and, many believed, a higher quality of juror.

Legal experts predicted that the California and Massachusetts high court decisions limiting peremptory challenges would immediately ripple through other states and be swiftly adopted on a federal level. But these two high courts were considered liberal activists, and it would take another seven years before the U.S. Supreme Court took action.

But finally, in 1986, the U.S. Supreme Court agreed to hear *Batson v. Kentucky*, a case in which an all-white jury convicted a Black man on charges of second-degree burglary and receiving stolen property. Relying in part on the *Soares* decision, the nation's high court ruled that excluding jurors by race was unconstitutional.

Like the *Soares* decision, *Batson* would never be a perfect solution. Prosecutors in other states began producing YouTube videos on how to get around the new federal jury selection standards with creative questioning techniques. And as Justice Thurgood Marshall, who had urged the U.S. Supreme Court to hear the *Batson* case, complained afterward, the "*Soares-Batson*" solution, which was percentage based, still allowed racial discrimination up to "an acceptable level." He and others argued that no level was acceptable, that the only real way to end discrimination against minority groups was to ban the use of peremptory challenges altogether—an argument still made today. But defense lawyers and prosecutors reject that solution in equal measure because it would leave jury selection almost entirely up to the judge.

Nonetheless, juries in Massachusetts are more racially diverse today, especially in Suffolk County, in part because of the *Soares* decision that resulted from the Puopolo trial. Its role in improving the perception of justice has been small but significant, said Norman Zalkind. "I think we fight our battles in very miniscule ways. If you get fair trials and you get fair results, it starts to move the culture in the right direction."

AFTERWORD
Progress and Struggles

TODAY, BOSTON STILL struggles with racism that is both subtle and glaring. The city's neighborhoods remain largely segregated, and its suburbs are overwhelmingly white. Income
disparities, among the highest in the nation, are jaw-dropping,
with the median net worth of Blacks in Boston at eight dollars,
according to the Federal Reserve of Boston's 2015 report *The
Color of Wealth in Boston*. This was so low, especially compared
with the $247,500 median net worth of whites, that when the
Boston Globe featured the number in its 2018 seven-part series
on race, a reporter had to do a follow-up story for readers to
clear up questions about whether it had been a typo. It wasn't.

Decades after the busing battle, 54 percent of Blacks sur-
veyed nationally in the *Boston Globe* series said they viewed the
city as unwelcoming to people of color, the highest percentage
of any other metropolitan area. The occasional sports fan who
shouts a racial insult at the opposing team reminds the nation
that despite the city's economic vitality and elite academic
institutions, Boston retains a reservoir of bigotry.

The *Globe* series documented several categories where racism was evident, including the low percentage of Blacks who
go on to college, the few who make it into the upper tiers of
management in Boston corporations or make partner at top law
firms, and the few who rise into any position of power, whether
business or government. But as *Globe* columnist Adrian Walker
pointed out in a 2018 column, economic inequality played a
dominant role in "nearly every ill the series talked about." The
wealth gap drives segregation in housing, educational opportunity, even medical care. In 2020, those gaps were underscored
by COVID-19, which disproportionately killed people of color.

One of Boston's ongoing problems is this: the national reputation it gained for racism during its busing years continues
to affect how the city's racial incidents are reported by the

national press, which discourages Black professionals from moving to Boston. In a catch-22, this inhibits the population growth of a middle- and upper-middle-income Black population, keeping the minority power base small and making the city unappealing to other Blacks considering job offers or admission offers from the city's colleges.

The racial slurs shouted out at professional sports events don't help matters, but as the *Globe* series noted, these incidents are rare today. When they do happen, they get significantly more media coverage than similar incidents in other cities.

In other words, Boston can't get past its own historical bad press. So, although it is important not to gloss over the city's ongoing racial problems, it's worth pointing out how far Boston has come—not to call it a resounding success, but to remember how ugly it once was and that change *can* happen. Today, Blacks may still feel uncomfortable in certain neighborhoods, but forty years ago, Blacks couldn't go to Carson Beach without being attacked by white sunbathers. Black children could not visit Bunker Hill Monument without being clubbed.

Racism in Boston rarely erupts into what was once everyday physical violence between whites and Blacks. In 2019, there were 170 hate crimes reported in Boston, as reported by the Massachusetts Executive Office of Public Safety and Security, which collects data from law enforcement agencies across the state annually. According to the statistics for Suffolk County, which is largely Boston, about one hundred of these were racially motivated, including anti-Black (52), anti-white (20), anti-Hispanic (20), and anti-Asian (7) incidents. This is about one-sixth of the 607 racial crimes in Boston reported in 1978.

Boston got its first African-American police commissioner in 2018, William Gross, although he retired in early 2021 for family reasons and an appointment of a successor was still in flux when this book went to press. Suffolk County also elected its second Black district attorney, Rachael Rollins, in 2018. And in the spring of 2021, Boston got its first Black and first woman mayor, Kim Janey, who took over for outgoing Mayor Marty Walsh, who was named labor secretary in President Joe Biden's cabinet. Although Janey is only acting mayor and must run in the fall 2021 election to permanently replace the mayor, the five leading announced candidates were also people of color.

This is not to say there aren't continuing challenges in Boston. Police reform, which has been contentious, was expected to be an ongoing issue in the mayoral race. But criminal justice has moved slowly in the right direction. In the 1970s, it was "white, racist, Irish and a closed system," according to Henry Owens, renowned for representing a good share of the Black defendants caught up in that system.

As the police force turned over and more minority cops joined the department and were put in positions of command, the tenor of law enforcement improved, he said. And although further progress is needed, Black defendants and victims of color get fairer trials from the criminal justice system. "During the progression of my career, things have been improving. It's a much, much different Boston today," Owens said.

The entire Combat Zone is different today too. The two strip clubs on LaGrange Street remain, but the building fronts are subtle now, minus the flashing neon and life-size seminude posters that once lured customers through the doorways. On a sunny weekday afternoon in June, two grandparents strolled a three-year-old in a designer carriage to their hotel by way of LaGrange Street, which was once the epicenter of prostitution. The grandparents neither hurried nor bothered to look over their shoulders.

The affluence of today's Boston has continued to creep down Washington Street in the form of trendy restaurants, upscale coffee shops, and wine bars. The Millennium Parking Garage replaced the Carnival Lounge, and the alley where Andy Puopolo was murdered backs up to luxury apartments, although the block remains in transition. Litter dots the sidewalks, and an addict is passed out on the wedge of cement on the corner known as Liberty Square Park.

The three men charged with the murder of Andy Puopolo are all dead. Richie Allen passed away in 1994, Edward Soares died in 1998, and Leon Easterling, who lived to 79 years of age in nearby Dorchester, died in 2014. Danny says he's glad he never murdered any of the three defendants, but even with their deaths, he hasn't found peace.

He and his family believe all three men should have served life sentences in prison for first-degree murder. While Danny recognizes that there were Black victims who did not get justice and that the practice of racially stacking the juries had to change, he's still angry that change had to come at his brother's expense— that his brother was denied justice to right other past wrongs. "It's difficult for people to hear Andy's name and not associate it with the Combat Zone and the city's racial problems," he said. "But Andy had nothing to do with the city's racial problems."

His brother was a victim not only of urban violence but also of a "perfect storm" of racial turmoil that preceded the second trial, Danny said. The all-white jury that acquitted a white Marine in the killing of Brian Nelson and the three white youths who shot and paralyzed Darryl Williams had nothing to do with Andy, but because of the timing, Danny believes Andy did not get the justice he deserved.

Standing at the mouth of the alley where his brother was stabbed to death, Danny said he will never be free of those long-ago events. There's nothing he can ever do to change what happened in the past, but he would like to change the city's understanding of his brother, who sacrificed his life to do what he thought was right.

"I want people to understand what Andy's life represented to those of us who knew him: goodness, respect, and loyalty . . . If it had been a Black kid getting beaten up, unable to defend himself that night, Andy would have been the first one to come to his aid, because that's how he was. He only cared about helping the underdog," he said.

Danny wants people to know that Andy was an intelligent, spiritual, twenty-year-old who would have contributed great things to the world as a doctor, as a husband, and as a parent. It was this realization that finally convinced him give up all plots for revenge: murder was no way to honor Andy's memory.

It has taken Danny nearly his entire life to realize revenge was a fantasy, an aspect of trauma and of grief. Whenever he had the opportunity, he thought better of it. Murder, he said, wryly, is just a lot harder than you'd think. "Everyone is a warrior until you actually put yourself in that spot, but you don't kill people easily, like in the movies. The only way you can kill someone is if you don't have a conscience."

Mostly, the family would like to clear up the misconceptions about Andy in Boston's history. The mistruths they still sometimes hear from random people on the street are that Andy charged into a Black neighborhood and attacked someone or that he got in trouble in the Combat Zone looking for sex. He was simply a college student who went out for a drink with his football team as part of a Harvard ritual. He tried to save a teammate and lost his life.

Later, in the North End, at the waterfront park that bears Andy's name, Danny remarks on how different the old neighborhood is today—how affluent and trendy. He looked back fondly on how poor and how tight-knit it used to be but also acknowledged its insularity.

Today, a Black woman on the other side of the baseball diamond walks a dog, something that would have been impossible in the North End forty-five years ago. The family would like to believe that Andy's death *was* the reason the Combat Zone was cleaned up and that he played some small role in improving the city and breaking down its barriers.

Danny visits this park like other people visit cemeteries. Of all the many tributes to his brother, he believes this park in the North End with Andy's name on it would have meant the most to his brother.

At midday in June, as the sun scorched the shadeless surface, the athletic fields and even the pools were empty, but in spring and fall, the park bustles with youth baseball and soccer games. Danny says that sometimes he stays to watch part of a game. He can remember when every single kid on his team had an Italian last name. Now kids of all ethnicities and races play together on the same teams. He thinks Andy would have liked that.

ACKNOWLEDGMENTS

This book is a product of more than ten years' work, with many highs, lows, and frustrations. It could not have been written without the help of many people who were generous with their time, their memories, and their support. It would not have been published without those who breathed new life into this project at key moments, prodding, poking, and moving it forward.

First of all, I thank Danny Puopolo and the late Francis "Dash" Tirella, who wanted Andy Puopolo's story to be told. They began collecting crucial documents, including the court transcript from the first trial, original newspaper clips, and television news videos and were willing to share them with me. I especially want to thank Danny, who gave so much of himself to preserve his brother's memory, and I am grateful for his honesty, generosity, and sense of fair play. I know it wasn't easy helping me with this book or reading it afterward.

I also thank Andrew Puopolo Sr., Fran Puopolo Sciaba, Karen Puopolo, Dr. Anthony Puopolo, Janice Brencick (formerly Puopolo), and the late Daniel "Boonie" Puopolo for the generosity of their time and memories.

Before I get to the many other people who contributed to the content of this book, I'd like to thank those who helped me shape it: most especially Barbara Shapiro and Frank "Spike" Santo for the developmental editing that was so crucial, and Claire McAlpine, Cathleen Keenan, and Beth Kirsch for their thoughtful suggestions and meticulous copyediting. And to Diane Bonavist for her editorial feedback and indexing, and Dante Bellini Jr. for his excellent ideas and generous support.

A very special thanks goes to Charles "Chuck" Walker, who provided so much insight into the law and the community and who championed this book when I needed it the most. I will never forget his kindness and ongoing support. I also thank him for sharing his memories as a young Black student in Boston during the 1970s.

I am grateful to the former Harvard football players who were willing to relive that traumatic night in the Combat Zone to provide me with a deeper understanding of what actually happened: Scott Coolidge, Dr. Malcolm DeCamp, Steven Saxon, Rev. Gordon Graham, and especially Dr. Tom Lincoln, who gave me so much of his time and offered so much clarity. Thanks also to Bill Wendel, to Bill Emper, and to former football coach Larry Glueck for their memories.

Thanks to Andy's classmates at Boston Latin School and Harvard (or both): Greg Mazares, Timothy Fitzgerald, Jimmy Ng, Greg McBride, Jim Byrne, Peter Senopoulos, Brian Rogers, Jim Hunter, and especially Kevin McCluskey, who was so helpful linking me to the right people. I'd also like to thank Danny's Latin School classmate and good friend Fred Rihbany.

A heartfelt thanks goes to all the prosecutors and defense lawyers who helped me understand this complex case and put it in historical context: Gerard Burke, Andrew Good, and especially Jack Dawley, Henry Owens, and Norman Zalkind, who were so candid and insightful. I am grateful to John Kiernan, Timothy O'Neill, Thomas Dwyer, and Tom Carey for helping me get to know Tom Mundy as a person as well as a prosecutor.

I thank Dr. Stephanie Hartwell, who helped me understand the trauma of losing a loved one or friend to murder and how the natural urge for revenge devastates not just individuals but also inner cities, and Maureen Wilson Leal, who updated me on the kinds of services families of homicide victims receive today. And to Jake Wark, formerly at the Suffolk Country District Attorney's office.

To Ray Molphy, Mark Pasquale, former Boston detective Billy Dwyer, and those who did not want to be named, thank you for providing memories of the three defendants—Richard Allen, Leon Easterling, and Edward Soares—as well as the Combat Zone in the 1970s. These sources were critical as family members could not be reached or, despite my many pleas, declined to speak. I am also grateful to Amanadina Feijo for her extensive and kind help to try to find Edward Soares's family members through the Portuguese American community, even if it was impossible.

My thanks go to Susan Wornick, Stanley Forman, former mayor and ambassador Ray Flynn, and Judge Nancy Gertner for helping me on important details, and to Stephanie Schorow, author of *Inside the Combat Zone: The Stripped Down Story of Boston's Most Notorious Neighborhood*, for generously sharing her vast knowledge of Combat Zone history.

I am grateful to Jay Senerchia, who remembered hearing me say at a Christmas party that I was searching for a story that needed to be told and connected me to Danny Puopolo so that I could begin to tell it. Also in the key introduction department, I thank Hank Phillippi Ryan and Jonathan Shapiro.

It might be repetitive to thank Cathleen Keenan again, but I must. I am so grateful to her and to Alan Roberts, as well as to the Institute for American Universities, for the once-in-a-lifetime opportunity to spend three months at a residency program in Aix-en-Provence, France, where I first completed the manuscript. Cathleen even sent meals to my apartment so I could work through the night to meet my deadline, and she and Claire McAlpine propped up my spirits when my original publisher announced, three weeks later, that it was going out of business.

Thank-you to Brian Harkins at the Social Justice Library for performing the miracle of finding what remained of the transcripts of the second trial, to Marcia Bovarnick for solving my technology problem, and to Bob Rush and Nancy Fisher for helping me connect some important dots.

I am grateful to Askold Melnyczuk, my adviser at my University of Massachusetts master's program, for inspiring me and letting me workshop a few of the early chapters, and my classmate Bella diGrazia for getting me in touch with her grandfather, the former police commissioner, who, shortly before he passed away, provided perspective and depth on the magnitude of police corruption in Boston in the early seventies.

I thank the University of Massachusetts, Boston, for its fabulous library database and the *Boston Globe* and *Boston Herald* for use of their morgues, with special thanks to the late Arthur Pollock at the *Herald*.

I want to thank my agent, Dan Mandel, for his support throughout this very long project, and Stephen Hull for prodding me into writing it five years after I'd put the book proposal aside. Thanks also to Rachael DeShano and Nancy Raynor at Bright Leaf for catching mistakes and putting up with my endless questions.

I especially want to thank my editor, Brian Halley, for rescuing this project and breathing new life into the book.

Most of all, I want to thank my husband, Bill Santo, whose belief never wavered, even when I wavered, and for keeping me sane through this entire process.

AUTHOR'S NOTE

The genesis of this book project came from Francis "Dash" Tirella's advice to Danny Puopolo to reject the idea of revenge and instead honor his brother's memory by telling Andy's story. The two began collecting documents, television video, court transcripts, and news accounts with the idea of making a film about Andy and the trials. They had an agreement with a film director and in 2007 were looking for a screenwriter. They had their own idea for a story, and I agreed to write the screenplay on spec on the condition that I could write a book afterward and have complete journalistic independence to tell the story as I viewed events.

Dash passed away in 2009, but Danny worked with me over the course of ten years, providing not only his own memories but also access to those of his family and friends. He connected me to key sources that made this book possible. The book I wrote was not the book he wanted, but he honored our agreement. I wanted to provide him with the opportunity to voice his objections.

STATEMENT OF DANNY PUOPOLO

It's been almost forty-five years since my brother was murdered in the streets and again in the courts. As a survivor of a murder victim and two highly publicized trials, I've seen many influences contribute to the perversion of justice. Deep down we all know right from wrong and good versus evil, but it's an unfortunate fact that justice can be compromised and manipulated.

My intent in participating in this book was to tell the truth about the perfect storm of events that led to the decision that set two of the three defendants free despite overwhelming evidence stated by the Massachusetts Supreme Judicial Court of murder by joint venture. My goal was to tell a story about my brother that was uplifting and could remove the dark cloud that hangs over the perception of this case. I'm not sure this

book accomplishes that—only time will tell. All I know is that
Andy was a true friend and hero who deserved justice in a court
of law and was denied that right.

I remain grateful to my departed friend, Francis "Dashy"
Tirella, for his devoted efforts, hard work, and wise direction
and to my family for their support and understanding despite
objections to participating in this book.

I thank Jan Brogan for her tenacity and professionalism,
but I wish the book had focused more on my brother, the sac-
rifices he made for family, friends, and ultimately a teammate,
and the life he did not get to live. Andy was a beacon of light,
color-blind to the injustices of the turbulent times in Boston
that this case is so often acquainted with.

To that end, I'd like to provide a tribute that was written
about Andy by one of his many friends and teammates who have
worked so hard to keep his memory alive. This tribute, which
I believe captures the essence of my brother, was read at the
dedication of Andrew Puopolo Park, which is in the North End
community, where Andy learned his sense of loyalty and respect.

TRIBUTE TO ANDY PUOPOLO
by Bill Wendel

There was something great about Andy Puopolo by today's standards.
Andy was always content to be last.

His teammates knew he was the last out of the
shower, and the last to training table.

His roommates knew he was last to complain,
and the last to talk about his many talents.

And every Harvard football fan knew he was our last
line of defense, and the last to give up.

I had the privilege of knowing Andy well and knew
he took religion seriously.

He understood in a special way that to be first was to be last, and to be last was to be first.

He understood in a special way that man hath no greater love than to lay down his life for his friends.

So on that tragic night many year ago, Andy Puopolo, the man who was always content to be last, was the first to come to the aid of his teammates.

Even unto death, he thought of himself last.

So it is fitting that we pay tribute to the man who refused to put himself first.

His humility was truly heroic.

NOTES

Unless otherwise cited, all quoted statements come from direct interviews conducted by the author between 2008 and 2018. Although not always directly quoted, the following people were interviewed for this book: Janice Brencick (formerly Puopolo), Gerard Burke, Jim Byrne, Tom Carey, Raymond "Scott" Coolidge, John "Jack" Dawley, Malcolm DeCamp, Robert diGrazia, Thomas E. Dwyer, William "Billy" Dwyer, Bill Emper, Tim Fitzgerald, Ray Flynn, Stanley Forman, Nancy Gertner, Larry Gleuck, Andrew Good, Gordon Graham, Stephanie Hartwell, Jim Hunter, John Kiernan, Maureen Wilson Leal, Tom Lincoln, Greg Mazares, Greg McBride, Melvin B. Miller, Ray Molphy, Timothy O'Neill, Henry F. Owens III, Mark Pasquale, Andrew Puopolo Sr., Anthony Puopolo, Danny Puopolo, Karen Puopolo, Fred Rihbany, Brian Rogers, Steven Saxon, Fran Puopolo Sciaba, Peter Senopoulos, Jonathan Shapiro, Stephanie Schorow, Charles E. "Chuck" Walker Jr., Jake Wark, Bill Wendel, Susan Wornick, Norman Zalkind, a former Combat Zone vendor who asked not to be named, a prison guard at Easterling's cell block who asked not to be named, and a close Easterling friend who asked not to be named.

CHAPTER ONE: A NIGHT IN "THE ZONE"
PAGE

2   *Picked as the favorite to win the Ivy League championship:* Deane McGowen, "Harvard Conquers Penn, 20–8, as Defense Excels," *New York Times*, November 7, 1976, 1; Joe Concannon, "The Nightmare Was Harvard's—It Never Awoke," *Boston Globe*, November 14, 1976, 104.

2   *They milled around, drinking draft beer:* Commonwealth v. Leon Easterling, Edward J. Soares, Richard S. Allen, Transcript of Evidence, Suffolk Superior Court, March 8, 1977 (dated for trial commencement) (hereafter Transcript1), vol. 2.

3   *they stopped cars and fondled men:* Richard Connolly, "Downtown Police Corruption Alleged: DiGrazia Ponders District 1 Report," *Boston Globe*, November 9, 1976, 1.

3   *Cassandra McIntyre, still a girl at sixteen:* Boston Police incident reports from 1975 and 1976, Naomi Axell and Cassandra McIntyre, and Police incident report from witness Malcolm DeCamp, November 1976, both obtained via the Freedom of Information Act.

4   *Rates were discussed:* Transcript1, vols. 2 and 3.

4   *they made it back to his Chevy Nova:* Transcript1, vols. 2 and 3.

CHAPTER TWO: COMBAT MEDICINE

8   *bad dreams about Andy:* "Once Cheerful, Happy and Outgoing, Times Have Changed for Puopolos," *Boston Herald*, March, 20, 1977.

11   *as far away as Butte, Montana, to Biddeford, Maine:* Data from the Newspaper Archive, www.NewspaperArchive.com; *Butte Montana Standard*, November 17,

1976; *Las Vegas Sun*, November 17, 1976, *Biddeford (ME) Journal*, November 17, 1976; *Anderson (IN) Herald*, November 17, 1976; *Delta Democrat Times* (Greenville, MS), December 17, 1976; *El Paso (TX) Herald Post*, November 17, 1976; *Pacific Stars and Stripes* (Tokyo, Japan), December 20, 1976.

12 *Linda Lovelace, of Deep Throat fame:* "The Porno Plague," *Time*, April 5, 1976.

12 *the increasingly violent content of these films:* "Porno Plague."

12 *Feminists objected:* Sam Meier, "The Time Feminists Tried to Outlaw Pornography," Splinternews.com, August 27 2015, https://splinternews.com /that-time-feminists-tried-to-outlaw-pornography-1793850316.

CHAPTER THREE: A SEXUAL DISNEYLAND

14 *The essence of Scollay Square:* Jonathan Kaufman, "From Scollay Sq. Tattoo Parlors to Combat Zone Porno Films," *Boston Globe*, December 27, 1984, 25.

15 *Chinatown, which had little political voice:* Michael Liu, *Forever Struggle: Activism, Identity, and Survival in Boston's Chinatown, 1880–2018* (Amherst: University of Massachusetts Press, 2020), 66–67; Tom Ashbrook, "The Zone Going the Way of All Flesh," *Boston Globe*, August 2, 1988, 53.

15 *The area, a hot spot for big band:* Stephanie Schorow, *Inside the Combat Zone: The Stripped Down Story of Boston's Most Notorious Neighborhood* (Boston: Union Park Press, 2017), 30.

15 *had more than quadrupled between 1960 and 1970:* "Massachusetts Crime Rates 1960–2016," compiled from FBI UCS Annual Crime Rates, www .disasterCenter.com/crime/macrime.htm.

16 *Others attributed the neglect to embarrassment:* Henry Jenkins, Tara McPherson, and Jane Shattuc, eds., *Hop on Pop: The Politics and Pleasures of Popular Culture* (Durham, NC: Duke University Press, 2002), 430–31.

17 *In a historic 1919 police strike:* "Boston Police Dept. Still Paying for 1919 Strike," *Boston Globe*, Aug 27 1972, 15.

18 *the 572-page secret document:* Richard Connolly, "Downtown Police Corruption Alleged: DiGrazia Ponders District 1 Report," *Boston Globe*, November 9, 1976, 1; "Partial Text of Report on Police District One" *Boston Globe*, November 9, 1976, 12.

18 *unnamed police officers drinking for free:* Connolly, "Downtown Police Corruption Alleged," 1; "Partial Text of Report," 12; Jerry Taylor, "17 Women Arrested in Combat Zone Raid," *Boston Globe*, November 26, 1974, 5.

18 *police allowed mobsters to double-park:* Connolly, "Downtown Police Corruption Alleged," 1; "Partial Text of Report," 12.

19 *dubbed the "golden boys":* Alexander Hawes Jr., "Report Ties Two Policemen to Kidnapping, Extortion, Rape," *Boston Globe*, November 10, 1976, 13.

19 *the "robber whore" scheme:* Connolly, "Downtown Police Corruption Alleged," 1; "Partial Text of Report," 12.

20 *"vindictive," parting shot:* Alexander Hawes Jr., "Jordan Tells Probe Unit to Proceed," *Boston Globe*, November 11, 1976, 1.

20 *doctors gave full credit to police:* Alexander Hawes Jr., "Harvard Athlete Is Stable after Combat Zone Melee," *Boston Globe*, November 17, 1976, 1.

20 *"He's a lucky kid":* Hawes, "Harvard Athlete," 1.

21   *the crime was pure larceny:* Hawes, 1.
22   *Early signs were encouraging:* Hawes, 1.

CHAPTER FOUR: YOU CAN'T BACK DOWN

24   *sprouting along the federally financed highways:* Ronald P. Formisano, *Boston against Busing: Race, Class, and Ethnicity in the 1960s and 1970s* (Chapel Hill: University of North Carolina Press, 1991), 12–14.

24   *in the midst of one of the city's worst recessions: School Desegregation in Boston: A Staff Report Prepared for the Hearing of the U.S. Commission on Civil Rights in Boston, Massachusetts, June 1975,* 31; Formisano, *Boston against Busing,* 12–25.

25   *the lines were drawn:* Jack Tager, *Boston Riots: Three Centuries of Social Violence* (Boston: Northeastern University Press, 2001), 182–85.

25   *highest concentration of white poverty in the entire nation: School Desegregation in Boston;* Francis J. Connolly, "Southie without Tears," *Commonwealth Magazine,* January 2000.

26   *when unemployment reached 15 percent:* Tager, *Boston Riots,* 195.

27   *a lucrative crime empire:* Ed Lion, "Boston Indictments Give Glimpse into Mob," United Press International (UPI) archives, September 25, 1983, https://www.upi.com/Archives/1983/09/25/Boston-Indictments -give-glimpse-into-mob/2143433310400/.

27   *the state's longest-ever organized crime trial:* Matthew Wald, "Four Convicted by U.S. Jury in Boston Rackets Trial," *New York Times,* February 27, 1986, A18.

32   *the 1965 Racial Imbalance Act:* Tager, *Boston Riots,* 191–93.

32   *disciplinary actions taken against a Black student:* Larry Dyne, "English High: Pride, Prejudice and Police," *Boston Globe,* February 14, 1971, 1.

CHAPTER FIVE: THE SLEAZE FACTOR

36   *to prepare for a murder indictment:* "Judge Denies Bail Hike in Puopolo Case," *Boston Globe,* December 1, 1976, 1.

36   *"God will answer our prayers":* Richard A. Knox, "Harvard Athlete's Brain Goes Silent," *Boston Globe,* November 25, 1976, 1.

36   *launched a grassroots campaign:* Earl Marchand, "Civic Drive On to Purge Combat Zone," *Boston Herald American,* November 18, 1976, 1.

37   *"notorious mode of robbery":* Dan McLaughlin, "Combat Zone Violence Hit by Cardinal," *Boston Herald American,* December 20, 1976, 1; "Protection in the Zone," *Boston Globe,* November 19, 1976, 22.

37   *"saturation" duty in the Zone:* John Cullen, "Prostitutes Invade the Back Bay," *Boston Globe,* November 21, 1976, 1.

38   *a huge mistake:* Paul Feeny and Peter Maneusi, "Officials Say Concept of X-Rated Zone Failed, Plan Crackdown on Violations," *Boston Globe,* November 30, 1976, 1.

38   *make it "dull and boring":* Feeny and Maneusi, "Concept of X-Rated Zone Failed," 1.

38   *a blind interest in one of the clubs:* "Dancer-Publicist for Combat Zone Reported Missing," *Boston Globe,* August 31, 1977, 35; "Zone Club Owners Criticize Police," *Boston Globe,* December, 2 1976, 49.

39   *she specifically blamed the Boston police:* Dave O'Brian, "Banned in Boston Again?," *Boston Phoenix*, November 14, 2006.

39   *Prostitutes Union of Massachusetts (PUMA):* "Prostitutes' Union Seeks Law Changes," *Boston Globe*, January 4 1977, 20; Cullen, "Prostitutes Invade the Back Bay," 1.

39   *"honest" prostitution and the "rip off variety":* Arthur Jones, "Hub Prostitutes Decry Violence," *Boston Globe*, November 21, 1976, 15.

39   *a retired prostitute:* John F. Cullen, "The Zone Devoid of Combat as Police Replace Hookers," *Boston Globe*, December 19, 1976, 3.

40   *"our white arrogance and naïveté":* Gordon Dalby, "Arrogance," letter to the editor, *Boston Globe*, November 24, 1976, 14.

41   *a springboard for higher political office:* Jack Tager, *Boston Riots: Three Centuries of Social Violence* (Boston: Northeastern University Press, 2001), 191–93; Ronald P. Formisano, *Boston against Busing: Race, Class, and Ethnicity in the 1960s and 1970s* (Chapel Hill: University of North Carolina Press, 1991), 1–21.

41   *clear patterns of segregation:* Formisano, *Boston against Busing*, 70–72.

42   *South Boston High School in September 1974:* Matthew Storin, "Japan Gets View of Boston Busing," *Boston Globe*, February 2, 1975, 2.

42   *They launched beer bottles:* Anthony J. Lukas, *Common Ground: A Turbulent Decade in the Lives of Three American Families* (New York: Vintage Books, 1986), 241.

42   *The violence only got worse:* James Ayres and Manli Ho, "38 Injured, One Seriously; 7 Arrested," *Boston Globe*, October 9, 1974, 1.

43   *Pro-busing forces countered with rallies:* "Freedom House Holds Pro-busing 'Assembly for Justice,'" *Bay State Banner*, October 7, 1974, 1; Arthur Jones and John Wood, "20,000 Join Integration Rally; Disputes, Clashes Delay March," *Boston Globe*, December 15, 1974, 1.

43   *burned in effigy:* Formisano, *Boston against Busing*, 1–65.

44   *highbrow towns with their exclusive school systems:* Mark Feeney, "Louise Day Hicks, Icon of Tumult, Dies," *Boston Globe*, October 22, 2003, A-1.

44   *helicopters flew overhead:* Michael Patrick MacDonald, "Whitey Bulger, Boston Busing, and Southie's Lost Generation," Schuster Institute for Investigative Journalism at Brandeis University, June 2014, https://www.schusterinstituteinvestigations.org/southies-lost-generation.

44   *disperse the angry white mob:* "Stabbing, 'Bridge Plot' and Contempt," *Boston Globe*, May 25, 1975, 5.

45   *antibusing plot to blow up five city bridges.* Arthur Jones, "Garrity Orders Stiffer Controls," December 14, 1974, 1.

45   *absurdities of the second phase of the plan:* Jim Vrabel, *A People's History of the New Boston* (Amherst: University of Massachusetts Press, 2014), 182.

46   *turned it into a spear:* Lukas, *Common Ground*, 322–26.

47   *Landsmark blamed the city politicians:* Lukas, *Common Ground*, 320–26.

47   *Poleet, a father of four:* Robert Anglin, "Man Near Death after Beating by Gang in Roxbury," *Boston Globe*, April 21, 1976, 1.

47   *leaders immediately blamed each other:* Marguerite Giudice, "Blacks, Whites Deplore Beating, Fear Tensions," *Boston Globe*, April 21, 1976, 1.

47   *the two coma victims:* John M. Langone, "Tragic Story of How 2 Live by Machinery," *Boston Herald American*, November 24, 1976, B3.

CHAPTER SIX: LOYALTY AND REVENGE

48   *the doctors had to be "extra careful":* Richard A. Knox, "Harvard Athlete's Brain Goes 'Silent,'" *Boston Globe*, November 25, 1976, 1.

50   *Revenge is not going to bring Andy back:* Associated Press, "He Was Like a Flower Cut Down," *North Adams (MA) Transcript*, December 18, 1976, 12.

50   *the pride of the North End:* Harold Banks, "Only Hope of a Miracle Remains for Puopolos," *Boston Herald American*, November 26, 1976, 3.

51   *business in the strip clubs was off:* Arthur Jones, "Hub Prostitutes Decry Violence," *Boston Globe*, November 21, 1976, 15.

52   *"an underworld plot to kill the men":* Associated Press, "Like a Flower 52 Down," 12.

53   *St. Leonard's, a late nineteenth-century Romanesque Catholic Church:* "Rites for Puopolo thronged," *Boston Herald American*, December 21, 1976, 6.

CHAPTER SEVEN: FEROCIOUS COMPETITORS

55   *distinguished twenty-eight-year career:* "Thomas Mundy Jr., 54," *Worcester Telegram & Gazette*, July 6, 1993, B5.

56   *"played hard, but he played fair":* Glen Justice, "Suffolk Prosecutor Thomas Mundy Jr. Claimed by Cancer," *Boston Globe*, July 5, 1993, 13.

57   *often managed to get a particular judge:* Andrew Blake, "A Job that Wields a Lot of Power," *Boston Globe*, May 2, 1982, 28.

57   *cranked up the heat on investigations:* Richard Connolly, "Probers Tracking the Real Owners in Combat Zone," *Boston Globe*, February 5, 1977, 1.

58   *Suffolk County Major Violators Division had won convictions:* Jonathan Fuerbringer, "Special Unit Charts Crackdown on Violent Crime," *Boston Globe*, April 24, 1976, 1.

58   *Critics say it can be a "lazy law":* "Joint Enterprise: First Murder Case Defendants Walk Free after Landmark Ruling," *Telegraph*, March 7, 2016; Owen Bowcott, "Joint Enterprise Law Wrongly Interpreted for 30 Years, Court Rules," *Guardian*, February 18, 2016.

CHAPTER EIGHT: A TERRIBLE WITNESS

61   *all their lawyers were white:* Thomas Shepard, "Black Lawyers, Blacks and the Boston Establishment," *Boston Globe*, October 12, 1969, 5; Maggie Rivas, "Centerpiece: The Problems of Black Lawyers," *Boston Globe*, February 18, 1982, 1.

61   *he was one year shy of meeting the criteria:* Corey Dade, "Civil Rights Champion Fights to Preserve Legacy Henry Owens Accused of Mishandling Funds," *Boston Globe*, August 25, 2002; Eric Convey, "Hub Lawyer Owens Facing Suspension," *Boston Herald*, May 31, 2001, 39.

63   *among the city's top criminal lawyers in 1976:* Nathan Cobb, "Who's Who in Boston's Legal Circles," *Boston Globe*, July 1, 1979, A-11.

65   *four stints in the house of corrections:* Edward McGrath, "Tough Gangs in Boston," *Daily Boston Globe*, September 27, 1959, 1; Criminal records from

the Boston Police Department for Richard Allen, Leon Easterling, and
Edward Soares, obtained in 2011 via the Freedom of Information Act.

65   *crimes escalated to larceny:* Criminal records.

67   *earning money from a prostitute:* Criminal records.

68   *a completely clean record for fourteen years:* Criminal records.

68   *by one witness account:* Commonwealth of Massachusetts v. Leon Easterling,
     Edward J. Soares, Richard S. Allen, Transcript of Evidence, vol. 2, Suffolk
     Superior Court, March 8, 1977 (dated for trial commencement).

CHAPTER NINE: PRIVATE LOSS, PUBLIC CONTROVERSY

71   *drastically altered worldview:* Ronnie Janoff-Bulman, *Shattered Assumptions:
     Towards a New Psychology of Trauma* (New York: Free Press, 1992), 49–72.

71   *the public nature of murder:* Lula M. Redmond, *Surviving: When Someone
     You Love Was Murdered: A Professional's Guide to Group Grief Therapy for
     Families and Friends of Murder Victims* (Clearwater, FL: Psychological
     Consultation and Education Services, 1989); A. Amick-McMullan, D. G.
     Kilpatrick, and H. S. Resnick, "Homicide as a Risk Factor for PTSD among
     Surviving Family Members," *Behavior Modification* 15 (1991): 545–59; E. K.
     Rynearson, MD, "Psychotherapy of Bereavement after Homicide," *Journal
     of Psychotherapy Practice and Research* 3, no. 4 (Fall 1994): 341–47; E. K.
     Rynearson, MD, "Psychotherapy of Bereavement after Homicide: Be Off-
     ensive," *Psychotherapy in Practice* 2, no. 4 (1996): 47–57; M. Thompson,
     F. Norris, and B. Ruback, "Comparative Distress Levels of Inner-City
     Family Members of Homicide Victims," *Journal of Traumatic Stress*
     11 (November 2, 1998): 223–42; K. Shear, E. Frank, P. Houck, and C.
     Reynolds, "Treatment of Complicated Grief: A Randomized Controlled
     Trial," *Journal of the American Medical Association* 293 (2005): 2601–8;
     Marilyn Peterson Armour and Mark S. Umbreit, "The Ultimate Penal
     Sanction and 'Closure' for Survivors of Homicide Victims," *Marquette
     Law Review* 91 (2007): 381.

CHAPTER TEN: WADING THROUGH THE JURY POOL

76   *fifty automatic exemptions:* "A Chance to Change the Jury," *Boston Globe,*
     February 3, 1974, 1; "Making Jury Duty Less Trying," *Boston Globe,* August
     29, 1991, 24.

77   *The desperately needed reform:* Diane Lewis, "New Jury Plan for 2 More
     Counties," *Boston Globe,* January 12, 1983, 1; William F Doherty, "Judge
     Wants Change in Jury Selection for US Courts in Boston," *Boston Globe,*
     November 3, 1982, 11.

78   *sentenced the manager of an X-rated theater:* Edgar J. Driscoll Jr., "Beacon Hill
     Memorial Service Set for Judge James C. Roy, 82," *Boston Globe,* September 21,
     1990, 19; Carolyn Clay, "'Miss Jones' Ruled Obscene, Cinema Manager
     Gets 2 1/2 Years, Fined $5,000," *Boston Globe,* October 6, 1973, 8.

78   *called "fair and impartial":* Driscoll, "Beacon Hill Memorial Service," 19.

78   *a full-page feature story:* "Once Cheerful, Happy and Outgoing, Times
     Have Changed for the Puopolos," *Boston Herald American,* March 20,
     1977, 22.

79   *New York Mafia was trying to buy:* Richard Ray and John Cullen, "N.Y. Mafia

Reported Eyeing Hub Porno Racket," *Boston Globe*, February 23, 1977, 3.

79   *Judge Roy decided to dismiss them:* Commonwealth v. Leon Easterling, Edward J. Soares, and Richard S. Allen, Transcript of Evidence, vol. 1, Commonwealth of Massachusetts, Suffolk Superior Court, March 8, 1977 (dated for trial commencement) (hereafter Transcript1)

82   *vague and confused answers:* Transcript1, vol. 1.

84   *"Go ahead, look brazen":* Al Sheehan, "Slain Athlete's Brother Lunges at Defendants," *Boston Globe*, March 11, 1977, 3.

CHAPTER ELEVEN: A NOBLE ACT

85   *edema of the brain:* Commonwealth of Massachusetts v. Leon Easterling, Edward J. Soares, Richard S. Allen, Transcript of Evidence, vol. 2, Suffolk Superior Court, March 8, 1977 (dated for trial commencement) (hereafter Transcript1).

88   *identify the clothing:* Alex MacPhail, "Harvard Player Describes Fatal Puopolo Stabbing," *Boston Herald American*, March 16, 1977, 3.

91   *"Quiet down, Mr. Owens":* Transcript1, vol. 2.

92   *wearing a sheepskin coat:* Transcript1, vol. 2.

95   *"There's one of them":* Transcript1, vols. 2 and 3.

96   *the judge overruled objections:* Transcript1, vols. 2, 3, and 4.

97   *Leon Easterling shocked the courtroom:* Transcript1, vol. 4.

98   *he worked as a street peddler:* Transcript1, vol. 4.

101 *"Since I can remember":* Transcript1, vol. 4.

102 *a spontaneous brawl:* Transcript1, vol. 4.

104 *wounds in Andy's heart:* Alan Sheehan, "Lawyers Dispute Reason for Attack on Puopolo," *Boston Globe*, March 23, 1977, 3.

CHAPTER TWELVE: STATE OF MIND

105 *the heat of passion couldn't apply:* Commonwealth of Massachusetts v. Leon Easterling, Edward J. Soares, Richard S. Allen, Transcript of Evidence, vol. 4, Suffolk Superior Court, March 8, 1977 (dated for trial commencement; hereafter Transcript1).

107 *struggled with feelings of hatred:* "Once Cheerful, Happy and Outgoing, Times Have Changed for the Puopolos," *Boston Herald American*, March 20, 1977.

109 *the air was so tense:* Alan Sheehan, "3 Guilty in Puopolo Slaying; Judge Imposes Life Sentences," *Boston Evening Globe*, March 24, 1977, 4.

110 *"Eddie . . . Oh, God":* Sheehan, "3 Guilty in Puopolo Slaying," 1; Alex MacPhail, "3 Puopolo Murderers Given Life," *Boston Herald American*, March 25, 1977, 7.

110 *took Eddie away in handcuffs:* Marvin Pave, "Justice, Relief Found by Some; Others Feel Pain," *Boston Globe*, March 25, 1977, 12.

110 *"ashamed for the jury system":* Alan Sheehan, "Puopolo Jury Goes into Second Day," *Boston Globe*, March 24, 1977, 3.

111 *"the verdict was just":* Marvin Pave, "Puopolo Sr.: 'Wife and I Feel Verdict Just,'" *Boston Evening Globe*, March 24, 1977, 5.

111 *Helen could not pretend:* Rich Bevilacqua, "3 Weeds Destroyed a Beautiful Flower," *Boston Herald American*, March 25, 1977, 7.

111   *they formed a pact:* Richard Ray, "Jurors Keeping Quiet about Delibera-
      tions," *Boston Globe*, March 25, 1977, 12; "Jurors Grim at Conclusion: All
      12 Refuse to Comment," *Boston Globe*, March 24, 1977, 4.

CHAPTER THIRTEEN: THE COLOR OF JUSTICE

112   *a Black kid from Roxbury:* Mary Thornton, "Attorney to Ask Judge for New
      Puopolo Trial," *Boston Globe*, April 3, 1977, 1.
112   *the fairness in sentencing three men:* "Harsh Justice," *Boston Globe*, March 26
      1977, 6.
113   *"three eyes for an eye":* Robert Jordan, "Perception of Justice Hurt by
      Puopolo," *Boston Globe*, March 29, 1977, 19.
113   *biggest names in civil rights law:* Thornton, "New Puopolo Trial," *Boston
      Globe*, 1.
115   *"The problem that won't go away":* Howard Husock, "Boston: The Problem
      that Won't Go Away," *New York Times*, November 25, 1979, 5.
116   *a symbol of the city's racial intolerance:* Arthur Jones and Timothy Dwyer, "14
      Arrested at Carson Beach after Refusing to Leave," *Boston Globe*, July 29,
      1977, 3.
116   *with a knife and a broken bottle:* Richard Martin, "Medford Man Slain After
      Traffic Dispute," *Boston Globe*, January 24, 1977.
117   *"no justice":* Robert Jordan, "Two Local Court Verdicts Show Scales of
      Justice Aren't Always in Balance," *Boston Globe*, July 13, 1977, 19.
117   *comparing the two verdicts:* Clarence Jones, "Two Views of a Trial: How Can
      We Not See a Racial Factor?," letter to the editor, *Boston Globe*, August 8,
      1977, 18.
117   *"angry and bitter whites":* Husock, "Boston," 5
117   *off the Boston City Council:* Ian Menzies, "Boston's Fate Lies in Public
      Schools," *Boston Globe*, November 16, 1977, 27.
118   *But intense racial battles raged:* Menzies, "Boston's Fate," 27.
118   *the violence did go both ways:* Husock, "Boston," 5; Joan Vennochi, "Police
      Probed 181 Racial Incidents in 1984," *Boston Globe*, December 28, 1984, 13;
      Jerry Taylor, "Boston's Smallest Police Unit; After 18 Months of Trying
      to Improve the Racial Climate, How Has It Done?," *Boston Globe*, August
      12, 1979, 8.
118   *visit the historic Bunker Hill Monument:* Peter Kadzis, "Black Group Attacked
      in Charlestown," *Boston Globe*, November 15, 1977, 1.
118   *"this lawless act of inhumanity":* Kadzis, "Black Group Attacked," *Boston
      Globe*, 1.
119   *an all-white jury acquitted:* "3 Men Indicted in Charlestown Assault," *Boston
      Globe*, November 22, 1977.
119   *Black victims could not get justice:* "The Charlestown Patriot: Beating Inves-
      tigation Should Continue," *Boston Globe*, December 19, 1978, 22.
119   *a press conference at City Hall Plaza:* Viola Osgood, "Black Leaders Call for
      Further Probe of Bunker Hill Racial Attack," *Boston Globe*, December 8,
      1978, 3.
119   *nine hundred incidents of racial violence:* "Rights Unit Urges US to Probe
      Beating," *Boston Globe*, December 30, 1978, 3.

120 *a new twenty-five-member interracial coalition*: Robert Levey, "Inmate Race Ratio Concerns Him," *Boston Globe*, October 29, 1979, 2.

121 *"by which a Black man can get a fair trial"*: Joseph M. Harvey, "Puopolo Case Appeal Argued," *Boston Globe*, September 12, 1978, 29.

121 *What the Boston Media Never Told You: Puopolo Defendants—Victims of Racist Injustice*, leaflet by Citywide Coalition for Justice and Equality, September 1978.

121 *an outcome of a spontaneous brawl*: "Say Brother; Case of Justice, A: African Americans and the United States Judicial System," GBH Archives, http://openvault.wgbh.org/catalog/V_9505CAA825F0444382DD673438C672E8.

122 *"the facts of the matter, as I personally viewed them"*: Edward Soares's letter from the legal files of defense attorney Norman Zalkind.

124 *dean of students, Archie Epps*: Sean Murphy, "N. End Park Named in Puopolo's Honor," *Boston Globe*, October 30, 1977, 17.

CHAPTER FOURTEEN: DEATH GRANTS NO APPEALS

126 *"saturation" enforcement strategy*: Jerry Taylor, "Police District Shake-up Cooled Combat Zone," *Boston Globe*, June 19, 1977, 33.

127 *a bill on Beacon Hill to legalize prostitution*: Andrew Blake, "Should Prostitution Be Legalized?; It's a Possibility in Massachusetts," *Boston Globe*, February 13, 1977, 2; Richard Hudson, "Combat Zone Plan: Shrink It," *Boston Globe*, August 22, 1977, 1.

127 *the true ownership of the nightclubs*: Taylor, "Police District Shake-up," 33.

128 *so empty one June evening*: Taylor: "Police District Shake-up," 33.

128 *stabbed him with an ice pick*: "Puopolo-Case Inmate Stabbed," *Boston Globe*, October 4, 1977, 12.

128 *"assassination squads"*: John F. Cullen, "4 in Walpole Execution Case Trying to Get Out of Isolation," *Boston Globe*, December 6, 1976, 1.

CHAPTER FIFTEEN: LANDMARK DECISION

134 *"ample" evidence submitted at trial*: Commonwealth v. Edward J. Soares (and three companion cases), 377 Mass. 461, September 11, 12, 1978–March 8, 1979, Massachusetts Supreme Judicial Court, Suffolk County, https://law.justia.com/cases/massachusetts/supreme-court/1979/377-mass-461-2.html. The three companion cases were one against Richard S. Allen and two against Leon Easterling.

135 *The percentage of Black potential jurors*: Commonwealth v. Edward J. Soares, 377 Mass. 461; "Puopolo: A Landmark Ruling," *Boston Globe*, March 10, 1979.

135 *California's Supreme Court*: The People, Plaintiff and Respondent, v. James Michael Wheeler et al., Defendants and Appellants, 22 Cal. 3d 258, Supreme Court of California, Opinion by Mosk, J., with Tobriner, Manuel and Newman, JJ., concurring. Separate concurring opinion by Bird, C. J. Separate dissenting opinion by Richardson, J., with Clark, J., concurring. September 25, 1978, Crim. No. 20233.

136 *fundamental unfairness for Blacks*: "Justice on the Jury," *Bay State Banner*, March 14, 1979, 4.

136 *"opens wounds and renews grief"*: "Justice on the Jury," 4.

140 *attacked and outnumbered*: "Statement by Citywide Coalition for Justice & Equality calling for Justice for Soares, Allen and Easterling, the Puopolo Defendants, and Condemning Assistant District Attorney Thomas J. Mundy's Efforts to Retry These Defendants by Appealing to Racial Prejudice and Slanders," Citywide Coalition press release, April 30, 1979, issued in Boston.

140 *Black defendants served longer terms*: Alexander Hawes Jr., "Deer Island Terms: Blacks Get More," *Boston Globe*, April 12, 1979, 1.

140 *away from the execution squads*: "Puopolo Defendants Denied Bail," *Boston Globe*, March 27, 1979, 28.

141 *they launched rocks, bottles, paint*: David Rogers and Charles Claffey, "Winegar Scolds Candidates for Silence on Southie," *Boston Globe*, September 20, 1979, 1.

141 *"they were not going to be pushed around"*: R. S. Kindleberger, "Racial Turmoil in Boston: At Southie High," *Boston Globe*, October 18, 1979, 1.

142 *for a pep talk*: Robert Rosenthal, "Player Shot on Field in Charlestown," *Boston Globe*, September 29, 1979, 1; ". . . And Good Reason to Heed It," *Boston Globe*, October 2, 1979, 34.

142 *securing the football field*: Dan Shaughnessy, "Nobody Won since He Was Shot on the Charlestown High School Football Field 11 Years Ago This Weekend, Darryl Williams Has Been Confined to a Wheelchair and a Life of Shattered Dreams," *Boston Globe*, September 30, 1990, 12.

142 *on life support*: Loretta McLaughlin, "Surgeon: 'All We Can Do Now Is Watch and Wait,'" *Boston Globe*, September 29, 1979, 27.

142 *The shooting of a fifteen-year-old*: "And Good Reason to Heed It."

143 *drunk and shooting at pigeons*: Al Larkin, "3 Teens Charged in Football Shooting," *Boston Globe*, October 1, 1979, 1.

143 *Not even the most skilled military marksman*: Richard Stewart, "The World Saw the Best and the Worst of Boston," *Boston Globe*, October 28, 1979, 1.

144 *three drunk teenagers on a rooftop*: Stewart, "World Saw the Best."

144 *could make them eligible for parole*: Alan Sheehan, "2 Are Sentenced to 10 Years in Darryl Williams Shooting," *Boston Globe*, March 27, 1980, 1; Judy Rakowsky, "For '79 Victim, an Unwelcome Reminder 'Code' Gunman Was Rooftop Assailant," *Boston Globe*, March 27, 1995, 13.

CHAPTER SIXTEEN: THE EDGE

146 *the same kind of sympathetic media figure*: Gayle Pollard, "Darryl's Mother Urges Prayer, Not Protest," *Boston Globe*, October 1, 1979, 21.

146 *a central issue in the mayoral race*: Alan Eisner, "Racial Conflict Becomes Campaign Issue," *Boston Herald American*, October 29, 1979.

146 *"illegal and unconstitutional" actions*: "Citywide Coalition for Justice and Equality Condemns Puopolo Prosecution's Attempt to Deny Its Constitutional Right to Support Defendants," Citywide Coalition press release, October 10, 1979, issued in Boston.

147 *Judge James McGuire presided*: Robert L. Hassett, "Puopolo Trial Judge 'Gets the Heavies,'" *Boston Herald American*, November 5, 1979.

148 *a running tally of the percentage:* Commonwealth v. Leon Easterling, v. Edward J. Soares, v. Richard S. Allen, Transcripts of Evidence, 9th Criminal Session, Thursday, October 25, 1979, Suffolk Superior Court 23-58-23-62, Social Law Library, Boston, MA (hereafter Transcript2).

149 *recommended by the governor's Judicial Nominating Commission:* "Governor's Letter Criticizes Screening Methods," *Boston Globe*, March 18, 1976, 18.

149 *"making me out to be a racist":* Transcript2, 19–14.

149 *knock off their "acrimonious remarks":* Transcript2, 19–22.

152 *carried a Bible:* Alan A. Sheehan "One Guilty, 2 freed in Puopolo Case," November 22, 1979, Transcript2, 24–44, and based on news photo by Frank Hill, *Boston Herald American*, November 22, 1979, A-16.

153 *"you never mentioned anything about cutting":* Transcript2, 23–60.

153 *"No I didn't":* Transcript2, 23–108,

153 *Pulling out the transcript:* Transcript2, 23-125-23-131.

154 *Stone: "That's right":* Transcript2, 23–66.

154 *"the Black students were seated in the rearmost section":* Transcript2, 23–83.

155 *"do you recall testifying in 1977":* Transcript2, 23-78-23-80.

158 *the man with the brown leather jacket:* Transcript2, 29–44.

158 *Coolidge stopped to regain his composure:* Transcript2, 29–45.

158 *ran from the courtroom in tears:* Alan Sheehan, "Story Silences Puopolo Court," *Boston Globe*, November 10, 1979, 17.

159 *compared to how he looked:* Transcript2, 29-77-29-79.

164 *the testimony was so contradictory:* Alan Sheehan, "Conflicts in Defense Testimony at Puopolo Trial," *Boston Globe*, November 18, 1979, 36.

164 *"endorse lawlessness":* Plaintiff-Appellate Briefs published by the Social Law Library following the 1979 trial, n.d., 52–53, Social Law Library, Boston, MA.

CHAPTER SEVENTEEN: BEHIND LOCKED DOORS

165 *windows overlooking Pemberton Square:* Anson Smith, "Searching for Justice behind Locked Doors," *Boston Globe*, August 6, 1978, 2.

165 *the only thing they initially agreed on:* Laura White, "Puopolo Case: Different Era, Different Verdicts," *Boston Herald American*, December 24, 1979, A3.

165 *but it was still confusing:* Transcript2, 38-5-38-20.

166 *The jury filed into the courtroom:* Alan Sheehan, "1 Guilty, 2 Freed in Puopolo Case," *Boston Globe*, November 22, 1979, 30.

166 *he sighed with relief:* Jim McFarland, "2 in Puopolo Killing Free, Third Guilty," *Boston Herald American*, November 22, 1979, A16.

166 *tears of joy in her eyes:* Laura White, "Tears of Shock at Puopolo Verdict," *Boston Herald American*, November 22, 1979, A3; Sheehan, "1 Guilty, 2 Freed," 1.

167 *red, cloth-covered Bible:* White, "Tears of Shock."

167 *swarmed by family members:* White, "Tears of Shock."

167 *in the light most favorable:* Jim McFarland, "2 in Puopolo Killing Free, Third Guilty," *Boston Herald American*, A16.

168 *the addition of three Black jurors:* White, "Puopolo Case."

168 *"Every middle-aged person with a pretty good job":* White, "Puopolo Case."

169   *"Let's say it didn't hurt"*: White, "Tears of Shock."

169   *the most damaging testimony*: White, "Puopolo Case."

170   *This guy changed his testimony*: White, "Puopolo Case."

170   *the verdicts came as a surprise*: Sheehan, "1 Guilty, 2 Freed," 1.

171   *reports that the football players were chased*: Commonwealth v. Leon
      Easterling, v. Edward J. Soares, v. Richard S. Allen, Transcripts of Evidence,
      9th Criminal Session, Boston, Massachusetts, Thursday, October 25, 1979,
      Suffolk Superior Court 23–58—23–62, Social Law Library, Boston, MA.

171   *riddled with contradictions*: Alan Sheehan, "Conflicts in Defense Testimony
      at Puopolo Trial," *Boston Globe*, November 18, 1979, 36.

173   *"a known pimp"*: Alan Sheehan, "Easterling Sentenced to 18 to 20 Years in
      Prison for Puopolo Death," *Boston Globe*, December 6, 1979, 25.

173   *"I have listened for many, many days"*: Sheehan, "Easterling Sentenced," 25.

173   *Jury nullification is the controversial action*: Arie M. Rubenstein, "Verdicts
      of Conscience: Nullification and the Modern Jury Trial," *Columbia Law
      Review* 106, no. 4 (2006): 959–93.

174   *Jury nullification has been defined differently among legal scholars*: Sonali
      Chakravarti, "Nullification and Black Lives Matter: The Power to Acquit,"
      August 5, 2016, https://publicseminar.org/2016/08/the-oj-simpson-ver
      dict-jury-nullification-and-black-lives-matter-the-power-to-acquit/.

174   *righting a past injustice*: Irwin A. Horowitz, Norbert Kerr, Ernest S. Park, and
      Christine Gockel, "Chaos in the Courtroom Reconsidered: Emotional Bias
      and Juror Nullification," *Law and Human Behavior* 30 (April 2006): 163–81;
      Hardeep Matharu, "Supreme Court Rules Controversial Joint Enterprise
      Law Has Been 'Wrongly Interpreted,'" *Independent*, February 18, 2016,
      http://Independent.co.uk/news/uk/supreme-court-rules-controversial-
      joint-enterprise-law-has-been-wrongly-interpreted-a6880981.html.

CHAPTER EIGHTEEN: A BROTHER'S RESPONSIBILITY

179   *new clubs had come in to take their place*: Stephanie Schorow, *Inside the Com-
      bat Zone: The Stripped Down Story of Boston's Most Notorious Neighborhood*
      (Boston: Union Park Press, 2017), 115–21, 132–33.

180   *family members of homicide victims*: Eric Schlosser, "A Grief Like No
      Other," *Atlantic Monthly*, September 1997; Mariëtte van Denderen, Jos de
      Keijser, Mark Huisman, and Paul A. Boelen, "Prevalence and Correlates
      of Self-Rated Posttraumatic Stress Disorder and Complicated Grief in a
      Community-Based Sample of Homicidally Bereaved Individuals," *Journal
      of Interpersonal Violence* 31 (?) (2016): 207–27.

181   *"near-consuming thoughts of revenge"*: Bruce Gross, "Life Sentence: Co-
      victims of Homicide," *Annals of American Psychotherapy Association* 10,
      no. 3 (September 2007): 39; Heidi Zinzow, Alyssa A. Rheingold, Alesia O.
      Hawkins, Benjamin E. Saunders, and Dean G. Kilpatrick, "Losing a Loved
      One to Homicide: Prevalence and Mental Health Correlates in a National
      Sample of Young Adults," *Journal of Trauma Stress* 22, no. 1 (February 22,
      2009): 20–27.

183   *"busing's true victims"*: David B. Wilson, "The Legacy of Busing," *Boston
      Globe*, November 9, 1981, 14.

184   *more popular in Black Roxbury:* Howard Kurtz and Michael Rezendes, "Heroics, Racial Harmony Boost Flynn's Popularity; the Public Metamorphosis of Boston's Mayor," *Washington Post*, September 20, 1987, A03.

184   *a good track record with the Black community:* Peter S. Canellos, "Roache Calls for No Preference in Police Hiring, Says He Would End Affirmative Action," *Boston Globe*, August 1993, 13.

184   *Neither police corruption nor Boston's racial troubles:* Spotlight Series, "Boston Police among Least Effective in the Nation," *Boston Globe*, October 12, 1980, 1; Joan Vennochi, "Police Probed 181 Racial Incidents in 1984," *Boston Globe*, December 28, 1984, 13.

185   *the success of the microcomputer and computer peripheral industries:* David Lampe, *The Massachusetts Miracle* (Cambridge, MA: MIT Press, 1988), 1–11.

187   *vacant upper stories of buildings:* Schorow, *Inside the Combat Zone*, 132.

CHAPTER NINETEEN: FURLOUGHS AND ESCAPES

191   *One October day on the job:* Kevin Cullen, "Convict in Puopolo Case Is Missing," *Boston Globe*, January 2, 1987, 17.

193   *eligible for furloughs:* Robin Toner, "Prison Furloughs in Massachusetts Threaten Dukakis Record on Crime," *New York Times*, July 5, 1988; Susan Forest, "How 12 Hours Shattered Two Lives," *Lawrence Eagle-Tribune*, August 16, 1987; T. J. Raphael, "How One Political Ad Held Back a Generation of American Inmates," *The World*, PRI (Public Radio International), May 18, 2015, https://www.pri.org/stories/2015-05-18/what-willie-horton-wrought.

193   *decided to turn himself in:* Peter J. Howe, "Missing Man Convicted in Puopolo Case Turns Himself In," *Boston Globe*, January 4, 1987, 25.

195   *all-night juice bars:* Stephanie Schorow, *Inside the Combat Zone: The Stripped Down Story of Boston's Most Notorious Neighborhood* (Boston: Union Park Press, 2017), 131–35.

195   *intravenous drug use:* Steve Marantz, "City Sets Policy on Services for AIDS Patients," *Boston Globe*, November 22, 1985, 1; "Downtown, August 9, 1994, 2 p.m.," *Boston Globe*, August 29, 1994, 14.

195   *Chinese community had gained strength:* Michael Liu, *Forever Struggle: Activism, Identity, and Survival in Boston's Chinatown, 1880–2018* (Amherst: University of Massachusetts Press, 2020), 66–67, 99, 107.

196   *leaning on existing property owners:* Richard Kindleberger, "Urban Development: The Combat Zone—Down but Not Out," *Boston Globe*, December 17, 1995, 1; Kevin Cullen, "The Shrinking Combat Zone: The Bad Old Days Are Over," *Boston Globe*, December 23, 1987, 33.

196   *earmarked for luxury apartment development:* Cullen, "Shrinking Combat Zone."

196   *aided by changing technology:* Paul Farhi, "Big Picture Reveals that VCRS Are Declining in Sales and Use," *Washington Post*, January 22, 1989.

CHAPTER TWENTY: HITMAN FOR HIRE

202   *engineering racial justice:* Ronald P. Formisano, *Boston against Busing: Race, Class, and Ethnicity in the 1960s and 1970s* (Chapel Hill: University of North Carolina Press, 1991), 223.

202   *urged Boston to abandon busing:* Ted Landsmark, "It's Time to End Busing in Boston," *Boston Globe*, January 31, 2009, A-11.

203   *a more diverse jury pool:* Nick King, "In Middlesex, When They Say Jury of One's Peers . . . They Mean It," *Boston Globe*, July 7, 1981, 1; Diane Lewis, "New Jury Plan for 2 More Counties," *Boston Globe*, January 12, 1983, 1.

204   *still allowed racial discrimination:* Randall Kennedy, *Race, Crime, and the Law* (New York: Vintage Books, 1997), 206.

204   *defense lawyers and prosecutors reject that solution:* Charles E. Walker Jr., "Inflicting Soares: The Continuing Viability of Peremptory Challenges," *Boston Bar Journal* 55, no. 2 (Spring 2011): 17.

AFTERWORD: PROGRESS AND STRUGGLES

205   *Boston still struggles with racism:* Ana Patricia Muñoz, Marlene Kim, Mariko Chang, Regine O. Jackson, Darrick Hamilton, and William A. Darity Jr., *The Color of Wealth in Boston*, Duke University, The New School, and the Federal Reserve Bank of Boston, March 25, 2015, https://www.bostonfed.org/publications/one-time-pubs/color-of-wealth.aspx; Todd Wallack, "11 Takeaways from This Month's Spotlight Series on Race in Boston," *Boston Globe* (online), December 29, 2017, https://www.bostonglobe.com/metro/2017/12/29/takeaways-from-groundbreaking-spotlight-series-race-boston/6C228SexjA7hGfyEsYMnjI/story.html; Akilah Johnson, "Boston. Racism. Image. Reality.: It Is the Hardest Question Hurled Our Way: Is This a Racist City? The Insult Is One We Want Badly to Reject. But a Spotlight Team Investigation Finds It Is Still Far Too Hard to Be Black in Boston, with Stark Inequities in Opportunity and Power," *Boston Globe*, December 10, 2017, A-1.

205   *The wealth gap drives segregation:* Adrian Walker, "A Year after a Groundbreaking Series on Race in Boston, Has Anything Gotten Better?," *Boston Globe* (online), December 16, 2018, https://www.bostonglobe.com/metro/2018/12/16/year-after-groundbreaking-series-race-boston-has-anything-gotten-better/MRxbVP6w9fWSQWkS2g81rL/story.html.

205   *One of Boston's ongoing problems:* Todd Wallack, "11 Takeaways."

206   *Boston rarely erupts: Massachusetts Hate Crime* 2019, Executive Office of Public Safety and Security, November 2020, Boston, MA.

INDEX

JAN BROGAN has been a journalist in New England for more than thirty years. She is a former staff writer at the *Worcester Telegram* and the *Providence Journal,* where she won the Gerald Loeb Award for distinguished financial writing. Her freelance work has appeared in the *Boston Globe,* several regional and national magazines, and two essay compilations. She is the author of four murder mysteries, one of which was purchased by Transactional Pictures for development into a television series. Originally from New Jersey, she's lived outside Boston since college. She has a BS in journalism from Boston University and a master's in English from the University of Massachusetts, Boston.